FINDING FEMINISM

Finding Feminism

Millennial Activists and the
Unfinished Gender Revolution

Alison Dahl Crossley

NEW YORK UNIVERSITY PRESS

New York

NEW YORK UNIVERSITY PRESS
New York
www.nyupress.org

References to Internet websites (URLs) were accurate at the time of writing. Neither the author nor New York University Press is responsible for URLs that may have expired or changed since the manuscript was prepared.

Library of Congress Cataloging-in-Publication Data
Names: Crossley, Alison Dahl, author.
Title: Finding feminism : millennial activists and the unfinished gender revolution / Alison Dahl Crossley.
Description: New York : New York University Press, [2017] | Includes bibliographical references and index.
Identifiers: LCCN 2016044890| ISBN 9781479898329 (cl : alk. paper) | ISBN 9781479884094 (pb : alk. paper)
Subjects: LCSH: Feminism. | Sex role. | Women's rights.
Classification: LCC HQ1155 .C76 2017 | DDC 305.42--dc23
LC record available at https://lccn.loc.gov/2016044890

New York University Press books are printed on acid-free paper, and their binding materials are chosen for strength and durability. We strive to use environmentally responsible suppliers and materials to the greatest extent possible in publishing our books.

Manufactured in the United States of America

10 9 8 7 6 5 4 3 2 1

Also available as an ebook

I smile at the arrogance of this; that we imagine that our work begins and ends with us.
—Cherríe Moraga, *This Bridge Called My Back: Writings by Radical Women of Color*

CONTENTS

ACKNOWLEDGMENTS

I wish to thank the participants in my research for their time and openness. Their enthusiasm was energizing. I continue to be reminded of the importance of their activism and their optimism for a more just and equal future.

Thank you to Verta Taylor. Her brilliant research inspired me to pursue a PhD. When I began the degree, little did I know how much Verta's generosity of time and thoughtful feedback would mean to me, or how her mentorship and friendship would enhance my life. Moreover, Verta lives her life with pizzazz to the max, uncompromising in both intellectual sophistication and fabulousness. She remains a bright light in my life.

I thank Leila J. Rupp and Maria Charles. Leila's intellectual openness and forward-thinking approach have encouraged me to think broadly and with nuance. Her deep knowledge and beautiful writing have driven me to be more thoughtful and precise in my work. I always remember how Leila sees the best in people. Thank you to Maria, who has consistently offered comments and support. Her considerable insight and analytic precision have been very valuable to me.

A number of people at the University of California–Santa Barbara were instrumental in their support and encouragement as I worked on this project. Thank you to Verta's community of students, especially Heather Hurwitz, Anna Sorensen, Ali Hendley, and the Gender Reading Group. Thank you to Bridget Harr. Thank you to Tracy Royce, Joan Budesa, Nicki Lisa Cole, and Brooke Mascagni for their laughter and fun, and also for their intellectual stimulation. Thank you to Cassandra Engeman, Greg Prieto, and Veronica Montes. I always felt loved and energized by my Santa Barbara people—Doug Stewart, Tonya Gill, Dasa Francikova, and the extended Kelso family—especially Carol, Susie and Matt, Missy & Co., Bo and Steve, Polly, Kyle, and Kori.

With gratitude I acknowledge the intellectual community and feminist workplace of the Clayman Institute for Gender Research at Stanford

University. It is my great pleasure to work with and learn from these inspiring people, dedicated to equality and inclusivity, especially Shelley Correll, Lori Nishiura Mackenzie, Ann Enthoven, Wendy Skidmore, Natalie Mason, Jennifer Portillo, Sara Jordan-Bloch, Marianne Cooper, Terra Terwilliger, Sandra Brenner, Shivani Mehta, Erika Gallegos Contreras, Becca Constantine, Caroline Simard, Jonna Louvier, Kristine Kilanski, Aliya Rao, Andrea Davies, and JoAnne Wehner. Many thanks to all of these smart women, who have enhanced my research and my life.

Thank you to those who have commented on and supported my work along the way: Pamela Stone, Angela McRobbie, Eileen Zurbriggen, Sarah Soule, Jo Reger, Nancy Whittier, Catherine Corrigall-Brown, Katrina Kimport, Kristin Thiel, Doug McAdam, and Rory McVeigh. I am also very grateful for the friendship and support of Ashley Farmer. To Ilene Kalish, Caelyn Cobb, and Alexia Traganas of NYU Press, thank you.

At Smith and in Northampton, thank you to Professors Nancy Whittier, Margaret Sarkissian, Marc Steinberg, and Fred and Lee-Ann Wessel. At the University of Minnesota, thank you to Shannon Stevens and Heidi Zimmerman. At UCSB, thank you to Paolo Gardinali and the Social Science Survey Center. For research funding, I am appreciative of the UCSB graduate division, the Flacks Fund for the Study of Democratic Possibilities, the UCSB Department of Sociology, and the Clayman Institute for Gender Research at Stanford University

Thanks to my friends from St. Paul Academy, who have been by my side through thick and thin since we were kids: Rhys Conlon, Hilary Gebauer, Matt Felt and Chad Kampe, Dena Larson, and Natalie Durk. Rhys, you have always been there for me in person, on the phone, and by USPS! That's love. To all of you, my extended family, you are the best. And to my brother, Kent, thank you for your quick wit and curiosity.

I thank my parents, Kent and Dee Ann, whose compassion for others and hard work inspire me. My dad has imparted an intellectual curiosity and openness throughout my life. And thank you to my mom for helping me be a better writer and for always looking on the bright side. Having parents who have been so supportive of and interested in my work has meant the world to me.

Tim, you are luminous. You make me happy to be alive. Your love, energy, and kind heart ramp me up every day. Who better to share life with?

1

Where Have All the Feminists Gone?

Millennials and the Unfinished Gender Revolution

If you were to hop on a beach cruiser for a ride around Isla Vista, California, you would see that it is a naturally stunning beachside community. Riding past Freebirds twenty-four-hour burrito shop, Woodstock's Pizza, and the Isla Vista grocery co-op, you would notice businesses interspersed with densely packed homes and apartment buildings, with the largely student and Latina and Latino family populations sharing bedrooms or illegally converted garages. As you rolled down Del Playa, the street paralleling the beach, the sun would feel warm on your face, and you would hear the music of a band practicing out of an open window. You would notice houses painted with brightly colored murals, someone rinsing off post–surf session in a wetsuit in an outdoor shower, and a 1968 VW van being slowly driven by a hippy sporting a huge beard. You would probably be incredulous that these tenants live in residences perched overlooking the Pacific Ocean.

On the evening of May 23, 2014, on the streets and in the homes of Isla Vista, twenty-two-year-old Elliott Rodger killed six University of California–Santa Barbara students and injured fourteen others before killing himself. His rampage—which included killing his two roommates and their friend, two Delta Delta Delta sorority members, patrons of local businesses, pedestrians, and bike riders—encompassed seventeen crime scenes across Isla Vista. It soon emerged that the rampage was driven by Rodger's hatred of women. In his last YouTube video, he said, "For the last eight years of my life, ever since I hit puberty, I've been forced to endure an existence of loneliness, rejection and unfulfilled desires all because girls have never been attracted to me. Girls gave their affection, and sex and love to other men but never to me. . . . I don't know why you girls aren't attracted to me, but I will punish you all for it."[1]

While grief and sorrow descended upon the beachside town and be-yond, there was a surprising turn of events. The news provoked an eye-opening surge of feminist activism. Fueled by the wide circulation of the killer's misogynist manifesto and his desire to exact "revenge" upon young women, feminists in Isla Vista and across the world clamored for a halt to sexism. Students and young people, online and off, success-fully shaped national discourse on the tragic incident. What started as a discussion of gun control and the killer's mental illness shifted into a broader debate about sexism. "Campus Killings Set Off Anguished Conversation about the Treatment of Women" (*New York Times*)[2] was accompanied by a photo of University of California–Santa Barbara femi-nist studies students marching through Isla Vista bearing placards say-ing, "Nobody is entitled to a womyn's body" and "Speak up! Every day." Major news outlets not known for their coverage of feminism or gender inequality blared headlines such as "Why It's So Hard for Men to See Misogyny" (*Slate*)[3] and "Hollywood and Violence: Is Misogyny a Grow-ing Concern?" (CNN).[4]

Online feminists shaped mainstream news coverage during this time, with #YesAllWomen drawing significant media attention. Born as a result of women's outrage over the sexist motivations of the killer, #YesAllWomen generated over a million tweets in four days. The tweets revealed, according to one CNN analyst, the "collective experience of what it's like to be a woman in a world where that can be dangerous."[5] Women around the globe shared 140 characters documenting their experiences with sexism, violence, and sexual harassment. Examples of tweets include the following: "Because I can't tweet about feminism without getting threats. . . . Speaking out shouldn't scare me," and "Every single woman you know has been harassed. And just as importantly every single woman you don't know has been harassed."

This feminist mobilization illuminated unexplored dimensions of feminism and gender inequality. Although the outcry may have been unforeseen by people who think that young women are uninterested in feminism or that sexism is no longer a pressing social issue, these events drew attention to the endurance of gender inequality as well as to the deep feminist networks rooted in the community. Social movement scholars know that this type of organizing does not appear out of thin air—it is the result of mobilizing grievances, preexisting social ties, a solidarity with other participants, spurious events, and a context that is, to some degree, amenable to movement organizing.[6]

Examples of surges of feminist mobilization are not rare. You may have read about Columbia University student Emma Sulkowicz, who carried her mattress around campus in protest of the way university administrators responded to her sexual assault report—or the widely used hashtag #RememberRenisha, commemorating murdered Detroit teenager Renisha McBride, bringing attention to the racism and sexism that erases the experiences of African American women. These campaigns, like the Isla Vista massacre response, point to the continued existence of feminists and relevance of feminism in the United States. Despite media attention to these events and much speculation about young women's interest in feminism, there is very little scholarship analyzing the state of the movement. *Finding Feminism* fills that void.

In the following chapters, I tell the stories of a diverse group of college student feminists from three different regions of the United States. By analyzing participants' intersectional feminist identities as well as the organizational strategies and structures of their feminist organizations, I elucidate the ways in which feminism has persisted and changed over time. The evidence in this book demonstrates how college students continue to be feminists and activists, despite speculation to the contrary, and how the meanings and tactics of feminism have changed over time. *Finding Feminism* contributes to broader conversations about the transformation and current state of the feminist movement, and the way these students are negotiating the strain borne by progress and stall.

This May Have Been the Best Year for Women since the Dawn of Time
—12/23/2014, *Huffington Post*

2014 Was a Bad Year for Women, but a Good Year for Feminism
—12/24/2014, *Huffington Post*

Oversimplified and contradictory notions of feminism and gender equality circulate widely in the media. This is not a new phenomenon. In the 1990s, the "feminism is dead" pronouncement had its heyday. Much to all feminists' chagrin (young and old mobilized as feminists during this time) the phrase was splashed across headlines and the covers of major magazines.[7] Media critic Jennifer Pozner called it the false feminist death syndrome, which, according to Bitch Media, is "a time-honored journalistic tradition."[8] While these obituaries continue,[9] there is now a counterpart to their narratives: "feminism is everywhere." At the same time that feminism is being declared dead or irrelevant, feminist ideologies are declared to be engrained in all our lives, like "fluoride in the water."[10] You may have noticed recent evidence of "feminism is everywhere." A number of celebrities who are especially popular with young women (i.e., Beyoncé, Taylor Swift, Lady Gaga, Emma Watson) have proclaimed to massive global audiences that they are feminists. Mass market books about feminism also abound.

The "feminism is everywhere" trope is a natural progression from the "girl power narrative" instilled early in many girls' psyches. That narrative espouses that girls can do anything they put their minds to. It is circulated in schools, books, the media, and even parenting manuals. Girls' apparently inexhaustible opportunities are touted in contrast to the limited experiences available to previous generations of women. In this individualist model, gender equality is the law of the land.

This trifecta of "feminism is dead," "feminism is everywhere," and "girls can do anything" is at odds with the well-documented pervasiveness of gender and other interrelated inequalities. The "stalled gender revolution" is the name sociologists have given to the events of the mid-1990s, when women's advancement was at a standstill following a period of improvements.[11] The stall continues today. Evidence for the stalled gender revolution is found in the continuance or worsening of the wage gap and the feminization of poverty (women are poorer than men in every state in the United States). Although it is widely heralded that in many public institutions of higher education women outnumber men, and that women on the whole are more educated than men, women ultimately will make less than men and have more barriers in advancing their jobs and careers. On average, women earn 78 percent of what men earn, while Latina women earn 54 percent of what White men earn. The pay gap, which sociologists attribute to the concentration of women in low-paying jobs,[12] has barely budged in at least ten years.[13] Even in women-dominated occupations such as nursing and teaching, men earn more—and are often promoted faster.[14] A *Washington Post* headline summed it up: "At This Rate, American Women Won't See Equal Pay until 2058."[15]

Given that the data supporting the existence of the stalled revolution is vast, the prevalent messages about feminism, women, and girls are superficial at best or erroneous at worse. They overstate the existence of gender equality. They reflect an inaccurate image of gender arrangements, and drastically simplify the complexities of inequalities and feminist movements. Cultural discourses such as these result in three interconnected impediments to feminist organizing. First, if gender inequality is not recognized as a social problem, when a woman does experience sexism she may interpret it as an individual problem rather than a systematic problem. Second, when the injustice of gender inequality and the need for redress is overlooked, the matter of gender equality lacks immediacy. Feminists may seem dull and outdated or as though they are overreacting. Third, as a result, feminist organizations and communities may be challenged in building membership or finding allies who are critical to the support of a movement and the cultivation of new feminists. At the same time, the feminist mobilization that is happening is disregarded and undervalued.[16]

Because of this confusion about the state of feminism and the simultaneous persistence of gender inequality, it is essential to closely examine the feminist movement. The lack of empirical research on the role of feminism in the lives of women today is disproportionate to the significant amount of speculation about the topic.[17] While it is sometimes argued that feminism is either dead or in abeyance around the globe, whether or not this is the reality for college students remains largely uninvestigated.[18] By introducing the voices of college student feminists and examining their experiences and opinions, I present multiple perspectives on feminism and gender inequalities, and further dismantle the rigid and exclusionary definitions of feminism and feminist protest.

This project provides rich data about the current state of feminism and how it has evolved. *Finding Feminism* also contributes to the body of literature that questions the usefulness and accuracy of the wave framework. I contend that in order to accurately analyze feminist mobilization and identities, and to discern the energy and impact of a long-lasting social movement, updated understandings of feminism are needed. These understandings should include feminism enacted in everyday, interactional, and intersectional ways, in unexpected locations, in online settings, and in organizations not solely concerned with gender inequality.

Finding Feminism highlights the nuanced and multifaceted nature of feminist movements—and how millennial feminists are mobilizing despite living in a culture that is not always supportive of women. This book asks, How has the feminist movement changed over time? Is the feminist movement alive, dead, or everywhere and nowhere? What are college students' experiences with and perceptions of social inequality? What are the forms, strategies, and tactics of college student feminism that allow the movement to persist? What are the factors that shape feminist cultures, and how are they influenced by institutional environments?

This study reveals the inaccuracies of the views that feminism is either a relic of the past or naturally within all of us, or that millennials are selfie-obsessed narcissists clueless about the inequalities all around them. Instead, in my diverse sample of students with varying racial/ethnic, class, and sexual identities, a more complex picture emerges about the state of the movement and the characteristics of young activists. However, I do not merely document the obstacles and successes of feminists, or simply record the evolution of the feminist movement. My findings build on extant literature about social movements, gender, and inequality. I connect with scholars who argue for the affirmation of the contemporary U.S. women's movement,[19] long after the decline of the second wave of mass feminism, and even as commentators continue to write about its demise.[20] I address larger questions regarding the consequences of the stalled gender revolution[21] and possibilities for its reinvigoration, the grievances and tactics of young activists,[22] the incorporation of social movements within institutions of higher education,[23] the dynamics of movements over many years,[24] and the multiple dimensions through which context alters movement culture.[25] *Finding Feminism* answers pressing questions about the present state of feminism, one of the longest-lasting social movements in modern history.

Feminist Mobilization and Continuity

Feminism, broadly speaking, is a movement to end gender and interrelated inequalities such as those that are race, class, and sexuality based. Feminist movements are diverse and vary widely according to national context and racial, ethnic, and sexual composition and the ideas and practices of indigenous groups and societies.[26] Because of this heterogeneity in women's life experiences, feminist mobilization has never been one-size-fits-all.[27] In *Feminism Unfinished*, Dorothy Sue Cobble, Linda Gordon, and Astrid Henry write, "[I]n a diverse country like the United States, we cannot expect different groups of women to have identical agendas. We cannot expect poor women feeding their families on food stamps to have the same priorities as female lawyers hoping to become partners in law firms."[28]

A number of structural preconditions that lead to mass feminist mobilization have been identified.[29] Large changes in the gender order have historically served as telling precursors to feminist organizing. For example, increased numbers of women in certain sectors of the labor force, the higher educational attainment of women, and a decline in women's fertility and reproductive roles create a climate in which women are politicized and consequently motivated to participate in feminist mobilization.[30] However, social movement scholars know that these shifts alone are not always enough to spur feminist organizing. Additional necessary factors include a sense of solidarity among feminists, the belief that change is possible, and adequate support or financial resources to facilitate activism.

Although studies traditionally focus on the state or politics as the main target of social movement participants, gender and social movement scholars identify a number of targets for change in addition to the state.[31] These include daily interaction or everyday life;[32] institutions such as the military and the church;[33] public and private higher education;[34] and the prevailing cultural milieu.[35] Through these scholars' analyses and expansive perspectives on where and how collective action takes place, we may understand the multiplicity of types and targets of feminism.[36]

On a personal level, feminists may create change by resisting expectations of women as dictated by the gender order. They may not participate in the institution of marriage, or may choose to live in a domestic arrangement other than a heterosexual nuclear family. They may avoid patronizing businesses that do not pay their workers a living wage, or those businesses that are known to contribute to antiwomen politicians or organizations. Feminists may eschew traditional standards of feminine appearance by not wearing makeup or clothes that draw attention to their bodies.[37] Or they may decline reconstruction after breast cancer surgery.[38] Mentoring other women is another form of feminism, such as when members of Black or Latina sororities encourage high school students to attend college. Regardless of the tactics or specific motivations, these examples draw attention to the politicization of everyday life or to the "personal is political" concept. Although focused on the individual level, these strategies seek overarching change by disrupting and reshaping the traditional institutions and practices that have emancipatory potential.[39]

The most famous examples of the "personal is political" were the consciousness-raising groups that were practiced widely among White, Black, Asian, and Latina women in the 1960s and '70s. In these groups, women learned to understand that their challenges in life were not specific to their individual lives, but were a result of broader structural inequalities that perpetuate the subordination of women and people of color. Consciousness-raising groups ideally involved four steps: self-revelation, active listening, discussion and linking individual problems and larger social forces, and connecting discussions to other theories of oppression.[40] Women came to understand their individual experiences within a larger framework of gender inequality. As a result, they shaped a distinct, powerful feminist culture. Loretta Ross described her experiences: "We may have formally called it 'consciousness-raising' but in essence we were telling each other stories to reclaim ourselves and our humanity. We created a feminist culture with these stories, not through narratives of logic and structure, but by creating verbal snapshots of the lived experiences of women."[41]

Personal issues such as intimate relationships, family, work, sexuality, and housework were shared among participants. The subsequent recognition of gender oppression drove much of the growth of the women's movement. Groups like the Combahee River Collective combined consciousness-raising and "high theory political education" to combine race and class considerations with feminism.[42] While some groups began without organizational affiliations, the process of politicization often led to such affiliations, as well as to additional feminist activism, or the maintenance of feminist networks.[43] Although consciousness-raising groups have largely died out, their function survives in the form of in-person women's groups or "circles," as well as online social media and feminist blog consumption and production.[44]

Feminists also work to create changes at the structural level. Through local and national organizing, they have used a dense network of advocates for feminist structural achievements. These networks include elected officials, lobbyists, members of social movement organizations, and on- and offline activists affiliated with community-based or grassroots groups. Working within legal channels, feminists have fought for a number of policies. They have come together to propose the Equal Rights Amendment,[45] as well as to implement policies that provide family and parental leave, ensure abortion rights,[46] and protect women from sexual harassment at work, to name a few. Means for achieving structural change have included civil disobedience, protest, and mass demonstrations, such as when African American women "stormed the gates of the capital demanding that the state, society and public servants acknowledge black women's humanity and suffering" prior to the 1963 March on Washington[47]—or, in 2004, when a reported one million women protested for women's rights and reproductive justice in the March for Women's Lives in Washington, D.C.[48] Student anti–sexual assault activists have built dense, nationwide networks to hold accountable their institutions of education for not adequately responding to sexual assault on campus.[49] Members of these organizations, such as End Rape on Campus (EROC), have traveled the country teaching other activists how to file Title IX complaints with the Department of Education.[50] Due to the success of much of this mobilization, in the past forty years feminists have made substantial inroads in institutional settings that have not typically been seen as feminist or even women-friendly. These include health-care, educational, religious, military, and corporate institutions.[51]

Feminists have reshaped norms, beliefs, and values related to gender, race, class, and sexuality, and have targeted cultural change more than participants in any other social movement.[52] The goal is to provide spaces and instigate practices that highlight the value of women's and girls' experiences and perspectives and the flaws of mainstream sexist culture.[53] Historian Anne Enke documented how the Detroit Motown Soul Sisters Softball Team, composed of predominantly African American women and organized in the 1960s and '70s, displayed "a non-normative gender performance through aggressive occupation of civic athletic space . . . and they worked to make public athletics more accessible to young girls and women."[54] These women scrutinized the male-centered world of sports, men's domination of public recreational space, and expectations of women to be demure and unathletic. Another example of cultural change occurred in the feminist self-help movement, in which, argues Verta Taylor, participants reshaped meanings of motherhood. Self-help groups aided women with postpartum depression in understanding their individual experiences as part of the oppressive and limiting expectations of women and mothers. They ultimately were "significant players in the redefinition of gender relations in American society."[55]

Feminists challenge the male domination of the streets and the Internet. Organizations such as Hollaback! are continuing the tradition of feminists taking back the night and rallying to make public spaces safe for women. The New York City group takes street harassment seriously, lobbying for local oversight of chronic street harassers, and publicly shaming men who engage in street harassment. Artist Tatiyana Fazlalizadeh's Stop Telling Women to Smile campaign, named after the common catcall, displays public art on streets across the world with messages such as "my outfit is not an invitation" and "my name is not baby." The Internet too has become an unsafe place for many women, as described in an article by journalist Amanda Hess titled "Why Women Aren't Welcome on the Internet."[56] Women report receiving life-altering threats and harassment online.[57] A Pew Research Center survey found that 92 percent of people ages eighteen to twenty-nine have been harassed online, and that young women are most likely to experience sexual harassment and stalking.[58] Organizations such as Women, Action, and the Media (WAM) have partnered with Twitter for an online harassment-reporting initiative, and Hollaback! has created the online platform Heartmob to support people who have been harassed online.

Feminists and the Media

A critical component of social movement participation is what sociologist Kathleen Blee calls the "intellectual work of activism—interpreting the world, developing a shared ideology, and shaping frames that will

translate the particular problems of an aggrieved group into universal conditions appealing to a broader public."[59] Feminists, like other
mobilized individuals, come to interpret their relationship to feminism
through their experiences with or observations of inequality, their reso-
nance with feminist ideology, their connection to other feminists, and
their contact with the media.[60] The mainstream news and entertainment media is particularly important to the feminist movement, as it has
created powerful frames and stigmas that influence the way feminists
and feminist ideologies are viewed.[61] For many people, the media is a
primary source from which individuals, feminist and not, learn about
feminism. For generations, feminists have fought for the mainstream
media to pay attention to issues of sexism. In their study of the wom-
en's rights movement from 1945 to 1960, Leila J. Rupp and Verta Taylor
found,

> By creating an inaccurate image of women's lives, by holding women who
> did not conform to the ideal responsible for the problems of the Ameri-
> can family, by focusing attention on individual women at the expense of
> the issues, and by ignoring the women's movement, the media helped to
> create an atmosphere in which it was difficult to put forth arguments for
> women's rights. Feminists understood, at the time, that this media treat-
> ment had important consequences.[62]

This is not unique to feminism, of course. Mainstream society always creates negative labels to detract participants from organizing and
challenging cultural and social mores. In previous research,[63] I found
that the bra-burning tactic first fabricated in 1967 remains a powerful
image from which young women of globally disparate geographical origins distance themselves.[64] The feminist bra-burner myth devalues and
sexualizes feminists, as it is indelibly etched into our cultural memory[65]
and narratives of feminism.[66] In a study of representations of feminists
and feminism in the news and public affairs media, Rebecca Ann Lind
and Colleen Salo found in an analysis of thirty-five thousand hours of
ABC, CNN, PBS, and NPR programming that feminists "are significantly more likely to be demonized" than the more general category
of women, and ten times more likely to be coupled with words such
as "jerks, bitches, radical or bad"[67] than the more general category of

women.[68] This is particularly relevant because several studies confirm that a positive attitude toward feminism is essential in order for an individual to adopt a feminist identity.[69]

Although these stigmas undoubtedly persist, gender inequality and public discourse about feminism and inequality have come to the forefront of mainstream news outlets. On any given day a reader may come across a number of articles in the mainstream press about gender issues or sexism. The *New York Times*, not known to be a feminist news outlet, has had a swell of coverage about gender inequality: In its "Economics" section, a headline reads, "A Possible Path to Closing the Pay Gap," and in its weekly "Your Money" section, "Moving Past Gender Barriers to Negotiate a Raise." On the west coast, the *Los Angeles Times* has featured articles about gender in Hollywood, such as "Battlestar Galactica: Moore, McDonnell Talk Sci-Fi Gender Equality." Books instructing women on how to rise above gender bias and embrace feminism have proliferated—including *Lean In*,[70] *Lean In for Graduates*,[71] *What Works for Women at Work*,[72] and *Wonder Woman*.[73]

On one hand, including the experiences of women and feminists in mainstream news outlets is significant. Through these outlets, we learn to negotiate whose opinions are valued, whose worldviews are respected, and what issues are of national and global significance. When gender inequality is presented as an issue of import, and feminism as a palatable identity, it paves the way for more people to understand the continued relevance of a movement focused on gender inequality. On the other hand, the feminism that has garnered attention in the mainstream media presents a limited scope of feminism, often glossing over the complexities within. The erasure of women of color in mainstream narratives about feminism specifically impacts public viewpoints and the central narratives of feminism: feminism is a White women's movement. The ramifications of this have been widely documented, and this "white-washing," as Benita Roth calls it,[74] portrays an inaccurate image of a complex movement with diverse participants. The white-washing of contemporary feminism encourages an incorrect image of the reality of the U.S feminism movement.

Women of color, young women, and others who are marginalized from the mainstream have found blogs and social media to be an effective platform for feminist communication, community, and mobilization.[75]

Blogs such as the *Crunk Feminist Collective* and *For Harriet*, authored by women of color, provide influential commentary and critique about current events. In conjunction with active social media presence, bloggers reach massive audiences with their commentary. These sites are especially trafficked by young people, as youth are likely to turn to these forms of media in lieu of legacy media. Prominent African American women have successfully organized online campaigns that have spilled to offline action. Feminista Jones is a mental health social worker who is a prolific writer and tweeter. She started the hashtag #YouOkaySis to call attention to street harassment and to encourage women to support each other during incidences of offline street harassment. Using #YouOkaySis, Jones shared her daily experiences of observing and experiencing street harassment in New York, and how she intervened. Even when she did not know the harassed woman, Jones would ask whether she was okay, or pretended to be a friend to the woman, often diffusing or stopping the incident. #YouOkaySis drew attention to the everyday sexism women experience in their daily lives. It also expanded the conversation about street harassment to consider how women of varying races and ethnicities experience street harassment differently and to encourage women to help each other. To provide another example, Kimberlé Crenshaw started #WhyWeCantWait in protest of President Obama's exclusion of Black women and girls in his My Brother's Keeper initiative. This resulted in a letter to the president signed by one thousand people, including many famous activists and intellectuals.[76]

Feminist mobilization has shaped all spheres of contemporary life. While different types of feminist mobilization abound, feminism and women's movements in the United States have withstood dramatic changes in historical, political, and cultural contexts. Although existing scholarship on the modern women's movement has focused on variations in mobilizing structures and dynamics, we know very little about the characteristics, identities, and tactical repertoires of feminist movements today. We do know that college students are in their prime for engagement in social movements, and that young feminists may help us learn about the future of feminism. Thus, understanding feminism among college students will paint a fuller picture of the continuation of the feminist movement. It is critical that we comprehend the changing forms and sites of women's movement mobilization.[77] As the stalled gender revolution reminds us, previous progress means neither that continued change is inevitable nor that advancements are everlasting.

The Stalled Gender Revolution and the Persistence of Gender Inequality

The "stalled gender revolution" is the backdrop against which young feminists develop their feminist consciousness and engage in feminist mobilization. The gender revolution, which created dramatic changes in the gender order, is currently "unfinished"[78] and "stalled."[79] The successes of feminism in the 1970s improved the lives of women and indelibly transformed the gender order. However, cultural and social attitudes toward women and their roles in society have not kept up with this transformation. Women flooded into male-dominated occupations, but without a concurrent flow of men into women-dominated occupations, much of the economic relationships of the gender order remained the same.[80] Indeed, following a period of increasingly forward-thinking perspectives, attitudes towards gender roles have plateaued and are not, as we might have expected, becoming more progressive.[81] The stall is a result of the opening of social institutions that allowed women advancement within previously closed labor sectors, combined with the inability to accommodate this advancement because of inflexible cultural expectations of paid work or care.[82]

Women may feel the effects of the stalled revolution at home and in the workplace. Marianne Cooper found that middle- and lower-class women are burdened with the emotionally taxing "worry work" of keeping the family afloat during insecure economic times.[83] Women of all socioeconomic and racial/ethnic backgrounds continue to be responsible for the majority of household and care work.[84] Care workers, who are disproportionately women, face a wage penalty, receiving "on average, lower hourly pay than we would predict them to have based on the other characteristics of the jobs, their skill demands, and the qualifications of those holding the jobs."[85] This inequality fuels the wage gap, which sociologists agree is due to the concentration of women in low-paying jobs.[86]

Expectations of women on the domestic and work fronts are simply at odds. Mary Blair-Loy calls these competing narratives "family devotion schemas" and "work devotion schemas."[87] Although there have been some positive adjustments, Blair-Loy found that even among younger cohorts of women there is still the sense that these schemas cannot be aligned.[88] Sociologist Brooke Conroy Bass found that even before becoming parents, 25–34-year-old women in heterosexual relationships "tended to downshift certain educational or professional opportunities in conjunction with anticipating parenthood," while the men in the relationships did not make any changes, thereby preserving labor inequality.[89] Research by Robin Ely, Pamela Stone, and Colleen Ammerman found that the careers of women of high socioeconomic statuses take a back seat to those of their men partners.[90] When women who have high aspirations for their careers and professional lives experience a dead end while trying to combine them with home responsibilities, they feel they have no choice but to quit their jobs.[91] In other words, although women may be moving up in some respects, the lack of change on the home front means that progress has stalled.[92]

Most workplaces have failed to provide childcare, flexible hours (for high-wage workers), or predictable schedules (for hourly workers) to accommodate the changing needs of its workforce. Hourly employees such as retail and service workers are disproportionately women, and a Pew study found that "[a]mong women across all races and ethnicities, hourly earnings lag behind those of white men and men in their own racial or ethnic group."[93] Hourly workers may not have predictable schedules or may even be "on call." While being "on call" was once reserved for physicians required to tend to a medical emergency, being "on call" is de rigueur for fast-food and retail workers. This practice saves the employer money by their not having to pay extra employees if business is slow, but in the process it places an often insurmountable burden on the millions of women hourly workers who have caretaking responsibilities. Women cannot leave their children at the last minute or pay for childcare when it is not needed. For professional workers, the rigid structure of many workplaces means that women are penalized for asking for flexible arrangements, such as working from home if a child is sick, so they may adapt to their children's needs. Many women are aware of the negative associations of being a working mother, so they do not even ask for accommodations. Sociologist Shelley Correll and her collaborators found evidence of a "motherhood penalty" in the professional workplace: women who have children are perceived as less devoted to their work and are punished by being compensated less than women without children, and less than all men.[94]

Women who do reach positions of leadership in their careers and professions have a higher risk of depression and worse mental health than their male colleagues, found a study by Tetyana Pudrovska,[95] with this stress probably caused by gender biases that penalize women for exhibiting characteristics such as assertiveness and confidence. Indeed, women who reach leadership positions experience backlash for behaving counter to dominant expectations of women.[96] Such are the ramifications of the notion that women are, above all, gentle nurturers.

As we can see, women experience deep cultural tensions with their advancement in society, combined with stagnancy in the institutions of work and family. This ensures the persistence of inequality and the stall of the revolution.

Events in politics and the gradual dismantling of reproductive rights also exhibit the stalled gender revolution and chilly attitudes towards feminists and women. Republican and Tea parties have introduced numerous legislative changes and proposed ballot measures that curtail family planning services and constrain women's reproductive rights. Planned Parenthood has been defunded or is in the process of becoming defunded in eight states, and ninety-two new laws against abortion went into effect between 2011–2012, including banning certain abortions and restricting access to abortion.[97] In June 2014, the Massachusetts Supreme Court struck down its abortion buffer zone law, which required antichoice protesters to stay away from clinic entrances. Pro-choice activists argue that these buffer zones are necessary in order to allow clinic guests safe access to abortion and reproductive-health services. Furthermore, religious institutions have fought President Obama's Affordable Care Act because they do not want to provide contraception to those who are enrolled in their insurance plans. Expansion of and access to reproductive rights were central victories of feminists in the 1960s and '70s. But the later flood of antiwomen sentiment and the political changes and discourses that were labeled the "war on women" showed how swiftly movement gains are reversed.

The shifting landscape of feminism and the push and pull of progress and inequality is the backdrop of *Finding Feminism*. The circumstances of the stalled gender revolution provide a glimpse into contemporary social inequalities, and point out the controlling forces in the structural, cultural, and interactional dimensions of women's lives. Many of these issues foreshadow the grievances that motivate the feminists in this study to organize. Given the seemingly change-resistant nature of gender inequality, it is imperative to know how feminists perceive these inequalities, what types of work feminists are doing to address these inequalities, and how they are perpetuating the feminist movement more broadly.

Concepts

Finding Feminism offers a multilevel perspective on campus feminism. I focus on individual-level feminist identities, the institutional contexts of feminism, feminist organizations, and the tactics that drive feminist mobilization on campus. Sociologists Suzanne Staggenborg and Verta Taylor write in "Whatever Happened to the Women's Movement?" that "[t]he women's movement survives to the extent that it has developed feminist 'fields' in a variety of arenas, devised tactical repertoires that have challenged numerous authorities and cultural and political codes, and permeated other social movements and public consciousness."[98] Expanding these ideas and other previous research on women's movements and social movements, I examine the contours of feminist "fields"—that is, how campus feminism is incorporated into a number of institutional settings. This addresses underdeveloped themes in social movement and gender literature—namely, how participants in a long-lasting movement find sustenance and support, and how their approaches to feminism alter and guarantee the movement's forward course. This book is arranged around two central concepts, social movement abeyance[99] and waveless feminism.

Abeyance and Waveless Feminism

AUTHOR: Do you think of yourself as a third wave feminist?

SOPHIA: I guess I don't, only because I'm constantly in this struggle—I think I see the movements of feminism as being much more fluid than the notions of these waves that we have.

AUTHOR: Do you think of yourself as a third wave feminist?

EILEEN: I feel like I'm supposed to. That's the impression that feminist scholarship has forced on me. So, like I'm a third wave feminist, but what will fourth wave feminists say about third wave feminists? And, are all of my ideas and philosophy totally aligned with third wave feminism? A lot of feminists, or women who you could categorize as third wave feminists, don't conceive of themselves or articulate themselves as third wave feminists though they may hold consistent beliefs with them.

Theoretically, some scholars have conceptualized contemporary U.S. women's movements as occurring in two or three waves. Using a global viewpoint, in a study completed in the early 1980s, Janet Chafetz, Anthony Dworkin, and Stephanie Swanson[100] divided women's movements into two waves (1850–1950 and 1960–mid-1980s) based on an analysis of forty-eight movements from around the world, including India, Latin America, the Caribbean, North and South America, Europe, Australia, and New Zealand.[101] What is widely called the first wave of U.S. feminism occurred in the late 1800s and early 1900s, culminating with women gaining suffrage with the ratification of the Nineteenth Amendment in 1920. Although feminist mobilization continued after 1920, many people consider the next major point of mobilization to be the 1960s second wave. In this second wave, during a time of major social upheaval, feminist energies focused on legal, economic, reproductive, and domestic equality, as well as issues of racism and homophobia in and outside the movement. In the mid-1990s, third wave feminism emerged with a vengeance.[102] Third wave feminists were invested in identifying with a movement of feminism that emphasized diversity of participants, ideas, and tactics.[103] Intersectionality and concentration on the complex nature of identity drove third wave feminists, who often rejected the gender binary and tenacious gender roles, embraced sexuality, and sought to include men in the movement. As Nancy Whittier argues, however, there were also many similarities between the second and third waves: "Third wave is distinguished by its attempt to engage younger women in working on many issues that are long-standing second wave feminist issues."[104] The fourth wave framework has not been theorized. It is ostensibly similar to third wave feminism, but with more emphasis on transgender issues and the value of online feminism.[105]

Although the wave framework correctly identifies time periods of heightened mobilization, gender and social movement scholars have more recently examined the different formations and strategies during nonpeak times. When movements decline, they do not always vanish. Instead, movement activities and participants may be nurtured and sustained in free spaces,[106] habitats,[107] social movement communities,[108] and abeyance structures,[109] or by cultural anchors.[110] As Polletta notes,[111] free spaces are consequential not only to the distinct roles they play in maintaining social movements but also as enduring outcomes of protest that can serve as pipelines to future mobilization.[112]

Verta Taylor first coined the term "abeyance"[113] in order to analyze the survival of social movements in hostile political climates, challenging the popularly held belief that the U.S. women's movement disappeared in the 1950s.[114] In abeyance, activists from an earlier phase of mobilization struggle to maintain the ideology and structural base of the movement in the absence of mass support. A movement in abeyance is primarily oriented toward maintaining itself rather than confronting the established order directly. Focusing on building an alternative culture, for example, is a means of survival when the political structure is not receptive to challenge. Social movement abeyance theorizes the properties of organizations and networks that contribute to movement continuity and long-term survival. Abeyance depicts a holding process by which social movements sustain themselves in a nonreceptive and antagonistic political environment. It also provides continuity from one stage of mobilization to the next. The concept of abeyance calls attention to previously unexplored phases of social movement development. It helps us understand the "carry-overs and carry-ons" between movements.[115]

One of the major outcomes of the abeyance theory has been for scholars to take a second look at the usefulness of the wave framework. The wave concept has been critiqued by many.[116] The wave framework implies that there is a monolithic feminism that may be categorized within one large swell. Although it is true that there are surges in feminist mobilization based on larger cultural and political events, the movement is more diffuse than the wave phenomenon captures, and the ebbs and flows are not reflective of the movement as a whole. For example, Becky Thompson argues that the decade that is characterized by mass mobilization of feminists (1972–1982) is the same time "scholar Chela Sandoval identifies as the period when 'ideological differences divided and helped to dissipate the movement from within.'"[117] This quotation illustrates how mobilization experiences are dependent on one's community of activists. What may be a time period of feminist flourishing for one group is the same period of difficulty and dilemma for another. We can see then how the wave framework encourages us to hear harmony where there is often dissonance and discord.

Social movement scholars know that all large-scale social movements have complex architecture and involve different ideologies, factions, communities, and grievances. Visions of feminism fueled by an allegiance to the wave framework do no service to the analysis of the feminist movement. Instead, they gloss over the interesting intricacies of a complex and multidimensional movement. The wave theory causes us to have blinders to the trajectory of movements, or to the dependence of mass surges on preexisting networks of activists who propel the movement.

Thus, in *Finding Feminism* I introduce the concept of *waveless feminism*. It emphasizes the persistence of feminism over time, the variations in feminism, and the interaction between feminism and other movements. As an extension of abeyance theory,[118] *waveless feminism* highlights how even in a downturn with seemingly low levels of feminist mobilization, we must not overlook the presence of activism, and the lively relationships between feminists and participants in other social movements. To be clear, "waveless" does not mean serene or flat. Rather, in keeping with the water analogy, waveless feminism is akin to a river. Sometimes there are rapids, sometimes it is very shallow or deep, sometimes there are rocks or other obstacles that divert its course, sometimes it is wide, at other times narrow, sometimes it overflows the banks, sometimes there is a drought. Waveless feminism captures the sentiment that "[f]eminism has been not a series of disconnected upsurges but a continuous flow."[119]

In *Finding Feminism* I ask, How have abeyance structures shifted over the years? What venues are abeyance structures for feminist movements today? Does waveless feminism reveal unexplored components of feminist activism? How are new generations of feminists invigorating feminism?

Methods

To address these questions, I gathered data at three college campuses, including the University of California–Santa Barbara, the University of Minnesota–Twin Cities, and Smith College. These campuses are not only in different regions of the country with different political contexts but also differ in terms of demographics, and their activist and feminist cultures. The University of California–Santa Barbara (UCSB) has a high percentage of Latino and Latina undergraduate students and a long history of student activism; Smith College (Smith) is an all-women's college founded on principles of feminism and women's advancement; the University of Minnesota–Twin Cities (U of M) has a close-knit community of student progressive activists who band together when antifeminists attempt to discredit or defund them. I employ a multimethod study to address the research questions, including interviews with seventy-five students of diverse backgrounds (including men and women, although women were the overwhelming majority of respondents). During interviews I probed students' experiences with inequality and engagement with feminism. I conducted participant observation in feminist organizations at each campus, during which time I learned about their grievances, tactics, and targets. Finally, a survey of students at each campus (n=1,400) paints a broad picture of respondents' perceptions of their campus climate, as well as their feminist identities, definitions of feminism, and variations in feminist identities by campus, race/ethnicity, and sexuality. See the appendix for a more in-depth discussion of methods.

Book Outline

In chapter 2, I ask, Who are these feminists and what do they believe? I analyze their feminist identities and the way they make sense of their experiences with intersectional inequalities. I focus on the grievances that motivate the feminists, and how they anticipate inequality shaping their lives in the future. This chapter also examines the perspectives of nonfeminists and those who were noncommittal towards feminism, allowing for an exploration of the feminist identity spectrum.

In chapter 3, I reveal the surprising variety of opportunities available to feminist students and student organizations, despite the sometimes antagonistic climate toward feminists. Openings for feminist activism include feminist organizing within student government, multicultural sororities, social justice–focused groups, and those college organizations with ties to national women's groups. Although literature on student activism primarily emphasizes street protest and anti-institutional organizing, the body of literature on student organizing has a theoretical blind spot pertaining to the way women's student activism varies from traditional conceptions of student organizing, which are largely based on men. My approach suggests that institutions of higher education are fertile grounds on which to educate new generations of feminists, to establish and nourish feminist consciousness and community, and to sustain a long-lasting social movement.

In chapter 4, I challenge the popular notion that feminist cohesiveness has diminished over time. I argue that there has never been a singular and unifying feminist movement. In analyzing the solidarity among feminists and the feminist collective identities on campuses and in student groups, I illustrate the contextual nature of feminism. I introduce a framework of three types of feminist organizational identities: *institutionally oriented feminism, oppositionally oriented feminism,* and *hybrid feminism.* I conclude the chapter with a discussion of solidarity and third wave feminism. Despite it being touted as the feminism for the new generation, participants in this study did not resonate with third wave feminism. This analysis supports the assertion that the feminist wave framework lacks utility, and highlights the expansive and forward-looking feminism embraced by participants.

In chapter 5, I elucidate the repertoires of contention used by the activists in this study, including the Internet, coalitions, and everyday tactics. The Internet augments existing face-to-face feminist student mobilization and is an important tactic for college student activists who have limited funds and who spend long hours online. Feminism is also incorporated in the everyday lives and interactions of college feminists. I introduce a typology of eight everyday feminisms. To illustrate the importance of coalitions, I then present examples of social justice collaborations on each campus that reached wide campus and community audiences. Feminist tactics are consistent over time in some dimensions but also change according to resource availability and technological advancements.

In the conclusion, I situate my findings within a larger picture of social movement continuity, producing a theoretical intervention applicable to all long-lasting social movements. I apply the theory of social movement abeyance[120] to the analysis in *Finding Feminism*. Social movement abeyance has been a significant theoretical framework for scholars' analysis of the persistence of long-lasting social movements. Many people argue that feminism is currently in a state of abeyance.[121] The theory emphasizes how movement participants draw inward and focus on maintaining movement culture during periods in which the movement is not supported. Notably, the abeyance theory has not been updated to reflect changes in organizing and social movement culture in the past twenty-five years. In this final chapter I systematically update the theory, arguing that during contemporary abeyance periods, social movement participants rely on *institutional, everyday*, and *online abeyance structures*.

In the methodological appendix, I discuss the methods of the study: participant observation, in-depth interviews, and a survey at three institutions of higher education. I provide participant demographics and profiles of the three campuses and the feminist organizations active on each campus.

2

Who Needs Feminism?

Gender Inequality and Feminist Identities

In the spring of 2012, the sixteen women students of Duke University Professor Rachel Seidman's Women in the Public Sphere course created a feminist campaign that caught on like wildfire. It has persisted to this day. In an effort to "fight back against these popular misconceptions surrounding the feminist movement" and the widespread questioning whether feminism is still needed, these women launched a Tumblr campaign and website "Who Needs Feminism?"[1] Since then, thousands of young women and men from across the world have submitted images of themselves holding whiteboards or paper broadcasting "I need feminism because . . ."

> I need feminism because my mother gave up her dreams for a family.[2]

> I need feminism because my adviser's only "advice" on my major was, "Are you sure you want to go into engineering? It's not exactly oriented for *females*."[3]

> I need feminism because the toxic masculinity which hurts me is a product of the same system that makes women submissive to men.[4]

> I need feminism because my mother told me to take cat calling as a compliment.[5]

The popularity of the website (hundreds of thousands of visitors from 164 countries) and the volume of submissions suggest that feminism is on the forefront of the minds of many young people.[6] It is an important site for visitors to learn about others' experiences with gender inequalities and to understand that they are not alone. Many of the recurring themes in the "I need feminism because . . ." campaign are echoed by the study participants in *Finding Feminism*. Participants spoke about incidents of sexual harassment and assault, street harassment, and a cognizance of intersectional inequalities. Participants in this study and contributors to the "I need feminism because . . ." campaign expressed a common disappointment in the overestimation of the status of women, and a desire to share why they think the movement is still relevant.

It is unsurprising that some millennial women wish to counter dominant narratives of feminism, which argue that a decline in feminism is provoked by young women's apathy and inaction. Nancy Whittier writes about this: "Second wave feminists often wrote as if there was no third wave, as if younger women remained apolitical or 'post feminist,' as if they were not part of the women's movement."[7] This dismissal of younger feminists was made clear in a recent study of 1970s-era feminists and their reflections on the movement: "[M]any respondents share emotions of dismay, anger, and sometimes even resentment about what they see as the loss of systematic or structural analysis of inequality among younger people, and in some cases, among younger feminists."[8] In the same study, sixty-year-old feminist research participant Tricia said, "I'm a bit surprised at the lack of real understanding about grassroots organizing and . . . I think it's because, in particular, young women think we have arrived. . . . I am kind of astonished by it."[9] To Tricia, young women are ignorant of the needs of social movement mobilization because they are clueless about unremitting inequalities. This is a common refrain in academic and mass market writing. In *The New Soft War on Women*, Caryl Rivers and Rosaline Barnett call it the "rose-colored glasses syndrome":

> Too many young women think that all the battles for gender equality have been fought and the future will just bring more progress. (The perception likely explains current low levels of feminist activism; as Barbara Epstein, a history professor at the University of California, Santa Cruz, says unequivocally, "There is no longer an organized feminist movement in the United States.")[10]

While Rivers and Barnett maintain that young women find progress inevitable as a natural condition, Epstein's academic viewpoint about feminism being dead implies that young women have failed to carry the torch. This narrative speaks to young women generally, as well as to young feminists, whose dedication to the movement is discounted.[11] It falls into four interrelated categories. First, it is thought that young women enjoy unprecedented access to opportunities and take for granted the rights attained through the gender revolution. As a consequence, they do not see their life experiences through the lens of inequality and fail to see the continued injustice that requires collective action.[12] Second, because young women are most likely not in the workforce full-time or do not yet have the responsibilities of running a home, it is thought that they do not yet encounter inequality, and would not identify with a movement to fight for it.[13] Third, those young women who do identify as feminist are thought to be focused only on themselves and their individual challenges and pleasures, and do not understand or mobilize against the persistence of systematic inequalities.[14] Fourth, it is assumed that young feminists are not as enraged as previous generations of feminists.[15]

This chapter asks whether the above assumptions are correct, through an examination of college students' perceptions of feminism, their experiences with inequalities, and their thoughts on women's status in the United States. To understand the boundaries between feminists and nonfeminists, I also include nonfeminist opinions about the movement. In exploring individual-level feminist identities, I ask, Who are these young feminists, and what do they believe?

Feminist Identities

Individual feminist identities potentially determine a person's orientation to the world, life choices, priorities, and participation in feminist collective action. In order to understand the individual nature of feminist identities, scholars of gender and social movements have investigated a number of factors, including rates of feminist self-identification, the nuances of embracing parts of feminism but rejecting other parts of feminism,[16] and the role of political generation, age,[17] and race.[18]

Literature on feminist self-identification helps us understand who feminists are, what they believe, and the state of the feminist movement. Scholars have shown that rates of feminist self-identification are higher and support of the feminist movement is greater than mainstream news narratives suggest, with 30–40 percent of Americans labeling themselves feminist.[19] Jason Schnittker and colleagues[20] found that men and women who were born between 1936 and 1955 have higher rates of feminist identification than younger men and women, suggesting a generational divergence. A different picture emerges when we also consider broader attitudinal changes, however. Even though young women possess increasingly progressive attitudes towards various gender roles and abortion, rates of feminist self-identification are lower than expected.[21] In a nationally representative poll of American adults conducted in 2013, 63 percent reported that they were neither a feminist nor an antifeminist, but 82 percent reported that women should be "social, political and economic equals."[22] These results capture feminist "fence-sitters,"[23] those individuals who identify neither as feminist nor as antifeminist.

Generation and age are key components of a person's knowledge of a movement and adoption of a movement identity. Whittier's theorization of political generations demonstrates that the time period in which a feminist enters a movement and her belonging to a "micro-cohort" affects her understanding of the movement, what issues are important to her, and in which organizations she participates.[24] These factors allow social movement scholars to ascertain how a long-lasting movement changes or stays the same, particularly as more established members' relationship to a movement shifts and as new members join. Another study about feminists suggests, "[T]he outcome of the various contestations regarding the meaning of feminism may be a *decreasing* consensus among younger cohorts about what identifying as a feminist implies."[25] A decreasing consensus could benefit the feminist movement in some ways, because it may help relax certain rigid boundaries that have been constructed about who feminists are and what they believe. At the same time, when it is unclear what feminism is exactly, feminist identification may be made less appealing, especially among young people grappling with their places in the movement and their experiences with inequality.

As a result of perceived incongruence between feminist ideology and identity, scholars of feminist movements find significant tension regarding an individual's adoption of a feminist identity. This "I'm not a feminist, but" phenomenon has been documented by a number of scholars.[26] They have found that women frequently expressed feminist sentiments immediately after denying a feminist identity; for example, "I'm not a feminist, but I support increased accessibility to reproductive health services" or "I'm not a feminist, but I work to eradicate sexism in whatever way I can." Reasons for choosing not to identify as a feminist run the gamut, such as the "feminist qualifier," in which women separate themselves from any "sanctions that they may perceive will result in associating themselves with feminism."[27] Long-standing negative stereotypes of feminists have been documented as important factors in hesitancy to identify as a feminist, with women feeling that there may be a social cost to identifying as feminist.[28] Even for those feminists who are involved in feminist organizations and communities, feminist identities are still not always straightforward. In Cheryl Hercus's examination[29] of Australian women's movement participants, for example, she found that these women were anxious about their own feminist identities, most notably the feminists' desire for both acceptance by the group and individual autonomy.

An individual's relationship to the movement has been found to vary by racial identity as well. Feminist politicization has been called a process or "click" moment for White women, who may learn about oppression at school or in women's groups, or encounter it in the workforce.[30] In contrast, because of deeply engrained racism and sexism, African American women and other women of color may experience oppression and racism their entire lives. Thus, they do not have a sudden realization of the pervasiveness of social injustice. Rather, it has always been a part of their lives.[31] Some have argued that the interaction between race and gender causes women to have "divided loyalties" between gender- or race-based movements.[32] However, research has found that Black women support feminist principles more than White women,[33] and that Latina women have greater levels of feminist identity development than White women.[34] This suggests that experiences with inequality—racial, gender, and otherwise—prime individuals to develop feminist consciousness and identities.

At the same time, we also know that an individual embracing a feminist identity is not the be-all and end-all of the movement. Boundaries between feminists and nonfeminists are not as important as they once were for two primary reasons, according to Whittier: "[M]any women I interviewed said that they are less likely to form negative impressions of people who do not identify publicly as feminists" and "[M]any long-time feminists reported that they are less likely to see themselves as part of a common group with someone simply because she calls herself a feminist."[35] Schnittker and colleagues underscored the complexities and multiple ways feminism is understood: "Because 'feminist' is premised on heterogeneous understandings of what 'feminism' is, the identity can be connected to manifold political agendas."[36] Indeed, White feminists and feminists of color have multiple grievances about war, the environment, and human rights issues, depending on their circumstances and social locations.[37] Given that feminism does not have one clear definition or political agenda, a continuum of feminist identities may make more sense than a binary.[38]

Although gender and social movement scholars have analyzed several dimensions of feminist movements and identities, the connection between young people's experiences with inequalities and their adoption or rejection of feminism is less understood. There is substantial popular attention to young people's experiences with inequality. You can walk into any bookstore and find a number of books about young people's opinions about feminism.[39] But, there is little empirical attention to the topic. Research by social psychologists helps us understand young people's experiences with inequalities more generally. For example, the high expectations and ambitions of young people are found to not always align with the realities of the social-structural constraints they will experience after college.[40] Shaped by culture and institutions, the cleavages between perceived strengths and constraints, or "biased self-assessments,"[41] are particularly detrimental to women's career paths, and may become most salient after women enter the labor market following graduation.[42] This undoubtedly is a component of curtailing involvement in feminist mobilization or adoption of feminist identities, because orientation towards feminism requires the recognition of inequality—oftentimes experienced in one's personal or work life. This also supports the portrayal of young people as not recognizing the inequalities they face. For scholars of the women's movement, the "lack of experience of overt discrimination and/or the resources to launch a feminist struggle" means that feminism is the "province of old (or middle-aged) women."[43] It may also mean that student feminism is unique, one that links what students learn in the classroom to what they observe in their own lives.

Women's Status: Not So Great

One criticism about millennial feminists is that they are unaware of the systematic and persistent inequalities that women experience.[44] To address this, I asked all participants their perceptions of women's status in the United States. Most feminist participants in this research agreed about the inequalities women face, unsurprisingly, although their answers in some way diverge from previous findings about feminists. Some fence-sitters and nonfeminists agreed with feminists about the status of women, but their subsequent thinking about the need for change was different.

Feminist participants' many comments about women's poor status highlighted the intersectional characteristics of inequality. U of M student Lauren simply called women's status "crap": "[W]e don't have choices over our body, over our health, White women are paid 70 cents to a dollar, it goes down for women that are not White." For Lauren, reproductive health, the wage gap, and racism and sexism was simple shorthand for the poor position of women in the United States. Brooke, also a U of M student, shared Lauren's negative feelings about women's status in the United States, but explained it with a greater emphasis on intersectionality:

> [W]omen's status is by no means any one thing. I think that it is incredibly affected by other issues like class, race, sexuality and ability; all these things shape what women's status is. . . . I know that if you look on a broad scale the opportunities available to women and the structural barriers are huge, I think, to varying degrees depending on all those other factors.

Brooke's knowledge about structural and intersectional inequalities was clear: women's status "does not mean one thing." Also stressing intersectionality, but adding gender identity and immigrant status,

Smith student Vivica said, "Well, I know it depends on race and class, and if they consider themselves cis gender or transgender. It seems like White women are more able to move into higher positions. . . . Immigrant women do most of the work." In these cases, feminist respondents provided a clear picture of their knowledge about inequality. The major inequalities feminist study participants identified as indicators of women's poor status were the wage gap, lack of reproductive justice, and lack of women's representation in the media. This is fitting given that these issues get a lot of attention in feminist media, and are important pieces of evidence supporting the existence of the stalled gender revolution.

Although feminist study participants themselves were well versed in intersectional inequality, one of the most common themes about women's status was that the inequalities are hidden. Participants described a disjuncture between metanarratives about equality and the on-the-ground experiences of women. UCSB student Cherrise pointed out the media's role in creating this discord: "In the media, you see the U.S. as a powerful place to be a woman. But when you are actually here, and you live here, you realize that you don't have that many privileges or rights. Especially as an African American woman." To Cherrise, it is clear that there is an inconsistency between messages about being a woman in the United States and her everyday life as a Black woman. In contrast, Smith student Frances's comment about hidden inequalities reflects her White privilege: "I think women are still very much controlled by structures, it's sort of hidden underneath things. I think a lot of women are unaware of their own inequalities, just because they are swept under the rug, and aren't noticed by men and women. Unless you are in an environment like Smith where you are analyzing that all the time." Although Frances herself is cognizant that women are "controlled by structures," her perception of inequality echoes the arguments that many women do not realize their subordinate position. She sets herself apart from that idea, however, by arguing that Smith students are in a context in which inequality is a topic of everyday conversations. U of M student Sophia concurred with the invisibility of gender inequality:

> I think that a lot of things are overlooked. I think that there's not as much of
> a consciousness, especially among women, of the problematic nature of op-

pression and all the forms that that takes, that there could be. I wish there was more of a consciousness around that, especially when I look at things like rape culture. I think that says huge things about the status of women within the United States that many women don't have a solid understanding of the ways in which that is a demonstration of how women have been oppressed and of how there is an imbalance in the system of power.

In some senses, Frances's and Sophia's observations of inequalities confirm the speculation that women are not aware of their own positions; although they themselves recognize inequalities, they feel as though other women do not see them to the same degree.

Smith student Sam believes inequality is so engrained in our everyday lives that we do not always notice it. She said,

> I think women are pushed into things they don't want to do, but a lot of times they don't see it. My friend has a boyfriend, and she views it as a burden to him to tell him her emotions. It's this underlying thing where the woman doesn't want to bother the man and she's afraid he'll reject her. A lot of women don't want to do something to upset the guy, but that doesn't prevent the guy from doing really messed up things to the woman. And that's what upsets me. Why don't you view yourself as equal. *If you were to ask them, do you think women are equal to men, they'll say of course, but in their daily life they don't live it. And that's what kills me inside.* (emphasis added)

This disconnect between the perceived existence of gender equality and everyday sexism experienced by her friend was upsetting to Sam, as is evident in her expressive description above. To her, this undercurrent of sexism was less visible not because we do not understand it but because it occurs in a routine, taken-for-granted, everyday way.

While some participants pointed to the media and interactional inequality as indicators of women's low status in the United States, Smith student Bea used the example of laws to support her point that there is a disconnect:

> I think that people don't realize how much stigma there still is against women because the problem is that we have laws that say that you can't

discriminate and people think that's good enough. They say, "Well we have these laws, women are doing just as well, there's 50% of women in med school, 50% are women in law school." So people want to say, "Okay, we're done. Feminist movement: it's over."

Bea concluded, "[P]eople don't realize that just because we're an advanced country they think that we don't have these problems when we absolutely do and they're worse because we ignore them." In her description, Bea repeated the often-used statistic about women and men's educational parity. Although this example typically buttresses arguments that we have achieved gender equality, Bea used it to show the rifts between perceived equality and reality.

Some fence-sitter and nonfeminist participants too noted that women in the United States have made noteworthy progress. Yet despite this, they also believed that women's status is not high. In what was a familiar theme, UCSB student and fence-sitter Mario said, "Women have gotten a lot of rights. Through the law we're equal, and the women who have come before me have fought so hard for that. In a way we have progressed, and we're coming up to par with equality of men. But the thing is, there is still so much to do." Similarly, fellow UCSB fence-sitter Bridget said, "[W]e've made progress, but it isn't where it should be." Those participants in this study who would not identify as feminist said that overall they thought women's status was good. Participants like UCSB student Lindsay said,

I would say . . . it's not necessarily as bad and as dire for everybody than all the academic journals and statistics may want to say. I think in the United States at least for the most part, women have a pretty good standing. I think there are lots of places in the rest of the world where the women are subjugated and kept under male control, and those countries have a lot more work to do.

Or Jessie, a U of M respondent said, "I always think of in comparison to others—I'd say very, very well off. I feel like it's acceptable to have women in leadership jobs and I feel like it's very, very well off here." Those respondents who do not believe gender inequality is a serious concern typically compared women's status in the United States to their status in other parts of the world, while the fence-sitters acknowledged both how far women have come in the United States and how much more work needs to be done.

Gender Inequality: Yes, But . . .

Since rates of feminism are not what we expect given such persistent inequalities,[45] it has been argued that young women are less likely to identify as feminist than older women because they have not yet experienced the inequalities they will probably face as post-college adults.[46] Others have declared millennials or younger generations to be out of touch or only focused on themselves.[47]

Regardless of their school and background, feminist and fence-sitter study participants were aware and observant of the structural and interactional inequalities that molded their young lives at home, at school, and in relationships. Feminist study participants reported experiencing gender inequality in their families from a young age. UCSB student and woman of color Diana said, "Growing up it was always girls belong in the kitchen, boys you can play. . . . Boys should not be washing dishes. From the get-go, my family upbringing was very cultural, machisto in a sense, very patriarchal. I know I challenged it all the time, and it usually got me in trouble." Although UCSB student Lisa recognized similar patterns, she was not as much of a fighter as Diana:

> I've always noticed how, in our family at least, the girls are always the ones who have to help the mom do the cooking, do the cleaning. Then the guys, my brothers, are always just sitting there and it always just frustrated me. That was always the norm. My mom wouldn't even realize that's unfair. It's interesting because she wants me to get out there and experience everything and build a career but then, at the same time, when we grew up it was always really apparent what the gender roles were.

Lisa was not the only respondent who experienced conflict between her mother's simultaneous modeling of the domestic gendered division of labor and her expansive hopes for her daughter's future. Smith student Eileen experienced a similar tension in that she was in many ways encouraged to be ambitious and goal oriented by her mother and father, but simultaneously experienced traditional gendering at home. Eileen spoke of how her parents taught her to be ambitious and "never taught me to limit myself," but at the same time,

> Increasingly I see the way that my father has these expectations for us because we're his daughters that he doesn't have for his son. The expectation that marriage should be on my radar, that I should be looking for someone to settle down with, even though I'm twenty. Kind of the more family-based goals that he thinks I should have but I don't.

To some participants, this push and pull was indicative of their personal experiences with inequality. This is evidence of participants' encountering the stalled gender revolution: they experience the tension between advances in gender equality and simultaneous continued inequality. Women and girls are told that the world is their oyster, yet at the same time, traditional gender roles in the home remain stagnant and loom large.

Participants of color shared long and detailed stories of the intersectional inequalities that were immutable parts of their lives. Diana, a UCSB student, said she noticed inequality in her upbringing: "I come from a predominantly Latino community, so in terms of racism, I don't think I felt it within my peers, but I would say maybe in terms of my school. It was low-income, it was one of the east LA schools, so there was a lot of systemic discrimination, lack of books, classes were crowded." Diana came to identify as a feminist at a young age, and was aware of how her individual life was shaped by broader structural forces. Similarly, Smith student Vivica spoke about growing up without many resources: "I mean, just the fact that I grew up in public housing, and I've read it, how Black people aren't allowed to live in the suburbs, and they are always pushed into these areas, and redlined them. And this continual lack of wealth building." Also addressing intersectional inequalities, UCSB student Ninjabi said of the anti-Muslim sentiments she's experienced, "I've been called Taliban. I think I've received more hatred because I'm a Muslim than because I'm a woman. But I think the combination is important, uh, yea. Sigh." When I asked about gender inequalities, respondents of color inevitably described the interaction of racial, gender, and class inequalities. In agreement with previous research, women of color reported perceiving more structural inequalities in their lives from a young age.[48]

Participants in this study also began noticing interactional gender inequality in high school—in the form of boys dominating the classroom and taking up more space than girls. UCSB student Camille said, "In classrooms, throughout my life I've always loved school. But males dominate every time. The class discussion or just putting forth ideas, and they are always validated, even by the women in the class. I've never realized it until high school, and I was the only female talking. I was perceived as aggressive, maybe masculine." On the other side of the spectrum, UCSB student Mary Ann was soft spoken and found that in high school she was doted on. She began to realize that women are underestimated and that less is expected of them:

> [W]hen I was in high school, I was really naïve and I didn't get the jokes, and they would be like, oh, you're so cute. But if one of the guys didn't get it, it would be like sissy or man up. I'm the woman, so I'm not expected to get the joke. And that's not okay, because you're expecting less of me. And that's what guys do.

For both Camille and Mary Ann, although for different reasons, their experiences in school led them to conclude that boys' experiences and voices were valued more than those of girls.

Despite my not asking the specific question, most participants in this study reported feeling as though little is expected of them because they are women. At each campus, feminist and fence-sitter respondents said that they feel, in different ways, as though men of all ages look at women as inferior. UCSB student Elsa experienced this at work, and noted its relationship to a larger historical trajectory of inequality: "In some cases I feel that people do expect less from me, especially at work. I work for an upper-class male, and he doesn't expect me to know much. . . . But if you assume that lower expectation, it's kind of submitting to a larger historical hierarchy of who's going to be subordinate and who's going to be dominant." Despite feeling this inferiority, Elsa was resolved not to let it make her feel as though she was less capable than a man. In the personal realm, Liz, a Smith student, shared her emotional experience of feeling as though a man devalued her:

It [feeling as though less is expected of her because she is a woman] even happens in relationships, like dating someone who is at a prestigious school. We're on the same track and doing the same thing, but that becomes a problem. It is okay for the man to do those things, but the minute you're on the same level, it becomes a problem for them. I've experienced that. Like you're not supposed to be doing as much as I'm doing, or more. Like I'm [the man] supposed to be the star in the relationship.

Liz, a bright and motivated person with high aspirations, did not think she was valued. It was clear that she was expected to downgrade her accomplishments and goals to make room for her boyfriend to be "the star." UCSB student Lola made the more general observation that in social interactions with men, if "I say something that's really interesting, they would be taken aback, and they'll be like, 'oh, I didn't know you knew that.'" Smith student Lily agreed: "When I'm interacting with men, they don't think I'm as smart as them or as determined as them, especially I'm not as competent as them, that's the big one, or I don't have the same skill set. I kind of have to be in their face to make them completely aware of my strengths and my own talents." Like Lily, U of M student Sam tried to contradict these sexist assumptions: "[I]n general society doesn't think that women can do certain things, and that's probably why I like being so handy, I like the fact that I as a woman can fix a lot of things that a guy maybe can't figure out how to fix. And it's my way to one-up their notions of what a woman can do." Although I was surprised initially at the number of ways in which participants reported experiencing feeling devalued in their social and work interactions with men, it became clear that to some other participants this experience was also a motivator to dismantle sexist categorization.

Participants in this study who worked part- or full-time to help pay for college tuition and expenses, and/or to send money to their families, had ample opportunities to experience sexism. Elsa, a UCSB student who worked forty to sixty hours a week as a caretaker, came to our interview surprisingly bright-eyed despite coming directly from an overnight shift. Clutching a paper cup of coffee, she looked at me and said,

There's not one day where I don't get discriminated against because of my gender. One, by me standing up for myself. By me being independent, by me, uh, advocating, you know, or pointing out gender inequality within my workplace, amongst my circle of friends, womanizing, degrading of women, I do speak up about it. I do in some ways restrict myself, as far as working with my clients, because my job isn't to educate them . . . and if I piss them off, then I probably would have a reduction in hours and I can't afford to do that. In my daily life, I write about it, I paint about it, I express it in my daily actions. Through this, I think I also influence my peers to think in the same way, and to be aware of it.

Elsa realized that although she was very angry about experiencing such inequalities, her paycheck relied on her not speaking up when her clients made sexist or racist comments. Perhaps this silencing added fuel to her fire. In her off time she found multiple avenues through which to express her dissatisfaction. Also employed outside of school, UCSB student Lola described being discriminated against because of her gender and sexually harassed while employed at a retail store. On these occasions, Lola said, "I'll look 'em in the eye and say knock it off, and they do." UCSB student Summer also said she experienced gender inequality in her summer employment. After speaking to a male colleague, she learned that she was paid less than her male coworkers who had the same qualifications and were doing the same job.

Other searing examples were when respondents reported incidents of street harassment as evidence of gender inequality. Smith student Gabriella felt that street harassment was not so bad in the broader scheme of inequality, while her comments illustrate the ubiquity of it: "I've been really lucky I think that the most discrimination or sexism I experience is walking down the street and sexual harassment. It still makes me angry, but understanding expectations about masculinity and why that happens was helpful in me not hating all men [laughs]. Because you can't walk down the street without getting catcalled." Shane, a queer woman from the U of M, was also harassed on the streets. In contrast to Gabriella, Shane attributed her harassment to her not having a conventionally feminine appearance. She said, "People see my body as a threat to [their] perceived notion of gender in society, and are going to react in a hostile atmosphere. Like, I was walking down the street, it was dusk, and I was feeling really good about my life, and these people drove by and yelled 'fucking fag!' and I was like, really?" Shane constantly felt as though her non–gender conformity made her an object for street harassment. Smith student Lily said she had a "million examples" of experiencing gender inequality. The most detailed description she gave, however, was of street harassment:

> The one that comes to mind the quickest to me is just walking down the street and have people in cars randomly shout things at me, because of something I'm wearing. That frustrates me to no end. I don't know why, but I have to stick up for myself and say something. I hope that if some-one shouts something that they'll be stopped at a red light, and if they do, I can give them a piece of my mind.

Smith respondent Anne W. called street harassment "socially ac-cepted" discrimination. All of these participants were angered by the normativity of catcalling. Being catcalled was an expected part of re-spondents' everyday lives and evidence of sexism. It was anger inducing and showed study participants how society devalues women.

Recent examples show that the frustrations with the omnipresence of street harassment are not unique to this dataset. They are expressed in society more broadly—for example, the hashtag #FirstHarassed emerged on Twitter in May 2015 (authored by @karynitha), and its popularity spread rapidly. The tweets were a powerful and popular reminder for women and girls to share their earliest encounters with street harass-ment. Other grassroots and national organizations such as anti–street harassment groups Stop Telling Women to Smile and Hollaback! con-firm that these sorts of interactional inequalities are a major concern among young feminists in the United States.

It is not astonishing that individuals who identified as feminist ex-pressed chagrin and consternation with gender inequality, but many of their experiences and the emotional nature with which they recounted these experiences were surprising. Feminist participants felt that sexism was an expected part of their existence. In school, on the streets, and in their familial and romantic relationships, sexism was part of the fabric of their everyday lives.

When I asked fence-sitter and nonfeminist participants whether they experienced gender inequality or not, a common refrain, "I haven't expe-rienced gender inequality, but . . . ," preceded their examples that could be described as gender inequality. For example, Jessie, a fence-sitter student at the U of M, said she had not experienced gender inequality, but then expressed frustration that "I can't go running on this nice trail behind my house alone because the parks department said that men hide in the bushes." As a follow-up I asked if she ran after dark, and she said a posted sign warned women not to go on the trail at any time of the day or night. She was annoyed with this, but did not relate it to power differences or inequality between men and women. Kendra, also a U of M student, expressed negative feelings towards feminists and thought that feminists get special treatment. The following exchange illustrates the "I haven't experienced gender inequality, but . . ." phenomenon:

> AUTHOR: Can you recall any personal experiences with gender inequality or any other inequalities?
>
> KENDRA: I guess there's little every day-to-day things. When I hang out at my boyfriend's house sometimes his roommates are just like, "Oh woman, go make me a sandwich" and stuff. I know they're kidding but they obviously say that for a reason. Sometimes in classes I feel like guys tend to talk over girls or they are always the first one to jump up and do the class activity or raise their hand and make sure their word is out there and their voice is heard. Where I just more sit back and let them because I don't really care, if you have that strong of an opinion and you want to talk, go ahead! I don't really care. But nothing major. I guess if you're running along Frat Row then some guys yell things at you, it's kind of like, "Ok, grow up." *But I wouldn't really call it inequality because to me they just look like bigger fools than I do so they're probably lesser, in that sense, than I am.* (emphasis added)

Kendra has certainly noticed instances when she has been treated poorly because she is a woman, and is able to rattle off examples from her day-to-day life with her boyfriend's roommates, in school, and on the street. But, as someone who is invested in not being a feminist, she would ascribe this not to any sort of inequality but rather to the immaturity of boys and men. Fence-sitters and nonfeminists observed the same sorts of phenomena as feminists—street harassment, not being safe in public, women being judged with harsher standards than men—although to some degree, as they anticipated this inequality, it was not a politicizing moment. This speaks to the sexist cultural context, in the sense that both feminists and nonfeminists expected either gender inequality or to be treated differently than men.

Unbounded Opportunities for Women?

The "rose-colored glasses syndrome," meaning that "too many young women think all the battles for gender equality have been fought,"[49] is a dominant narrative among feminists of older generations.[50] Despite literature demonstrating that young women are aware of inequalities[51] and are mobilizing against them,[52] the assertion that young feminists and young women more generally are out of touch with the reality of gender inequality is commonplace. In order to ascertain their feelings and views towards feminism, I evaluated whether survey and interview study participants felt they would have any barriers in achieving their goals in life. All but eight of the seventy-five interview participants, feminists and nonfeminists, expected to experience structural inequalities. In the survey, over 65 percent of study participants agreed or strongly agreed that "in the future, I am concerned that gender inequality will influence my career" and "in the future, I am concerned that gender inequality will influence my personal life." These questions captured participants' feelings about the stalled gender revolution—and what they think about the opportunities and challenges in their lives.

Consistent with the evidence supporting the stalled gender revolution, a number of feminist students expected difficulties balancing their careers and personal lives. Smith student Maddelena was just as assured about her future career as she was worried that she would have to give up her career for her family: "I know that's the nature of things, to sacrifice career for family." She continued,

> I think it's going to be hard to find the family/career balance. I don't know what's looked down on more now, a woman who gives up her career to have a family, or if a woman gives up someone she loves for a career. I don't know if it's one or the other, and maybe there are ways to do both, but I don't know if it's selfish to choose your career over another person. But I definitely think that's the stigma and I just don't, I don't know what's going to happen there, but I see it as a problem.

Maddelena was in many ways resigned to the fact that she would have to change her career in some way if she wanted a fulfilling personal life. Sylvia, a Smith student, worried about her employers seeing her in a negative light because she was a woman: "There's always that anxiety in the back of my head, when I am older . . . that employers will see me as more disposable in a way. Maybe they'll be thinking, soon she'll be going on maternity leave." This anxiety was less about home life and more about discrimination on the part of her employer. UCSB student Isabela concurred, and was worried about how getting master's and doctoral degrees would fit in with her plans for a family: "Yes, I want kids, and I want a family, and I think it's like, when do I have kids, when do I have a family, how is the responsibility going to come about? As a mom, you have to be there a good amount of time." Isabela was worried about managing the responsibility of a home and how it would fit into work. Eileen, a Smith student, told me in great detail about an emotional conversation with her mother. To this day, her description of this interaction is etched in my mind:

> I remember once I was driving in the car with her, and I was probably like fifteen or sixteen, and starting to think about college and what I wanted to do with my life and becoming more aware that my mom was a stay-at-home mom. . . . I just asked her one day in the car if she was happy with her life, I just asked her point blank.

Although her mother said she was happy to be a mother, she also told Eileen that she "regretted not having more to show for herself." Eileen sensed with sadness that her mother was sorry that "she didn't have a career, or a passion, she was just so consumed with being a wife for so many years." In that moment, Eileen "became very resolved to not . . . make a choice [like this], [to not have to] talk to my children and not be able to say that there was something I really thought was missing from my life." Even though most of the participants in this project were single and child-free, on the basis of their experiences with their families and their observations of the world around them, they had anxieties about how to live a fulfilling and balanced life. Although it is yet to be seen whether these women will indeed alter their careers, research on adults who were recently married or engaged found that women were likely to change their careers or downshift their professional lives in anticipation of the difficulties of balancing family and work, in turn fueling gender inequality.[53]

The wage gap, which has received a lot of publicity in terms of the stalled gender revolution, was a familiar concept to feminists and non-feminists alike. Christina, a Smith student, talked about the wage gap:

> Once I get a job, income disparities and the wage gap is something that really concerns me. I know at [large university name redacted] in the political science department, women weren't getting as much as men, and they had to sue the school, to get their retroactive wages . . . and that really worries me. Men are more likely to negotiate wages, so I have to keep that in mind, to negotiate, and barter, but even if I do that, I still think I'll be paid less than a man.

UCSB student Isabela said, "[W]omen are more likely to get a lower salary than men, and that pisses me off, like I'll work hard for my MA or PhD!" In some ways, these respondents are resigned to the fact that they will not be as well paid as their male colleagues. They were angry and anxious about it but also knew that, with the continued wage gap and the stalled gender revolution, it was an inescapable circumstance.

More generally than the wage gap, participants in this study were very worried about finances and the economy. They were nervous about paying for school, about making money, about being in debt, and about not having the cultural capital of a good school to make connections to get a job. UCSB student Janet, a feminist who lives in a co-op and spoke with me quite a lot about global inequalities, had recently been accepted at Berkeley and the University of Chicago for graduate school:

> I actually really wanted to go to Berkeley and the University of Chicago, but couldn't afford it, and didn't want to take out a hundred thousand dollar loan; I didn't want to put myself in the position where I couldn't ever buy a house. I think I'm automatically cut off from economic resources . . . [B]etter schools lead to better jobs.

In addition to being knowledgeable about feminism and interrelated inequalities, Janet knew that she would be missing out because of her lack of financial resources. UCSB student Elsa said, "The biggest barrier would be financial" and worried about getting grants and a job. Smith participant Sylvia had more immediate concerns about her family: "I do worry financially. My father works overtime, almost every other night, and growing up I would only see him on Sundays. He would leave for work at 6:00 a.m. and come home around midnight. . . . I worry about his health, and now that he's getting older, and if something happened, I don't know how we'd survive." Like Sylvia, UCSB student Cherisse is worried about her family. She tried to be upbeat and positive, but her stress was evident. She said, "It's not easy. Family barriers, that's a big barrier, 'cause my family members need financial assistance," and later she told me that she barely got by as a student, but still paid her mother's bills.

Not conforming to conventional gender expectations was a shared apprehension about their futures. Shane, the U of M student who was street harassed because of her non-gender-conforming attire, thinks this will be a barrier in her life.

> Yes, I want to work with youth, but most people will question my body, and my gender norms. Already interviewing for jobs . . . my resume looked good, but after I went to an interview in slacks and button ups, they were like "oh." There's some conservatism, especially when it comes to youth. . . . Obviously, I could grow my hair out, dress more feminine and cover my tattoos, but I don't want to.

Transgender male Smith student Rueben worries about his gender appearance:

> I'm afraid of being denied housing, jobs, and love, because of my gender identity and sexual identity. It can be confused and misunderstood. It's really weird to think that people have seen me as a straight guy . . . and so . . . I might be booted from a queer community because I'm not lesbian or gay anymore.

Those who did not conform to stereotypical gender displays were fearful of how their appearance would affect their work and personal lives. Overall, I did not find evidence supporting the existence of the "rose-colored glasses syndrome," and participants from a variety of racial and socioeconomic backgrounds easily reported the inequalities and power hierarchies they had experienced and expected to experience.

Feminism: Activism, Inclusivity, Intersectionality

Participants' feminism was shaped by their experiences with inequality, their perceptions of women's status in the United States, and the barriers they expected to face in their lives. What did feminism mean to the participants in this study? Where did feminists learn about the movement? How was it related to their grievances? Much of participants' feminist identities was consistent with previous versions of feminism.[54] In the survey, the people and activities that were most influential in inspiring a self-identification as a feminist were mothers, friends, and websites or nonschool reading. Overall, self-identified feminist participants described feminism as a concern for women's rights, equality between men and women, and an emphasis on the intersectional nature of oppression. Their responses were on a spectrum from very detailed descriptions to more general comments about the movement. For example, Smith student Eileen said simply that feminists strive for women to be "treated equally both by individuals and structurally by law and policy." U of M student Maxine said passionately that feminism is a "constant vigilance to protect and defend the rights of women from the history and current manifestations of patriarchy." UCSB student Anselmo, along with a number of other participants in this study, spoke generally of feminism as a movement that is concerned with equality between men and women. These themes were similarly reflected in the survey, in which the most common definitions of feminism included the terms "gender equality," "activism," "social/legal rights and equality," and "intersectionality."

Feminist study participants not only spoke of their personal thoughts about feminism but also emphasized mobilization around gender inequality and injustice in general. U of M student Zan said, "[M]y feminist identification is very interrelated to my activist identification. . . . [I]t's not *just* [emphasis added] aligning with political views of feminism." She continued: "People who identify as feminist are oftentimes the people who are more vocal and open about their beliefs, and they're really passionate about that, otherwise they wouldn't have that identification that people disagree with." In this respect, Zan feels that it is the responsibility of feminists to point out incidents of inequality and injustice. Similarly, Smith student Liz said feminism must include speaking and being active: feminism is "taking a stand against gender roles and gender inequality, and not only believing that it's wrong but also speaking about it and being active." UCSB student Lola said that feminists are

> opinionated in a positive way. Having their voices be heard. Straightforward. If there's an issue, or discrimination, it would be taken care of. I feel that being feminist means that you are outspoken. And if something is keeping you back, you'll do anything to fight it. You are more aware of others around you, you notice inequalities between men and women, but inequalities in general.

A central feature of many of these participants' feminism was action or activism, which meant speaking out when they encountered interactional inequality and collectively organizing around feminist grievances. One criticism mounted against young feminists is that an individual focus comes at the expense of perpetuating a broader movement, so it was noteworthy that so many emphasized acting upon their feminism.

Participants in this study also spoke of the expansive features of the feminist movement. Regardless of their race, class, or sexuality identities, they carefully included considerations of differences in race, class, and sexuality in their descriptions of feminism. Said Smith student Liz, "[N]ot everyone, not every woman experiences the same types of problems," which to her meant that women practice different types of feminism. Smith student Anna P. said, "Feminism is . . . not only searching for oppression but acknowledging it exists because you are a woman. And then to take that further, not just being a woman, but looking at class and race, and how that intertwines with gender, and also acknowledging your privilege as a White woman." Anna P. highlighted that although White women are oppressed because they are women, they also have racial privilege, which is denied to other women. Participants also emphasized the nonmonolithic nature of feminism. Smith student Vivica simply said, "Not assuming that one feminism is the same for everyone else." Bette said, "I feel like the word 'feminism' is different for everybody. . . . On one hand, I feel that I should be about lesbian rights, but for me, race and class issues are more important." After speaking about the patriarchy, U of M student Maxine said that feminism is "different for everyone." To Vivica, Bette, and Maxine, the broad reach of the movement was assumed and not particularly noteworthy. UCSB student Anselmo stopped himself after he began to define feminism:

> A caveat that needs to be added . . . there are different interpretations of feminism, and people use "feminism" differently, there's a third world feminist critique of Euro-American feminism as a justification of cultural imperialism, a Middle Eastern critique of Western feminism, is, for example, people using the idea that Muslim women are slaves to their husbands as a justification for war.

Anselmo here carefully points out how one person's feminism is another person's oppression, introducing power and privilege into the conversation about intersectionality. This is an acknowledgment of the contextual nature of feminism, and of its direct relationship to an individual's interests and worldview.

Race, Sexuality, and Gender and Feminist Identity

Race

In the survey data there was little difference in feminist identity whether the respondent identified as White or of color. Thirty-four percent of the respondents identified as persons of color. In contrast, although many interview participants, both White and of color, embraced dynamic and intersectional versions of feminism, women of color at all campuses also modified their feminism. Smith student Bette said, "I think feminism is different for people depending on their social position. White feminism is different from Black feminism and if you take class into account, your ideas of feminism are going to change. I guess I consider myself a feminist." Chicana UCSB student Diana said that she embraced feminism at a young age, but "ever since, I've been finding my own place within the feminist movement. 'Feminist' is still accompanied by other words, whether it's a 'Salvadorian feminist' or a 'Mexican feminist,' or 'Chicana feminist' or 'third world feminist.' I've always used those words." Diana was not hesitant to identify as a feminist, and was confident and straightforward about describing feminism. However, when I probed further, she also felt the need to modify her feminism. UCSB student Ninjabi said that although she was a feminist, "I think there are different types of feminism, and I typically disagree with Western feminism, because I feel like it is so limited and its analysis is so narrow." Although these women ultimately identified as feminist, their identifications included other identities such as race and ethnicity.

In other ways, women of color, similarly to White women, as cited in previous research, hesitated to identify as feminist because of the high standards and expectations associated with feminism.[55] Smith student Vivica, a working-class Black heterosexual woman, said that she read numerous feminist blogs, specifically by Native American and Latina feminists, and is interested in womanism and feminism. She provided a detailed description of womanism: "The liberation of women of color is the liberation of everyone else. Everything rests on them, because without them, the whole system couldn't exist." But when I asked if she identified as a womanist she said, "I guess, I don't know. I don't think I could call myself that until I take a feminist course, and cite different cases. I don't think I'm well read enough to say what I am." Black UCSB student Summer, a feminist studies student, said that she didn't think she earned the label "feminist" because she listened to gangster rap with sexist lyrics.

> I feel like there's still music that I'm listening to, like say that I'm at a party, like I'll dance to it, and I won't even think about it. And I'll even listen to it at my house, and I'm like, this is so disrespectful . . . like, it goes against how I really feel or what I feel is right. I feel like I'm just struggling with being a feminist.

In contrast, UCSB student Camille spoke at length about her Armenian heritage and the tensions she felt embracing the identity "woman of color." When I asked her whether she identified as a feminist, she said,

> Yes. I think our generation is actually embracing this more. Women of color are embracing it more as it becomes more inclusive. It's talking about intersections. I don't think any other framework is talking about

intersections. I think that's why feminism is going to be successful. That's what our generation is going to add to it, you know, it's not about women, it's about gender, and class and race, and nationality and ability. So many identities. That's what I love!

In this description, Camille added nationality and ability to the description of feminism and intersectionality. Her excitement and optimism about feminism was palpable. Despite the fact that women of color frequently modified their feminism, most of them used the word "intersectional" to explain their feminism and felt positively about the overlap between feminism and intersectionality.

Sexuality and Gender

Lesbians have historically played a major role in perpetuating feminist organizations and nurturing feminist culture.[56] Survey data indicate that gay/lesbian, bisexual, and queer study participants were more likely to identify as feminist than heterosexual students. Those survey respondents who identified as queer were the most likely of all participants to identify as feminist. This makes sense, in that queer theorists stress social change and emancipatory politics, particularly in challenging heteronormativity and gender binaries.[57] Queer theorists' and queer activists' emphasis on intersectionality and coalitions also closely match the feminist ideologies of the students in this research.[58]

Feminists were motivated by their interest in queer issues. White, lower-middle-class queer U of M woman Shane called herself a queer feminist: "But I feel like a feminist, because I'm a big promoter of equality. I like this new wave of feminism, that instead of saying women's equality, it's gender equality. And I also like this idea of breaking away from gender norms, which is really problematic." Shane was involved in the queer student organization as well, and throughout our interviews underscored the limitations of the gender binary. Michele described Smith students as "definitely geared to LGBTQ issues, a lot of the popular events on campus are the ones that focus on that issue. This is a huge issue here, I guess because it's more accepting of LGBTQ people, to find themselves. I think that definitely makes a difference in the atmosphere or personality of Smith." Smith student Anne W., who identified as queer and was in a relationship with a transgender man, created a boundary between feminist and queer life on campus: "I tend to be in a minority that's more interested in the feminist life on campus, and I think the queer life tends to dominate." In some ways, Anne W. found that queer topics had surpassed feminist topics in popularity at Smith, particularly in terms of interest in transgender issues. Most participants did not make such a clear distinction between queer and feminist issues. Gilgamesh, a member of the U of M feminist collective, said that the organization was intersectional "because feminism is very much oriented to not only empowering women, but trans individuals as well." For most feminist participants, advocating for both feminist and queer issues was important.

Participants in this study were very interested in speaking about transgender issues. When Smith student Sylvia described her campus, she said, "Smith is a small school, it's a woman's college, but it doesn't mean we just have women, we do have people who are transgender and who are transitioning." The interest in transgenderism was most striking at Smith. Anne W. reported, "Here, you have a lot of influence of queer life. And lots of terminology you wouldn't hear as much on other campuses." Smith students frequently initiated discussion of queer politics and transgender inclusion in our conversations about feminism. Students spoke carefully about Smith not as a women's college but as "a college for woman-identified people," and those who were not transgendered discussed their experiences as those of "cis gendered" women. In comparison, among those in feminist organizations, this language was used either sporadically (at the U of M) or never (at UCSB).

When I attended the National Young Feminist Leadership Conference, I observed that a focus on transgender students and feminism was a core interest of students and attendees. At the panel "Confronting the Gender Binary and Creating Safe Space on Campus," every seat and standing-room space was filled, which was not the case in the other sessions I attended. A panel of young feminists spoke about their experiences as transgender students and creating trans-inclusive policies at their schools. The audience members were very excited and animated; the room had an electric energy. After the panelists shared their challenges and successes as transgender organizers, audience members asked questions such as "I'm in a trans group on campus, but we have no trans members, how should we get them to attend?" and "I'm not trans, but how can I be a good SOFFA [significant other, family, friend, ally]?" We see among this population that feminism and transgender inclusion coexisted and in some senses complemented each other.

Social Problems That Concern Feminists

Feminist participants in this study were distressed by a number of social problems. Their primary concerns were rape culture, the gender binary, and reproductive justice. One of the issues they spent considerable time talking to me about was rape and sexual assault. They had several explanations as to why this issue was so important, often describing personal experiences and linking them to a broader rape culture. Anne W. at Smith connected feminism to rape culture:

> [A] lot of feminism to me is making the world safer for women, because a lot of that has been dictated by men, like rape culture, it's been like don't wear this, don't do this, and that's really not how it should be. . . . [I]t shouldn't be about victim shaming. For me, feminism is about equalizing a lot of things.

Anne W. made a strong connection between her feminism and rape culture, particularly the commonplace blaming of women for what is ultimately a sexist culture. Ninjabi, a UCSB student who spoke at length about how wearing her hijab makes her a target for harassment when she enters UCSB student community Isla Vista, described in detail an incident she learned about while being trained to work for an antirape community organization in Santa Barbara:

> [W]e were told this story of how this girl was drunk and this guy was taking her behind this dumpster and started pulling down her skirt and was going to rape her. The IV foot patrol [police force] witnessed this. When they went to court the woman didn't remember anything, but the IV foot patrol had testified. The judge said, in front of the girl who was almost raped, said to the man, "I'm sorry we wasted your time," and let the man go.

She continued to tell how Isla Vista is unsafe for women and to explain why she keeps her distance from the community, especially during prime party times. For both Anne W. and Ninjabi, blaming women for sexual assault was a common point of anger. Christina, a Smith student, spoke more generally about rape culture, which she said "becomes more and more apparent to me everyday." She recalled not wanting to walk her dog because of the verbal harassment she inevitably receives:

> I just ignore it, because the few times I've reacted, I get yelled at, like "I was just trying to compliment you," "Calm down, you're overreacting," and that's a huge part of rape culture; they see a woman's body and they think it's theirs to say whatever they want to. And it takes no account as to how it makes me feel and maybe my past experiences with men. So that is something I'm reminded of every day, that we live in a rape culture.

While a number of students linked street harassment to feminism, Christina also connected it to a broader rape culture, and treating women like objects. UCSB student Diana explicitly associated sexual assault with gender inequality when she said that she thinks about how "sexism perpetuates rape." Study participants were well versed about rape culture and feminism, and explained it from the perspective of personal experience as well as from a global view. For example, although Diana was very involved in sexual assault prevention on campus, she also started a new student organization with fellow feminist student organizers to raise awareness about sexual assault and femicide in Juarez, Mexico.

Regardless of how participants thought about feminism, they had a lot to say about the constraints associated with the gender binary. For example, Smith student Elizabeth identified as a radical feminist—she said that she was proud to be a cis gender woman, but her primary feminist concern was "smashing the gender binary." She continued, "I have many features and behavioral aspects that don't fit into the sexism associated with the gender binary. I do think the gender binary is incredibly oppressive." Mary Ann, a UCSB student, spoke of her discomfort with expectations for women's roles and appearances, and simply said her feminism was about "trying to degender our society." Some participants spoke about the gender binary and that we should not only focus on women when we discuss gender inequality. U of

M student Shane felt that "both genders are harmed by our society's notion of what is male and female, and how these genders should act. And everyone in between is left behind. And I also like this idea of breaking away from the gender norm, which is really problematic." Although I did not specifically ask about the inclusion of men in the feminist movement, participants spoke about gender inequality affecting both men and women. As Smith student Vivica said about feminism, "you know, freeing everyone from gender inequalities, because if a woman has to be a woman and a man has to be a man, that denies feelings that he should have too." UCSB student Diana said feminism is "equality for all genders," and she continued, "And, in the beginning [feminism] began as a woman's space, but with my development, my definition has encompassed all genders, it has come to include more than just women." Smith student Bea said, "I think feminism has also changed in that it's no longer about women; it's about just equality for gender." Smith student Eileen said, "[A] feminist is a man or woman, doesn't matter." At Smith and the U of M, much of this concern for the gender binary was about transgenderism, but all respondents cared about including men in the movement.[59]

The third major concern of feminists was reproductive rights and justice. At the time of data collection, Planned Parenthood was at risk of having its funding eliminated. Indeed, women's health-care funding is an ongoing debate and point of contestation. Students at all campuses were mobilized on- and offline—which I address in depth in chapter 5. Smith student Hazel connected reproductive rights to larger issues in the gender order. She said, "I think women's reproductive rights and abortion rights [are] rooted in power struggles between men and women." Although UCSB student Janet said, "As a feminist, of course reproductive rights are a huge deal," overall UCSB students were not as concerned with reproductive rights as the other research participants were. This is unsurprising because California is a state that has led the nation in legislation for reproductive rights, and the state has even expanded reproductive services during a time when they are eroding in the rest of the country. As an instructor at UCSB, I noted that many of my students (who were mostly California raised), were not aware of the national scope of reproductive rights infringements, and seemed confident in the accessibility and affordability of reproductive health care.

Fence-Sitters

Pamela Aronson coined the term "fence-sitters"[60] for those individuals who would not completely identify with feminists but who would not completely reject feminism. Students at the three schools had different ways of distancing themselves from feminism. The specific ways in which the U of M students denied their feminism speaks to the conservative nature of the campus. The U of M students who said they were not feminist claimed that feminists were irritating and extreme. Denying the importance or relevance of feminism seemed to be part of their dominant discourse. This diverges from the reasons students at other campuses resisted feminist identities. The Smith students who were not feminists had adopted a feminist identity early in their lives—many of them were raised by feminists and had feminist friends in school—and were "over it." Thus, when they arrived at Smith, they felt that feminism was already a comfortable part of them. Anne S., who is not a feminist but who was raised by feminists, said, when I asked if she thought of herself as a feminist, "I definitely did when I was younger, and I like the ideology. . . . When I was younger, it helped me assert my individualism, my cultural icons were feminists. I don't think I need the label now." When I asked why, she said, "It is just a part of me now. . . . It comes out in my speech and how I hold myself and how I live my life." Alternatively, Bea said, recalling her feminist past,

> I did change over high school. I think my senior year was really the peak of my feminism in terms of the way I was representing myself and it's actually died down a lot since I've gotten into college. Although, my ideas have changed and I think my ideas have gotten more extreme. The way that I represent myself has gotten less extreme.

The few UCSB students who resisted a feminist identity were, interestingly, leaders of feminist organizations, but did not feel that they were ready for the title yet. This reflected their positive view of feminists and the open-mindedness attributed to the student culture. When I asked UCSB student Mario whether she was a feminist, I was surprised by her response:

MARIO: I don't know, I'm normally labeled as a feminist because of my involvement in [feminist student organization]. But that word has a lot of weight behind it. *I don't think I've earned the title of calling myself a feminist* [emphasis added]. Yes, I'm active, but I'm not active enough. I haven't felt like I've earned that title yet. I'd love to be able to call myself a feminist one day, I just have to earn it.

AUTHOR: What would you have to do to earn it?

MARIO: I don't know, something significant. More action. Especially in Santa Barbara, UCSB, calling yourself a feminist, there's a lot of weight behind it, and you can't just go up to anyone and say "I'm a feminist." People looking in will say "what have you done?"

Similarly, UCSB student Summer told me about her favorite feminist writers like Barbara Smith and bell hooks—but although she admires feminists, she feels as though she cannot quite adopt the label because she behaves in some ways that could be problematic.

I did notice a bit of the well-documented "I'm not a feminist, but" phenomenon. For example, U of M respondent Eleanor said, "I think that the basic ideas of political and social equality are good, and we should have those things, but I feel like feminists oftentimes get so whiny." Similarly Ezra, a thoughtful dance major, said, "I wouldn't call myself a feminist, but I would say I'm an avid supporter of gender equality." Lara similarly said,

> I would not describe myself as a feminist. Just because I agree with equal rights and all that, it's a strong point with me, but mainly I see myself as myself. Not just as a woman, not just Native American. I know what I can do, and I know what women can do. My whole thing is being independent, just that I can do it!

Smith student Alex said, "[O]bviously, I strongly support women's rights and equality. I just think of a feminist as more extreme than I see myself." She recounted a recent social gathering:

> [W]e were at an apartment with a bunch of my friends. And [one friend] said [later] "I just wanted to get out of that heteronormative apartment."

[laughs] . . . Smith is a feminist cesspool. [laughs] People are just so into the, like . . . the no gender binary, and just so against it, I'm like come on. It is taken to a whole other level here.

There were commonalities between nonfeminists and fence-sitters. For example, Bette, who knew a lot about feminism and was in a feminist organization, said,

> I think I thought I was more of a feminist before I came to Smith, because I seemed very, way too left for my community growing up. But, like in comparison to feminism here at Smith, I don't know if I'm on that side of the spectrum necessarily, because I think feminism is different for people depending on their social position.

Consistent with Smith students who said they weren't feminist because of the perceived anti-man tone of feminism, Michele said, "I'm for women. But, I feel like 'feminist' has a negative connotation in terms of really drastic anti-men. And if that's what it is, I'm not. I'm definitely aware of social inequalities between men and women, and I feel like that is important to acknowledge and can be correct." U of M student Eleanor, who was not a feminist, said,

> Watching all of the attacks on women's health care especially has really made me realize that the fight my mother and grandmother fought is still very much being waged. . . . Watching as Susan G. Komen—a group with which my family has a personal connection, and a group that is supposed to be advocating for women's health—hire a "pro-life" VP and then proceed to play pawn in a war on Planned Parenthood, the largest advocate for women's health care through all social classes, as well as watching the Catholic Church's continued attempts to deny women access to affordable birth control has really made me realize how much there is left to fight for.

The ways in which students distanced themselves from feminism were complex. They did so not only because there was a stigma attached to feminism, as has been well documented, or because they were not aware of the pressing issues of import to feminists. Rather, some of them felt that they had not engaged in enough activism to embrace the feminist label, further evidence of Chris Bobel's findings regarding the "perfect standard" required of activists.[61] Others felt that they had already incorporated feminism so deeply into their lives that it was no longer necessary to claim the identity.

Chapter 2 Conclusion

I opened this chapter with an account of the "I need feminism because . . ." campaign, highlighting young people's experiences with sexism and connections to feminism. Many of their grievances—about sexual assault, street harassment, and the myth of gender equality—were common to the college students in this study. Like participants in the campaign, feminist participants were frustrated that representations and discussions of women's position in society underestimated the presence of inequalities. Many feminists were aware of the central components of the stalled gender revolution—such as the wage gap and work/family life balance—and were concerned that these inequalities would become problems in their lives. While most feminists were irritated with what they saw as a pollyanna-ish media depiction of gender equality, the nonfeminists and fence-sitters agreed that women's status in the United States is not great, but in comparison to how bad it could be, it was acceptable.

Talking about their experiences with inequality was easy for many participants in this study. Feminist and fence-sitters from all schools easily rattled off all the ways in which they experience inequality, regardless of their backgrounds. Although they are young and in college, they are not immune to inequality. The injustices they experienced and described with great passion and emotion were primarily interactional—exchanges in which they felt devalued or overlooked because of their gender. These interactions occurred at school, in relationships with their families, peers, and dates, and on the streets. Although many of these observations were part of a larger landscape of structural inequality, which some of them acknowledged, feminist respondents at all schools recognized how everyday inequalities shaped their everyday lives. This is consistent with research by sociologists Cecilia Ridgeway and Shelley Correll, who argue that the gender hierarchy is perpetuated in large part through interactional inequality.[62] The notion that young people think they can have it all, or that feminists think there's nothing left to fight for but individual change, is not the narrative that resonates with participants in this study. Their experiences with gender inequality foreshadowed their allegiance to feminism and the issues that compel them to mobilize as feminists.

The nonmonolithic and contextual nature of feminism was of utmost importance to participants. A focus on intersectionality is nothing new to feminism. It has been a salient feature of feminist movements for generations,[63] as participants have always negotiated their interconnected racial, class, sexuality, and gender identities. However, as Nancy Whittier writes, this approach is distinct in some ways: "[F]eminist organizing and theorizing by women of color certainly predates the third wave. . . . However, activism in the late 1990s and after *was* distinct in its reluctance to generalize about women or make claims on women's similarities as the basis of solidarity."[64] I found a similar occurrence in my research, in that participants emphasized differences among and between women without acknowledging solidarity or feelings of mutual interest based on gender alone. While a focus on intersectionality is not new, it is different in some ways for these participants because of their emphasis on including men.

Study participants were clear that feminism is not a one-size-fits-all movement, and in particular that there are different types of feminism practiced and embraced by various racial/ethnic communities. Elsewhere it has been suggested that women of color may feel as though an overarching feminism is not relevant to their experiences or identities,[65] due to the white-washing of the feminist movement and the overlooking of the "pluralistic reality of feminist organizing."[66] These findings suggest, however, that participants' adoption of expansive and inclusive ideas of feminisms and the intersectional nature of inequalities means that for women of color and other women, feminism may suit them all. Although they did feel as though they had to modify their feminist identities, none said that they could not identify with feminism because it did not reflect their experiences.

Feminists were not preoccupied about creating boundaries between who is or who is not a feminist—they emphasized the extensive and varying definitions of feminists by individuals with different backgrounds and experiences.[67] This supports the argument by Schnittker and colleagues[68] that there is less of a consensus today in feminists' definition of feminism than there was in the past. But, this is not necessarily a negative prediction for the future of feminism. When the nuances of feminism are equally emphasized by White and people of color participants, it opens a greater and more inclusive discussion of feminism. The wave framework is too limiting to accommodate these movement complexities.

These findings suggest that those who do not embrace feminism do so for complicated reasons. It was not simply that feminism carried some negative connotations or that broader concerns about the movement were not important. Fence-sitters or nonfeminists had two main reasons for resisting feminism—either because of the stigma associated with feminism, or because they put feminism on a pedestal and felt as though they could not live up to the movement's high standards. Moreover, it is important to note that the nonfeminists did not believe that all was fine in the world or that equality reigned supreme.

This chapter suggests that college students' experiences with gender inequality could be shifting. First, the mainstream press has given unprecedented levels of attention to sexual assault and the wage gap, issues that were at the forefront of participants' minds. Whether or not they knew a lot about gender inequality and feminism, participants in this study were quick to list these as issues affecting women's status. Second, young people today are incredibly media savvy and observant of trends in their media-saturated world—street harassment, gender norms, and sexual harassment get a lot of attention on social media and blogs, such as the "I need feminism because . . ." website. As I explore later in the book, much of their knowledge about feminism and the pervasiveness of gender inequality comes from online sources. Third, because of rising educational costs and an economy in a downturn, many college students today do not have the luxury of being full-time students without additional employment. Some need to work in order to pay for their tuition or living expenses; others need to send money to their financially strapped families. Because of this, they may experience some of these workforce inequalities early in their lives. Perhaps the speculations about young people not experiencing gender inequality come from a past era in which young people were shielded from many of life's injustices.

In the beginning of the chapter I noted four assumptions that guide popular interpretations of young women and their relationships to feminism: young women take for granted the rights attained through the gender revolution and fail to see their own experiences through the lens of inequality; young women who have not experienced any obvious inequality will not identify with a movement to fight for gender inequality; young women who do identify with feminism are focused only on their individual challenges and pleasures; young feminists are not as angry or as organized as previous generations of feminists were. Although it is true that nonfeminist participants did not wish to acknowledge their experiences with gender inequality and that some feminists believed other women did not understand the extent of gender oppression in the United States, overall this chapter exposes flaws in each of the above four assumptions. The phenomenon of "rose-colored glasses," in which young women fail to see sexism in their lives,[69] was not exemplified in many of my respondents' lives. They have experienced inequality, they do see obstacles, and they are not only focused on their own lives and circumstances. As I will show in subsequent chapters, feminists are organized. All participants in this study had more complex answers to questions about feminism, inequality, and gender than the four assumptions would allow.

So what are we to make of the popular conceptions of millennial women based on what we know from the women in this study? The arguments that feminists do not exist or that they are not active are based on a one-dimensional understanding of feminism. We know that generalizations about an entire generation of feminists are too vague to accurately explain the spectrum of feminism and different approaches to inequalities. Expectations by older generations about younger generations of activists are probably incongruent, since movement participation in large part depends on the time period when an individual enters a movement.[70] Moreover, as literature by feminists of color has found, it is a privilege not to recognize inequality; for many women injustice and inequality are presumed and inevitable. The perceptions driving the dismissive opinions about young feminists rely on narrow definitions of feminism—a feminism that has probably never existed and that has also failed to change with the times.

3

Multicultural Sororities, Women's Centers, and the Institutional Fields of Feminist Activism

As a result of the organizing by a coalition of student and feminist organizers, New York State governor Cuomo passed an "Enough Is Enough" bill in June 2015. The bill will grant New York students who are reporting sexual violence immunity from being punished for violating drug and alcohol rules. The legislation also requires schools to be transparent with their data on the outcomes of disciplinary actions in sexual assault cases.

At St. Olaf College in Northfield, Minnesota, students gather for a Take Back the Night March and speak-out, followed by a party in Ytterboe lounge. For over twenty-five years, the school's Sexual Assault Resource Network has provided students with support and emergency care.

At Boston College, members of the group Students for Sexual Health recently garnered national media attention for distributing condoms and information about safe sex to students from their dorm rooms and other locations convenient for students. Because Boston College is a Catholic institution, college administration threatened the students with disciplinary action if the college received any formal reports of such activity.

At San Francisco State University, women's and gender studies majors are required to intern in a community organization their senior year. Students have interned at the GLBT Historical Society, Jewish anti–domestic violence organization Shalom-Bayit, and Girl Ventures.

Across the country, feminist students are making changes on their campuses and in their communities. Institutions of higher education provide students with resources and opportunities to learn about feminist ideologies, to engage in feminist mobilization, and to address inequalities inside and outside their institutions. As a result, students gain leadership skills, evident in the calm confidence many participants displayed while running meetings and events. They become deft at public speaking, even in not always welcoming contexts, such as in front of a group of fraternity brothers who were required by the university to learn about sexual assault. They also gained organizational skills through these activities and planning events, ranging from very small to very large. Campus feminist mobilization is initiated and sustained in part by the preexisting feminist networks at each institution, including women's, gender, and feminist studies programs/departments, women's centers, and feminist student organizations.

In this chapter, I analyze how the three institutions of higher education in this study are largely friendly habitats[1] for feminist organizing. I illustrate the unexpected opportunities for feminist mobilization, and the support feminist students receive from women's studies departments and women's centers. I also show the drawbacks of organizing in institutional contexts because of administrative oversight and restrictions on student mobilization. I draw on the literature on women's movements, student activism, and institutional movements to highlight the challenges and possibilities of campus feminism. I ask, Are institutions of higher education fertile grounds for growing social movements? In what ways do feminist and women's studies departments and women's centers shape feminist student culture, and how do they vary by campus? How is feminism nurtured and/or challenged inside institutions? Does the institutional context effectively prolong the waveless feminist movement?

Institutional Feminism

Most social movements target the state;[2] however, all institutions are potentially subject to the pressures of social movements.[3] The structure of power in families, inequalities in the workplace, the operation of the military, the limiting or expansion of religious authority, the regulation of the media and entertainment, the system of local, state, and federal taxation, the acquisition of human capital in education, medical authority, and practice—in other words, the exercise of power in any institutional arena—becomes a site of political and movement contestation.[4] Scholars have only recently begun to analyze the dynamics of social movements inside institutions.[5] Elizabeth Armstrong and Mary Bernstein have proposed a "multi-institutional politics approach"[6] to social movements that extends the insights of state-centered approaches by directing attention to the distinctive institutional fields in which a social movement mobilizes and to the ways this influences mobilization processes and movement tactics.[7]

Scholarship on student activism has remained largely separate from the literature on social movements within institutions. However, scholars are intrigued by the case of student activism because of its energetic young participants, novel tactics, and ubiquitous nature. According to social movement scholar Nick Crossley,[8] students tend to become mobilized because they have flexible schedules and belong to large and dense networks of young people. He writes, "University students act upon their values and identities, and they do so because and to the extent that the shift to university allows them to hook up with a sufficient number of likeminded others to reach the critical mass necessary for activism."[9] Others have echoed these sentiments and found that movement participation, and more specifically exiting a movement, has less to do with changes in personal political ideology and more to do with changes in the personal lives of mobilized participants.[10] Although there is quite a lot of literature about student organizing, we know very little about feminist student activism specifically.[11]

Analysis of institutional organizing and social movements suggests that "[i]t is too easy to presume that what occurs on the streets is disruptive and what occurs within institutional contexts is accommodative."[12] Although we know a considerable amount about student activism,[13] little attention has been paid to social movements in institutions of education. Fabio Rojas's *From Black Power to Black Studies* is one of the few texts that sheds light on the relationships between institutions and social movements.[14] Rojas's analysis reveals the connection between the Black Power movement and academia and the institutional contexts in which Black studies programs were started and survived. A systematic study of the integration of women's movements into women's studies, similar to Rojas's treatment of Black studies, could be useful for understanding the benefits and drawbacks of institutional organizing. Asking some of the same questions about the relationship between feminist movements and academia would be germane to understanding the evolution of both women's studies programs and the women's movement.[15]

In this chapter I examine the incorporation of feminism in institutions of higher education. My comparative approach between three institutions of higher education examines how feminist mobilization is shaped by institutional settings. I employ an approach to feminism that is considerate of the institutional specificities of feminism, emphasizing the dynamic and multidimensional nature of the movement. Although there are some similarities among institutional feminism on the three campuses, particularly related to the age group of the participants in this study and the conditions of the stalled gender revolution, I demonstrate how the institutional context influenced the types of organizing on each campus.

The Impact of Women's Studies

Women's studies programs emerged from the energies of the women's, peace, and civil rights movements.[16] Since the 1970s, women's studies programs and departments have proliferated on college campuses, many of them closely connected to the women's movement and feminist activism.[17] According to a National Women's Studies Association report, in 1977 there were 276 women's studies programs in the United States, and in 2007, there were nearly 650 women's studies departments.[18] Because these are interdisciplinary programs or departments, the lives and experiences of women are placed at the center of women's studies' intellectual projects. The field of women's studies revolutionized the male-dominated academy and shifted what was deemed acceptable as valuable topics of study. An Association of American Colleges and Universities study found that "women's studies creates a link between voice, empowerment, self-esteem, and critical thinking"; that students regard "women's studies to be more intellectually rigorous [than non–women's studies courses] because it challenges them to incorporate new knowledge into their lives"; and that they "continue to translate that sense of empowerment after graduation into citizen action."[19]

Because of their placements in institutions of higher education dominated by White men, many of which were elite, people responsible for the early development of women's studies were racially and socioeconomically homogenous.[20] In *All the Women Are White, All the Blacks Are Men, but Some of Us Are Brave: Black Women's Studies*, Gloria Hull, Patricia Scott, and Barbara Smith write that in addressing the populations enrolled in institutions of higher education, women's studies "focused almost exclusively upon the lives of white women."[21] For example, V. P.

Franklin writes that not only were African American women invisible in women's studies curricula in the late 1960s and 1970s but African American women were also "critical of the ideological and intellectual thrust of the women's studies programs."[22] During this time period, mobilized participants in institutions were forming women's studies, Black studies, and Chicano/Chicana studies simultaneously. This meant that, at best, feminist activist attentions were diffused within area studies, or that, at worst, racist and exclusionary practices kept women of color from being full participants in the discipline of women's studies. Other challenges to women's studies have resided in the tension between the objectives of a feminist movement and those of an academic institution.[23]

One of the main learning outcomes of women's studies has been to educate a new generation about the history and precepts of feminism.[24] Students who take women's studies classes learn about the history and ideologies of women's movements around the world, the inequalities that shape women's lives, and how women are agents of social change. Research has found that the discipline of women's studies fosters personal change and transformation among faculty,[25] and imparts awareness of gender inequality and intention to participate in social justice activism among students.[26] A 2011 study found that women's studies majors cluster in certain professional fields, particularly "higher education administration, entrepreneurship, law, academe, the health professions, and nonprofit work," presumably bringing feminist principles to feminist and nonfeminist spaces.[27]

Women's studies programs have changed their approaches and perspectives over the decades. Many have also changed their names from "women's studies" to "feminist studies" (UCSB), to "study of women and gender" (Smith College), or to "gender, women, and sexuality studies" (University of Minnesota). All three campuses in this study grant bachelor's degrees in the major. Currently, both UCSB and the U of M offer a PhD in the field—two of sixteen universities in the United States that do.[28] Attacks on and devaluation of women's studies departments, their faculty, students, and staff are commonplace. Examples include hostile phone calls, letters, and e-mails to faculty and staff objecting to feminist classes and programs serving women; demands to fire or investigate faculty members who espouse feminist beliefs; and appeals to defund women's studies programs at the state level.[29] From within universities, it means that departments are used to precarious and/or reduced levels of funding, many operating with faculty members whose time is split between two departments. From outside universities, individual faculty members have experienced attack and serious conflict as a result of their scholarship, teaching, and viewpoints on women.[30]

In the survey, the strength of the women's feminist identity was clearly related to whether or not the respondent had taken a women's studies class. Although students who are more inclined to sympathize with feminist ideologies may be more likely to enroll in women's studies classes, 43 percent of those who had taken a feminist studies class agreed with the statement "I use the term 'feminist' to describe myself." This is a high number given the unpopularity of claiming a feminist identity and the conflicting and nebulous interpretations of feminist ideologies.[31]

Interview participants discussed the importance of women's studies courses in their development as feminists and activists. Majors and nonmajors spoke about how women's studies courses had influenced their perceptions and understandings of feminism, and their involvement in feminist student groups. At UCSB, for example, Diana knew she wanted to be a feminist studies and Chicana/Chicano studies double major before she arrived. She was inspired by what she heard about the activist history of UCSB and said that feminist studies aided her in "finding out what type of feminist I am." Because Diana knew she was a feminist from a young age, she looked to feminist studies classes to help focus and hone her personal understandings of feminism. On the other hand, other participants had not previously given much thought to feminism. Through taking such courses they began to understand the significance of the movement in their lives. Sociologist Jo Reger calls this "surfacing"—the process by which an individual comes to realize his or her feminist identity.[32] U of M student Brooke, a gender, women's, and sexualities studies major, exemplifies this phenomenon:

> I started thinking about the word and actual movement of feminism in my first intro to women and gender studies class. I didn't really think about whether I identified as a feminist before then. As soon as I took that women and gender studies class, then suddenly the word "feminism" was everywhere. As soon as I started reading about it, of course, identifying as a feminist was instant.

While Brooke had not previously thought much about feminism, UCSB student Camille sounded like a budding feminist prior to taking her feminist studies courses: "I definitely had the passion, but I didn't know the terms or the way to frame it [before matriculating at UCSB]. Feminist studies, and all these organizations, gave me the tools to communicate." Although students like Camille are understandably drawn to feminist studies classes, many students are in feminist studies courses in order to fulfill a degree requirement (i.e., writing, critical thinking). Thus, students who may not already be interested in or passionate about feminism may become engaged while learning about the movement.

These classes also provided important contextualization for students who had experienced inequalities. Elsa, a feminist studies major at UCSB, was a working-class Mexican American and Native American woman. She said that she began to associate with feminist ideologies during her second year at UCSB while in feminist studies class. Working forty to sixty hours a week to support herself through college, Elsa experienced sexism at her place of employment, and she emphasized that sexism is an everyday and expected occurrence. For her, feminist studies provided a much-needed perspective on her own life: "Initially I went in to just take [feminist studies] courses, and I didn't identify with it, but learning about the gender dynamics, minority dynamics, domestic violence. . . . I was abused as a child, and learning that academic perspective is very useful, learning where it came from and from a historical perspective." Elsa's process of "surfacing" as a feminist was striking. Feminist studies courses allowed her to understand her individual life in a broader context of structural and institutional inequalities. In fact, Elsa had a notable maturity to her. She discussed structural and personal inequalities deftly and calmly, and she recognized that this lucidity about her experiences was first cultivated in the feminist studies classroom. This resonates with the transformative potential of feminist studies courses documented in the literature.[33]

This process of "surfacing"[34] in women's studies inspired students to participate in feminist organizations. Mary Ann recently transferred to UCSB from another university in Southern California, and immediately gravitated towards the Feminist Studies and Theater departments, as well as to several feminist organizations. She said that her feminist studies major allowed her to pursue the "activism aspect" of her interests and to "spread the word" about feminist studies. Likewise, UCSB student Summer said she was able to "host an art and activism workshop that was inspired by my feminist studies class. And the art was in the women's center, and I'm proud that it is hanging up." All but one of the feminist studies majors I interviewed were in feminist student organizations. Survey data show that the students who were involved in such organizations were more likely to have taken a feminist studies class (14.4 percent) than not (4.4 percent). As students learned in these classes about race, class, and gender injustices and about different forms of organizing, feminist student groups benefited. These groups afforded outlets for students to organize around the inequalities and grievances they studied in their classes.

The Feminist Studies Department at UCSB had a powerful pipeline to student organizations—there was an activist context at UCSB that facilitated student involvement and gave numerous opportunities to be involved in feminist and social justice causes. In fact, the UCSB Feminist Studies Department was very activist oriented—students in one feminist studies course told me they were required to do an activist project for their final grade. Also, the feminist studies faculty on that campus is known to be outspoken. While students at the other two schools had similar experiences, they did not experience such an enveloping activist context as at UCSB. Although some people state that activism and scholarship should not go together, it is shown that many students became politicized in women's studies departments. In my research, I found little evidence that women's studies was seen as directed primarily to White students or was exclusionary—in fact, at UCSB, the most ethnically and racially diverse school in this study, students of color were very devoted to the women's studies program and spoke highly of the course offerings and faculty.

The qualitative data, combined with the survey data, affirm the influential relationships between women's studies departments and feminist student organizing. In the survey, students who had taken feminist studies classes acknowledged the existence of sexism at higher rates than those who had not, an important precursor to feminist activism. Students who had taken feminist studies classes were much more likely to be concerned that gender inequality would affect their careers. Nearly

69 percent of all students agreed that "the gendered wage gap (women being paid less than men for the same job) will affect my earnings at some point in the future." However, those students who reported that they had taken feminist studies classes were more likely to agree with the statement (82.5 percent) than students who had not taken feminist studies classes (64.5 percent). Students who had taken feminist studies classes were also more likely to report having participated in actions or events devoted to promoting gender equality (52 percent) as compared to those students who had not taken feminist studies classes (28.1 percent).

Those individuals who take feminist studies courses may be predisposed to feminist perspectives. Others take these classes simply to fulfill general education requirements. From both views, many of my interviewees said that feminist studies classes changed their lives in unforeseen ways. Students with feminist inclinations also may have been more likely to take the survey, which could have led to a selection bias. I was cautious to avoid using the words "feminist" or "gender" in the advertisement and description of my survey, and because I did not target feminist studies students in my survey advertisement, I did not have many feminist studies majors respond to the survey. (It is worth reiterating that the advertisement for the survey was distributed among math, science, humanities, and social science majors.) Thus, given the breadth of survey respondents' majors, the strength of students supporting feminism was surprising.

The survey data reveal that most students learn about feminism in courses outside of women's and feminist studies courses, although 38.9 percent of the survey respondents had taken at least one feminist studies class at their home campus. Of all the students who took the survey, 78.6 percent indicated that they learned about feminism in college classes. This suggests that feminism is taught in numerous classes outside the feminist studies department and suggests a strong institutional position. This phenomenon was particularly strong at Smith College, where 85.3 percent of its students learned about feminism in college. Students at Smith told me that elements of feminism were integrated into most of the classes they had taken. Regardless, the majority of survey participants, whether or not they had taken a feminist studies class, had learned about feminism in college.

Women's Centers and Feminist Students

In the 1960s and '70s, feminists founded women's centers in colleges and universities throughout the United States. These feminists sought to counteract the male domination in institutions of higher education and to provide resources for women students, staff, and faculty.[35] Women's centers were typically managed and organized by students or faculty, depending on the size of the institution. The centers provided programming and support for women students, specifically at a time when rates of women's enrollment in college escalated and when many formerly all-male colleges were becoming co-ed. Services provided by women's centers included advocacy for victims of sexual assault and domestic violence, distribution of information pertaining to women's health, and assistance navigating university culture. The feminist leaders of women's centers, often in conjunction with women's studies departments, were successful in addressing the needs of feminists and women within the academy.[36] They fundamentally changed the university experience for women.

Because of the historical role of women's centers in perpetuating feminism within higher education, I speculated that they would also play a substantive role in the lives of feminist students. This was true to varying degrees. Although it is clear that these women's centers continue to maintain "feminist habitats,"[37] or environments in which feminist claims-making may occur, my research suggests that these centers are not as essential to contemporary feminist groups and activists as they were in the past.

The U of M women's center, founded in 1960, has the distinction of being the first university campus women's center in the country. Its present mission is to advance equity "for women students, staff, faculty and alumnae across identities by increasing connections for women's success, cultivating socially responsible leaders, and advocating for organizational culture change toward excellence for all."[38] As it is such a large university, the mission statement reflects the expansiveness of the institution's reach. The center continues to build on this history but with some constraints. Currently the women's center is limited by its small space in the ground floor of a mainly academic building, with little walk-in traffic. They do not have room for a library, resource center, or gathering area. However, their dedicated staff and students make the most of what they have. Their programming runs the gamut from workshops on eradicating the glass ceiling and on work-related negotiation to awards recognizing women faculty and students to women's leadership summits.

The staff and students associated with the women's center had little involvement with campus feminist groups. A women's center staff member serves as a liaison to feminist student organizations, but there was little success in this relationship. Students reported that feminist organizations and the women's center were on friendly terms, but the connection was unimportant. Because groups like the feminist student collective receive funds from student service fees (the feminist organization at the U of M had a $27,200 budget for the 2011–2012 school year), they typically do not request funds from the women's center. Nonetheless, they do cosponsor and collaborate on presenting panel discussions and well-known guest speakers. One example of a cosponsorship by the women's center and the feminist student collective was an event held at the student health center called "Women's Self-Defense Class: Discover the Strength within You!" Despite such collaborations, the women's center and feminist student organizations face similar problems, such as struggling for office space and decreasing support from the university.

The UCSB women's center was founded in 1975, fifteen years after the U of M women's center. However, the center played more of an active role in student life and was more encouraged by the university than the U of M women's center was. The UCSB women's center is in a highly visible location immediately inside the main doors of the new student resource center on the principal bicycle and skateboard thoroughfare from Isla Vista to campus. The student resource center also houses student organizations, student affairs offices, and computer labs. With an open layout and modern industrial feel, it is constantly abuzz with activity, as students study and hang out. Because of its central location, the women's center has an obvious presence on campus. Moreover, its students and staff members plan a large number of programs, advertise well, and have created a welcoming space. The women's center offices include a library and computers, a meeting room/art gallery, and spaces for a number of career staff members. Student workers cheerfully greet visitors at the front desk. Students are conducting group meetings in the library, lounging in the massage chair, or checking e-mail on the center's computers. The women's center at UCSB has recently changed its institutional position and mission statement to more directly include students of color and queer students. The women's center is now under the umbrella of "women, gender, and sexual equity" and offers programs for non-traditional-age and queer students, and for sexual assault prevention. Its mission statement emphasizes the "feminist approach to provide support, advocacy, resources, and education to the UCSB community," its respect for all gender expressions and sexual orientations, and its desire to create a campus that is "safe, equitable, and just."[39]

At the time of my study, the UCSB women's center had a more central role in student feminist organizing than the U of M center did. Staff members at the UCSB center were the hosts, funders, and primary organizers of two feminist student organizations. Students applied to the women's center for the leadership positions in each organization, and were paid a modest stipend. A women's center staff member sat in on each meeting and appeared to play a prominent role in the daily business of running the student groups. During some meetings it seemed as though student participants had little input on programming for the organization, with the staff member(s) primarily in charge of events. The student activists who were affiliated with the women's center, however, were talented and committed leaders. It seems that at least some of this is due to the fact that they were trained to be student leaders by the women's center staff, and had a notable camaraderie with other women's center student leaders.

Although UCSB women's center did sponsor two feminist organizations, they were neither the most energetic nor the primary campus feminist organizations. Members of these women's center student groups were accountable to university administration and the motivations of the women's center staff. Perhaps it was because of this that the meetings often felt stiff and stilted. In contrast, when I went to feminist student group meetings outside the center, I was struck by the enthusiasm and creativity exhibited. I also found that members of the other UCSB feminist organizations had more room to push against the university policies (for example, in protesting the increase in University of California tuition or the lack of educational accessibility to low-income Latina students). Women's center staff and students were not in a position to ruffle any feathers because of their institutional embeddedness and position as part of student affairs administration. As one university employee explained to me, a university event or policy deemed objectionable or sexist by the women's center staff would be addressed through institutional channels only. In contrast, outside feminist organizations had more leeway in how they addressed injustices, and could even have been disruptive or confrontational. In this comparison, we can understand how feminists are constrained within institutions.

Smith College has no women's center per se. According to one student, there is a space designated for feminist and queer organizations' meetings in the basement of an on-campus house. While Smith lacks a singular women's center, it houses other centers whose programs promote women. Smith's Center for Women in Mathematics includes a post-BA program for women considering graduate school in mathematics but who need more preparation, an intense math program for junior-year undergraduate women students from any college or university, and weekly gatherings or lectures for Smith students interested in mathematics. Smith's "Women's Narrative Project" hosts workshops and panels to foster a dialogue about women and work-life balance. Smith also has a center for women and financial independence, which educates Smith students about financial planning and literacy and managing debt, including workshops and noncredit courses. In essence, Smith sustains many different women's centers, each with specific foci. I did not find any relationship between these centers and feminist organizations on campus.

The U of M and UCSB women's centers were not impervious to the widely circulated tropes that gender equality has been achieved and that feminism has declined. Employees of both centers reported frequently being questioned about the purpose of a women's center. Feminist students who worked at the UCSB women's center said that they had to repeatedly describe to questioning male students the relevance of the women's center. At the U of M, one staff member said, with exasperation, that male students often asked her where the men's resource center was. The U of M has responded to negative attitudes towards feminism and gender equality by directly addressing why women's centers remain important. Its women's center has an extensive website with an illuminating "About us" page: "At the Women's Center, we are often asked questions about who we are, what we do, and if the work we do regarding women's and gender equity is still necessary. To that end, we created a document entitled 'Why Do We Still Need Women's Centers?'" That document details the gender and racial inequalities that persist in higher education, including gender segregation in math and science ("[T]he highest median starting salaries for college graduates are in the fields of computer science and engineering, fields that have the lowest percentage of women."), athletics ("Each year male athletes receive over $136 million more than female athletes in college athletic scholarships at NCAA member institutions."), and faculty appointments (Women are "only 36% of associate professors and only 21% of full professors. And only 2.4% of full professors are women of color.").[40] These facts and figures shine a light on the continued relevance of women's centers and the feminist movement more broadly.

Feminist Student Organizations: Local, National, Greek

Loud dance music played as I entered the "Speak Out! Against Abusive Relationships" event, cosponsored by a large multicultural sorority and the UCSB women's center. Strawberries, pita, and hummus were on the table in the back of the room, with blueberry acai juice to drink. Both men and women were in attendance, a boisterous and fun-loving group shouting across the room, teasing each other, and laughing. Attendees appeared to know each other from their sororities and fraternities, judging by the copious number of Greek letters emblazoned on students' clothing. Many Latina students I recognized were adorned with their sororities' logos—Greek letters gleaming from mirrored pendants hanging around their necks or in hot pink fabric embroidered on the front of their hooded sweatshirts. At six o'clock in the evening, when the event began, about forty people were crowded in the small multipurpose room near the center of campus.

As the group settled in, the chipper emcee taught us about power and control in intimate relationships, emphasizing how abusive relationships may affect people of all race, ethnic, class, sexual, and gender identities. She then spoke about myths and facts regarding abusive relationships. At the conclusion of the opening discussion, the student moderator said enthusiastically, "Congratulations! We are all part of a community that supports healthy relationships!" She then introduced two student musicians, an

Asian American man and an African American man. As one played the guitar and beautifully sang Otis Redding's "Try a Little Tenderness," the other accompanied him on the saxophone. As the event progressed, men and women students read poetry about feminism and relationships, and performed spoken word about the exoticization and abuse of women of color. One student performed a Tahitian dance. At the end of the evening we all signed certificates called the "dating person's bill of rights" and shared what we learned during the course of the evening.

Student organizations are ubiquitous on college campuses, particularly those with on-campus socializing opportunities and those where most students live on or near campus. At campuses like these, students create widespread networks that facilitate organizing and protest. Student organizations are often overseen by student affairs offices, an arrangement that recognizes the extracurricular learning that happens in these organizations, and also allows monitoring of their activities. On the three campuses in this study, members of student organizations contributed to an equitable campus community, organized against inequality, imparted feminist ideology among their peers (much of which they learned in feminist studies classes), provided services to community members in need, and learned leadership skills. In some striking examples, members of feminist organizations also stepped forward when university budgets were cut. The most common student groups were part of student government, sororities, and national feminist organizations, or were affiliated only with their campus's student affairs office.

In order to be a registered student group, members must have three or four student leaders, a staff/faculty advisor, and an organizational constitution, and must attend an orientation session in which they learn rules, policies, and expectations of student organization conduct. In exchange, members of student organizations receive a few benefits, depending on the campus. Students may reserve meeting rooms on campus, apply for internal grants, obtain the support of the student engagement office, or receive funds to get started ($250 at UCSB, for example).

Multicultural sororities, including predominantly Latina and Black women members, were active sites of feminist organizing at UCSB. Although the White fraternity/sorority system traditionally has been a site of racism and sexism and is known to emphasize social elements of group membership,[41] those fraternities and sororities serving communities of color have more activist and service orientations.[42] My research indicates that multicultural sororities created feminist networks and contributed to a larger feminist social movement community on campus. Members of multicultural sororities also reported that feminism was implicit in the collective identities of their organizations.[43] When I asked UCSB student Ayaliza about her involvement in a multicultural sorority, she spoke about how it allowed her to live out feminism in her day-to-day life, and provided an important feminist community. This is consistent with Latina and Chicana feminist ideology, which emphasizes the importance of community.[44] They worked to empower members, provide professional and social opportunities, and serve their community through volunteer work and outreach. Members also spoke about how their sororities articulated feminist goals and cosponsored events with other feminist organizations, demonstrating the degree to which feminist networks have diffused in institutional settings. A major concern of Ayaliza and her sorority is encouraging other Latina women and girls to pursue their education and learn leadership skills. For example, Ayaliza and her sorority members hosted a fall leadership conference for high school Latina girls, "[w]ith workshops and guest speakers . . . [W]e want them to pursue higher education." Multicultural sororities held campus fundraisers and collected nominal membership fees. They also received funding from grants and internal sources, as did all registered student organizations. These organizations seemed to be more inclined to do off-campus outreach than other student groups, such as when a UCSB sorority member recently visited a local high school to talk to young women about the importance of higher education.

Several student groups at each campus supplemented their student service fees with resources from extra-institutional organizations such as the National Organization for Women, the National Abortion Rights Action League, the Feminist Majority Foundation, and Planned Parenthood. The national groups generally provided resources such as pamphlets and ideas for campus programming. Students with national associations attended lobby day at the state capitol, tabled with banners from national organizations, and served as student branches of these nonprofits. Representatives from some national organizations encouraged students to get involved in politics and national conversations on women's issues, and also urged the students to get involved in local and national organizing. Although Nancy Whittier found that third wave feminists are more interested in grassroots than national organizing, these young feminists had some degree of interest in connecting with national feminist organizations.[45]

Smith student Marie is a member of a Smith feminist group with a national affiliation. Her friend started the group because a Smith alum was involved in founding the organization. The students wanted to pay tribute to this history by starting a student group affiliated with the organization. Marie said, "We're going to be more of a political lobbying group. . . . [W]e'll support [the national organization] goals, like we might have a phone bank and call senators. The ERA is one of the main issues right now, and to convince people to talk to their congresspeople and get it passed." Although the national organization does not fund the Smith students and the Smith group pays no dues to the national organization, Marie understood that it is expected of their group to "go to events that [the national organization] hosts, to show there are fresh young people interested in the feminist movement." Other young feminists have said that this national organization has a not-so-stellar reputation for including young people; perhaps this effort with Smith students was meant to remedy that reputation. From my conversation with Marie, it remained unclear what the groups were doing for each other, but it appeared that these students had a more traditional view of feminism and the concerns of feminists than their peers, and were not having their needs met by the existing feminist groups at Smith. There was also some tension brewing because students formed a campus chapter of the national organization without consultation with those feminists already engaged in activism. Said Gabriella, a member of another Smith feminist group,

Why would you start a chapter of [national organization] without coming to this long-standing feminist organization? I know they took members of ours because right when they started up two of our members disappeared. And I'm bitter about it! It completely made no sense to me! And then they send me e-mails like, we want to collaborate, blah blah blah.

Gabriella said of the national organization,

[I]n the past it was the second wave, it was this White, very middle-upper-class organization that didn't include a whole lot of people. And it's part of why a lot of people don't consider themselves feminist, because these feminists of the time didn't represent them. And now to have a chapter on campus, when we already had a feminist org that was intent on including everyone is redundant, but also . . . stupid [laughs].

Gabriella later said that the feminist organization she belonged to is "sort of connected with the Feminist Majority Foundation [FMF]." This meant that the FMF gives them discounts on t-shirts (which they sold at a large campus event) and solicits the student group for money, which is kind of humorous given that this student group had been allocated only seventeen dollars for its events the previous semester. At other campuses, the FMF used local liaisons to reach out to already-mobilized feminists, but did not start a new group at any of these schools.

The national pro-choice organizations were very successful in their mobilization of students, and without them, it seemed that pro-choice groups might not have existed on these campuses. In one case, a UCSB student told me that the pro-choice group had died out when its members graduated, but a friend restarted the group with the guidance of the local Planned Parenthood office where she was interning. This national organization had a very active UCSB chapter, as well as a Smith chapter. Anne W., a member of a nationally affiliated pro-choice organization at Smith, said that many colleges have similar groups. The national organization funds them—meaning, said Anne W., "They send us all of our condoms, our lube, a lot of our resources, we go to rally day in Boston, like the New York and DC rallies." In exchange, the Smith group "has to report a log of their meetings every week, just so they can continue to ensure to do what we're doing." With this organization, it seems as though they oversee the group to make sure it continues and to hold it accountable to the organization's plans and goals. This makes sense, given that many student organizations regularly struggle to survive after a dedicated group of students graduate. Although there were a few students who expressed off-handed dissatisfaction with the micromanagement by the local organizational employees, overall, students appreciated these connections.

Another type of student organization was the womyn's board at UCSB, which was part of the student government. Members planned a large number of events, and due to their ample budget, many were large in scale and scope. In addition, members distributed money to other campus groups that shared their mission of empowering women. In this respect, it was both a civic and a political organization. During the weekly meetings of the womyn's board, members of other student groups presented their proposed events with a budget. The board voted on whether or not to fund these events, with the amount of allocated funding dependent on the extent to which the event empowered women. The maximum amount of funding per request was three hundred dollars, for "any program or event that is centered around womyn or girls [sic] issues with the intention of education, promoting, or celebrating womyn (locally, nationally, and/or globally)" or that sought "to support any organization that further empowers womyn's causes directly."[46] Sometimes it also funded other campus feminist organizations. The term "empowering women" was broadly defined by the board; it funded La Raza college day, a day at UCSB for underrepresented high school students, as well as the anti–Valentine's Day improv and playwriting festival.

Support and Funding of Feminist Groups

Student organizations received varying levels of encouragement and monetary aid from their institutions. It may seem at first glance that the private, feminist Smith College would provide a bounty of resources to feminist activists, and that the U of M, with antifeminist students in a more conservative region of the country, would fund little. This was not the case. The differences and nuances in organizational support and funding speak to the complexities of institutional activism, and the variations are surprising.

At all three campuses, most of the registered student organizations were funded by student service fees. All full-time students are required to pay a set amount of student service fees per semester or quarter, which is shared by organizations and other campus student services. The amount allocated to each group was determined by a committee of students (U of M, Smith) or by an all-campus vote (UCSB). The students I spoke with at the U of M and Smith were highly dissatisfied with the fee-allocation process, citing a lack of transparency, confusing and contradictory procedures, and an overrepresentation of student committee members with conservative political views. The exception to this is the womyn's board at UCSB, a feminist organization that is part of the student government. The board also received student service fees, with the allocated amount voted on every other year in an all-campus election.

Smith College and U of M activists expressed frustration with the lack of backing from the schools. At the U of M, their funding levels were acceptable, if fragile. The Women's Collective at the U of M had contentious relationships with administrators, and was not hesitant to confront institutional policies it deemed objectionable. For example, during a convocation speech by the university president, an individual associated with the organization unfurled a large banner decrying the low pay of university clerical workers and the high pay of the president. The university's pushback was perhaps impacted by a history of disruptive student protest, and led to the organization's members feeling ostracized and demeaned. Women's Collective members told me that the university threatened to take away their considerable office space and resource center on the second floor of the student union. The collective was also forbidden from allowing other progressive or radical groups to use its space. U of M student Lauren, however, felt that the professors who were teaching her classes were supportive and encouraging of their activism: "It's really frustrating and I don't feel supported by the university at all because of that. I think that my professors, absolutely, they support me but I think the university, in general, doesn't."

At Smith, feminist students were also disappointed with the lack of funding and advocacy from administrators, especially the staff overseeing student organizations and/or student affairs staff. Activists at Smith thought that the college was a little *too* interested in the women of color student groups. Smith students told me that this was the case because, to the administration, the groups indicated the diversity of the student body. Smith student Michele, a member of the Black student organization, described the tense relationship between her group and the college:

I think Smith wants to take control of [our student organization], or like they'd put our [Black student organization] name on something without asking permission. There have been a couple instances where they've just put the name on it. Smith wants to use it in their corporate ways, in terms of marketing and advertising, to seem like we're diverse, but the students want to keep it under student control.

Smith student Bette shared a similar story about her involvement in the Black student organization and the college's striving for the image of racial diversity. I asked Bette whether her organization would die out when students graduate, since this is a challenge facing student groups. She said of Black, Latina, and Asian student organizations, "Those orgs have to be here, for the brochures, for advertising. I don't think it will ever be erased, because that will look pretty bad I think, if they talk about diversity and there are no orgs to reflect that. I'm sure they'll step in."

Students at Smith also found their funding inadequate, indicating that private institutions do not necessarily provide substantial resources for their student organizations. Gabriella, who was a leader of the Smith feminist activists, said,

I mean, we got seventeen dollars as our budget last semester, and we wanted chalk and spray paint, but they wouldn't give us money to spray-paint banners. So we got seventeen dollars for chalk and something else. This semester we got more, because we had an event already planned. It's always a hassle. It's like begging them for money every time you want to have an event.

Students at both Smith and the U of M had the perception that many of the students who were involved in allocating funds gave preference to conservative student organizations. Anne W., in a pro-choice organization at Smith, said, "We try [for funding] every year, and they deny us. It's been a sore spot for a while. It's pretty limited who gets funds, and they do not like to give us funds, we fight for anything. We normally submit a budget proposal of several thousand dollars, and we're lucky if we get $200 every year." When I asked her why she thinks her organization is continually denied funding, she did not know: "[T]here's really no reason they don't give it to us, especially when they gave the Republicans fifteen thousand dollars this year. They brought this speaker to campus for two days, I don't know, apparently it cost fifteen thousand dollars. It's been a little irritating, it can be hard to keep your organization up and running when nobody gives you any money." At Smith, the students did not push back against their levels of funding, except for continuing to ask for more.

At the U of M, students involved in feminist organizations said that conservative student groups received disproportionate funding levels in relationship to their membership base and event attendance. Lauren, of the feminist collective, discussed at length the latest student service fee allocation:

> Students for Human Life [antichoice student organization], they get a ridiculous amount of money. They are one of three groups that get a third of the money allotted to the student groups for this year. There are three conservative groups that get 30 percent of the funding. CFACT [Collegians for a Constructive Tomorrow, a conservative student organization], they get $200,000 for next year. They normally get $100,000 but because they want to bring George Bush to campus next semester, the university has to pay for it and that's $200,000.

The U of M supported many conservative organizations, in contrast to the other research sites. These included antichoice organizations, an organization for conservative men in fraternities, and a conservative student newspaper. The interview participants' perception was that the conservative students spearheaded a campaign to remove the student "cultural centers" that occupied the majority of the offices and resources on the second floor of the student union. The "cultural centers" included student organizations for women and for African American, Muslim, disabled, international, and queer students. According to an article in the U of M student newspaper, the conservative-leaning student service fees committee led the reallocation campaign and accused the cultural centers of not being "viewpoint neutral." The article also stated that the vice provost of student affairs was influenced by this rationale.[47] Although the details continue to be debated, it seems the conservative students have amassed some institutional power, which the feminists found frustrating.

The feminist students at the U of M coalitioned with other progressive student groups to object to the removing of their space and affirmed the importance of marginalized groups having spaces on campus. They protested and had meetings to ensure their continued funding and space in the student center. Their objections turned out to be relatively successful. Although many of these progressive organizations were given smaller resource centers and offices in the remodel, most of them continued to have space (although they pointed out that their artwork was removed and that the new space was sterile). Since I gathered the data for this book, the feminist organization's level of funding has continued to decrease while the conservative students have continued to get additional funding.

Unlike Smith and the U of M, UCSB feminists said that they felt their university administration and fellow students supported their activism. Lisa, in an antirape organization, said, "I think there's a general climate among UCSB faculty and students where it's very inviting. I feel like [feminism] could be a difficult thing to encourage and it might even be shunned. I think on this campus it's a lot more inviting, I think it's very encouraged." Summer, who was in a Black sorority as well as a non-Greek student organization, said that she feels that UCSB is supportive of both of her organizations:

As far as people we request funds from, Greek affairs is very, very, very supportive. Anything we need, any resources they can direct us to, we have a really good relationship with them. The Community Affairs Board, they're super supportive, and try to come out to our programs if we have them. [Student government] is usually funding our programs no matter how big or small our events are. In that sense, I feel like people recognize we really are trying to do something positive.

UCSB student Eliana described the creative ways the members raised funds for their feminist organization, and also how the student government funded their special presentations. Recently, they held a program to benefit the low-income families who live in their neighborhood. She said, "[W]e went to [the student government] funding committee, and told them about our event and stated how much we needed, which was around four thousand dollars, and they funded us for the event. So, it was for a good cause, they funded it completely." Ayaliza described how her multicultural sorority raises funds because, as first-generation college students, they cannot afford to pay the dues that typically sustain Greek organizations. When I asked her whether she felt that the UCSB administration supports her multicultural organization, she was positive: "I feel so, definitely. You know, holding events on campus, the fact they let us use their rooms, I feel that's support in and of itself. They're very open to people attending events that are educational and [are for] a good cause." Members of student organizations at UCSB reported that the university was amenable to their organizing and that their peers' relaxed demeanor and "live and let live" attitudes allowed student organizers to mobilize with few obstacles. This also nurtures an extensive network of feminists who are supported by their community and capable of mobilizing rapidly when necessary, such as in response to the killings of UCSB students in Isla Vista. Feminist UCSB students gained national attention for immediately drawing attention to the sexist motivations of the killer. This dense network also activated more recently, when UCSB students mobilized against the administration for not adequately responding to sexual assault complaints.

The Institutional and Personal Benefits of Campus Feminism

The feminists in this study reaped numerous benefits from their university or college. The institutions fortified their activism and allowed them to hone valuable leadership skills. In turn, feminist student organizations contributed to the college or university by supporting the mission and goals of the institutions, as well as by stepping in when funding shortages emerged. In the economic downturn, student organizations occasionally filled in the gaps that other institutional entities could not cover. For example, during their presentation to the UCSB womyn's board, members of the anti–Valentine's Day improv and playwriting festival organization requested money for the two-day event because the theater department had stopped financing such events amid budget cuts. Since the students planning the festival were from the Theater Department, and it was being held in a theater on campus, they were very discouraged. They turned to the womyn's board, where in a weekly meeting the theater students presented details of the event, its connection to women on campus, plus a detailed budget. The festival was funded. In another example, at the U of M a coalition of students, including many from feminist organizations, planned a day for students from low-income neighborhoods to visit the university in hopes of encouraging greater numbers of underrepresented minorities to matriculate. The students were in part motivated to protest the university administration's defunding of services that would encourage such students to enroll. Nonetheless, they took responsibility for a diversity event that would typically be planned and funded by university administration.

Feminist student organizations contributed to institutional missions by training leaders, engaged citizens, and critical thinkers. The students learned a multiplicity of skills through their participation in feminist groups. Members gained experience running meetings, planning events, and communicating with other students and administrators. They also wrote detailed grant proposals to sustain their organizations. Students at all three schools were impressive in their abilities to run a meeting and plan an event with confidence and composure. Members of the U of M feminist collective presented their budget and organizational records in front of a student committee and open audience every year, for example. The leaders of the UCSB antirape organization were also very skilled at public speaking. For example, during Stalking Awareness Month, the student leaders led workshops about the dangers and seriousness of stalking. To a group of seventeen to eighteen attendees of all races and genders, the group leaders created ground rules for the meeting ("One mic, one diva"), facilitated discussions, and educated those who attended the meetings. In my field notes I wrote, "[Two leaders] gave a very polished and professional presentation, it was clear they took it very seriously. It was really clear that for them, education was activism. They must have been trained quite a bit because they were so good." But these students not only spoke to students who attended their meetings; they also conducted outreach with students who were not necessarily seeking out their message. Their leaders were required to educate their peers about sexual assault by speaking in dorms, fraternities, and sororities. They were not always greeted with the respect or enthusiasm they would have liked. Lisa, a UCSB student in the organization, reflected on their antirape presentations given to fraternity members.

> Some of the challenges we've faced throughout the year were frat presentations. For the most part, they're really just supportive. But sometimes we've had challenges where they ask really offensive questions about what we do and what rape is. It's really disheartening and really disappointing sometimes but it's a good challenge and usually in the end I think it's important for them to really hear what we have to say. It's challenging but it's not going to stop us so it's okay.

Students in this organization and others were also expected to "table" regularly, and they sat at a table in a main thoroughfare on campus and advertised their upcoming events to passing students. The students were coached by their advisors on how to respond to difficult or combative questions about sexual assault. Members of student organizations felt it was important not only to work for social change broadly speaking but also to contribute to creating an inclusive and welcoming college campus. In turn, their activism also taught them indispensable lifelong skills.

Institutional Oversight

Administrators at the U of M and UCSB imposed restrictions that curtailed feminist activism in compliance with their status as publicly funded institutions. Because Smith is a private college, organizers there did not face the same restraints. Because feminist students at all three colleges were very interested in activism around reproductive rights, the fact that this is a highly contested and political issue meant that they could not always mobilize in ways they considered the most effective. Student government affiliation at UCSB prevented feminist organizations from mobilizing around any topic related to abortion because of campus policies that forbid the use of student money to fund "political issues." Isabela said that her feminist organization was prohibited from mentioning "any political ideologies or anything to do with politics. So that's why a lot of times, [the womyn's board] has to step back. Like with the whole Planned Parenthood [controversy], we can only take a certain stance on it. We can't endorse Planned Parenthood."

Similarly, UCSB student Ayaliza, in a nationally affiliated pro-choice organization, shared her experiences applying for a stipend from the student government to attend "capitol day" in Sacramento. During "capitol day" young people would have the opportunity to meet with legislators and learn about and discuss reproductive health care: "We support reproductive services for women, but a lot of people think it's about abortion. Like when we applied for funding for capitol day to [student government], they voted no, because they said they didn't support political issues and abortion is a big one." Because funding for all proposed events depended on following these rules, students took the restrictions seriously, despite their concern, even outrage, over the inaccessibility of women's health care and reproductive health services and the national threats to Planned Parenthood. At the U of M, mobilization related to abortion had been particularly problematic for the student service fees–funded feminist collective during political elections. At these times, debates around reproductive rights are often most heated, and the organization was forbidden from engaging in partisan politics.

Institutional surveillance of student organizations ensured adherence to university policies. The weekly meetings of the UCSB womyn's board were attended by a long-time university administrator and advisor who was there to clarify rules and decision-making procedures. Her presence as a university official seemed out of place at the casual student-run meetings. She was older than anyone else in the room, professionally attired, and although not unpleasant, she was mostly silent during meetings. However, the students in the organization expressed appreciation for her guidance because they had to acquiesce to numerous university policies and procedures. Of their advisor, Isabela said, "I think she's a feminist, and she makes sure we abide by [university] policies, if we have any questions she's there for us. She'll say you can't give money to that, you might want to get away from that. On Planned Parenthood, she just told us, you can't take a stance." Institutional fields shaped grievances, and students responded to these restrictions in varying manners. Feminists in this research were limited by their institutional contexts in some respects. Some students objected to these limitations, while others were grateful for their opportunities to engage in feminist mobilization.

Chapter 3 Conclusion

I opened this chapter with descriptions of how institutions of higher education are homes to feminist organizing and integral to feminist movements. Student involvement in women's studies departments, sexual assault centers, women's centers, and student organizations undoubtedly perpetuate the movement on campuses all over the country. This chapter took a closer look at how exactly these three institutions of higher education are related to feminism.

So are multicultural sororities moving up in popularity while women's centers are declining? Due to the increasing opportunities for feminists inside institutions of higher education, students are finding outlets to expand their feminism other than the ubiquitous women's studies/women's centers duo. The women's centers were less central to feminist organizing than many other organizations to which students brought their feminist ideology. In part because of the success of women's entry into all academic areas of higher education, feminist students are learning about and applying their feminism to a number of unexpected fields.

Feminist students in this study had a multiplicity of opportunities to engage with feminist ideologies and to obtain funding to support their organizations. These included involvement with women's centers, women's studies departments, registered student groups, student government, and multicultural sororities, as well as affiliation with large, national feminist organizations. The history of feminism within institutions of higher education is steeped in women's centers and women's studies departments, which laid the foundation and continue to spur the mobilization of feminist students. In this research, I found that registered student groups were central to student feminism, and that women's studies departments and women's centers provided activist networks and feminist frames that nourished the movement, even when culturally out of favor. Despite being in an institutional context, the dynamic interaction among women's studies departments, women's centers, and a number of feminist student organizations created robust feminist mobilization opportunities.

At the same time, institutions of higher education both enabled and constrained feminist mobilization. The college and universities in this research allowed, at the least, or facilitated, at best, feminist student organizing. Research participants found numerous opportunities to mobilize and forge feminist cultures and to engage in protest and other forms of contentious claims-making. Feminist habitats[48] were nourished by women's centers and women's studies departments. Student activists mobilized in unexpected places, such as student government, sororities, and nationally affiliated organizations. While students learned valuable leadership abilities and contributed to their institutions' missions, they also faced oversight and restrictions on their mobilization.

The variations in feminism I encountered were unforeseen. For example, Smith College has a history of cultivating women leaders, as their mission is to "educate women of promise for lives of distinction."[49] While the college housed numerous institutional entities to encourage student success, this did not always translate into promoting student leadership in feminist student organizations. UCSB, which did not have a feminist history or structure, provided significant support to its feminist organizations, and also had the most diverse types of feminist student groups, including the very active multicultural sororities. The U of M feminist organizations, which faced considerable antifeminist sentiment, were able to hold on to their substantial resources and a large office in the highly sought-after student union. This elucidates how institutions of higher education have different degrees of receptivity to feminist claims-making, depending on the political environment, university structure, and presence of oppositional groups.[50]

The feminist "free spaces" on campus—women's centers, women's studies departments, and feminist student organizations—form an institutional social movement community.[51] This community "suggests a variety of loosely connected actors—including individual activists, movement organizations, institutionalized supporters, alternative institutions and services, and cultural groups" who support social movement goals.[52] The concept of social movement community shifts our focus from specifically organization-level analysis to cultural analysis. That, in turn, allows us to understand the persistence of social movements.[53]

These findings confirm that social movement participants may generate organizational and institutional change while also realizing the broader goals of a movement.[54] This perspective views institutions as being in a dynamic and interactive relationship among individuals, movement participants, and organizations. It provides a more optimistic view of the process of social movement institutionalization than the dichotomies of institutional versus noninstitutional social movements, or success and failure.[55] As the survey data indicated, campus feminism teaches students about feminist ideologies and movements, activates their feminist identities, and stimulates student participation in feminist student organizations. The majority of feminist students I interviewed also reported that they anticipated feminist ideology would influence their future career paths and personal lives, contributing to movement continuity. The leadership abilities students acquired in feminist student organizations, their positive experiences in feminist classes, and their desires to contribute to the betterment of their communities are optimistic counterstatements to those feminists who doubt the existence of feminism among young women.

The levels of mobilization and opposition at each institution complicate the argument that student activism is most likely to occur at small and highly selective institutions.[56] Although that may remain the case for student *protest*, student *organizing* diverges from this formulation. Student organizing is more ubiquitous than student protest, and the generalizations based on institutional type obscure the variety of opportunities available to students to participate in feminist social change in different settings. The student organizing in this study was much more limited in scope at the small, highly selective liberal arts college than at the larger institutions. A closer examination of the context and social movement communities at each institution reveals unexpected openings for feminist claims-making, such as within sororities and student government. It also highlights the contextual nature of movements within institutions.

4

The Bonds of Feminism

Collective Identities and Feminist Organizations

It was a crisp spring evening at UCSB. As the ocean fog crept onto campus, a long line of students formed outside the doors of the student center. UCSB students, staff, and faculty waited for the doors to open for the annual Womyn Unite Banquet. The event was organized by the womyn's board in order to celebrate women and feminist student organizations, and the chosen theme was "building a collective consciousness through creating community." It was no small organizational feat for the students. They invited a prominent feminist of color to give the keynote lecture, planned an extensive program featuring performances by a number of students, and provided dinner for the 250 attendees. Their budget for the evening was approximately fourteen thousand dollars. As I looked around the crowded banquet hall, I noted that a majority of the attendees were women of color, with everyone seated at tables covered in bright purple tablecloths and topped with centerpieces featuring photos of Frida Kahlo, Angela Davis, Erica Badu, Mother Theresa, and Lady Gaga. Prior to the keynote speaker, the "herstorian" of the womyn's board gave a detailed presentation about the history of activism and feminism on the UCSB campus. The accompanying PowerPoint presentation included documentation about women's activism at UCSB and images of feminist organization minutes from the 1980s and other artifacts that described the activist history of UCSB. Following the historical presentation, another student read poetry, dancers from the Armenian women's student organization performed, and a women's a capella group sang. Although the event was funded by one feminist organization, students from other campus feminist and women's organizations contributed to the evening's festivities. These groups were a support group for undocumented immigrant students, a women of color student conference organizing committee, a pro-choice organization, a human rights organization, the campus queer resource center, and a community organization that empowers low-income Santa Barbara residents. Representatives from these organizations set up informational tables around the perimeter of the banquet hall, and several made announcements at the end of the banquet about upcoming events. The members of the womyn's board wanted the evening to provide an opportunity for networking and fellowship. As I circulated around the room, I saw many familiar faces from a variety of feminist organizations on campus, revealing significant membership overlap between feminist and progressive organizations. When the event was over, those of us who helped plan it cleaned up and took group pictures. The students glowed with excitement and chattered about the successful evening.

This banquet represented the unique institutional specificities of UCSB's feminist collective identity. In contrast to the feminist collective identities at the University of Minnesota and Smith College, UCSB feminists spoke about the importance of the activist history of their campus, and how it influenced the shape and forms of their own feminism. Similar to the other campuses, however, feminists at UCSB "carried over" their feminism to other student groups that were not necessarily centered around gender concerns.

In this chapter, I discuss the solidarity among feminists and the feminist collective identities on campuses and in student groups. I present three types of organizational collective identity: *oppositionally oriented feminism, institutionally oriented feminism*, and *hybrid feminism*. I discuss the centrality of intersectionality to the students' organizations on each campus. Finally, I consider movement-level identities and third wave feminism. I ask, How do feminist collective identities shift in different locations? How do we "find" feminism when it is diffuse and when boundaries between feminists and nonfeminists fade? How does the institutional context generate different types of feminism? How do participants link their feminism with their intersectional concerns in feminist organizations? Do movement-level identities unify participants?

Collective Identity

Collective identity is "the shared definition of a group that derives from members' common interests, experiences, and solidarity"[1] and is critical in creating cohesion and momentum in a social movement. How is collective identity created and maintained? It is an interactional process, and is reconstructed and renegotiated among movement members in a continual process.[2] Verta Taylor and Nancy Whittier present three elements paramount to the formation of collective identity: (1) a process of boundary creation between social movement actors and those outside the movement, (2) the establishment of collective consciousness, and (3) negotiation, or the incorporation of movement politics and practices in everyday life.[3] In addition to the establishment of a framework to analyze mobilization and identity, Taylor and Whittier direct social movement scholars' attention to the importance of individual actors and everyday actions in the shaping of collective identity.

Although the difficulty in establishing clear boundaries around who or what can be counted as feminist is at times posed as a post-1970s phenomenon, feminist identities have been contested since the inception of the movement.[4] Responding to conflicting definitions and strategies of feminists, Leila J. Rupp and Verta Taylor developed a collective identity typology amenable to analyzing a variety of feminist identities, specifically related to differences in geographical and/or historical locations. The authors identify interrelated layers of "organizational, movement, and solidary" identities, and highlight how each of these levels of analysis interacts with and shapes the others.[5] Because this framework allows us to understand differences between and among feminists and to recognize the continual process of collective identity formation, it provides the overarching reference for this chapter.

Evaluating feminist collective identities is challenging due to the imprecise nature of feminism.[6] "Because 'feminist' is premised on heterogeneous understandings of what 'feminism' is, the identity can be connected to manifold political agendas."[7] In this era of "everywhere and nowhere" feminism,[8] in which it is argued that feminism is at times imperceptible because of its incorporation in mainstream ideology and a range of institutions, the boundaries between feminists and nonfeminists are conceptual challenges. However, as Melucci argues, "[T]he ability of a collective actor to distinguish itself from others must be recognized by these others. Therefore it would be impossible to talk of collective identity without referring to its relational dimension."[9] Not only is collective identity reliant on a relational development between mobilized participants and outsiders; it is also contextually specific.

Third wave and young feminists have expressed consternation with a feminist movement premised on solidarity and "we-ness." In their effort to distance themselves from older feminists who were thought to rely on an exclusionary sisterhood, young feminists are thought to be focused on themselves in contrast to being bound to a collective feminist movement. In her discussion of third wave feminism, Astrid Henry writes, "In both forms of this new writing, feminism, as well as women's experiences generally, are not described using a collective 'we' voice, but rather with what I would term first-person-singular definitions of feminism, in which each author tells her *own* story and provides her *own* definition of what feminism means to her."[10] This individualist feminist approach is often categorized with neoliberal or empowerment feminism, in which feminists believe any choice they make could be considered feminist, simply on account of their being women.[11] These forms of feminism are criticized due to their lack of political focus, or because they uphold capitalist systems' subordination of women.[12] If this individualist notion of feminism is true, was there a dearth of feminist collective identity among campus feminists?

Feminist Organizations

Feminist organizations are critical elements for the construction of feminist collective identities. These groups have historically perpetuated feminist ideologies, advanced feminist grievances, and created feminist solidarity. Feminist organizations take various forms, and are nationally affiliated, institutionally affiliated, grassroots, or a combination of all.[13] Myra Marx Ferree and Patricia Yancey Martin argue that feminist organizations are in large part overlooked or taken for granted, "*seen but unseen* and rarely acknowledged as successful mobilizations of a movement that continues to press for change. . . . A more accurate measure of the health of the contemporary women's movement can be made by taking stock of feminist organizations."[14] Indeed, feminist organizations tell us a lot about the movement—and in understanding feminist organization members' strategies, tactics, grievances, emotions, and solidarity, we can understand the state of the movement more broadly.[15]

We know very little about feminist student organizations, although we know a lot about feminist organizations[16] and student protest.[17] Mem-

bers of feminist student organizations have led protests against community violence, pressed a university for change in sexual assault policies,
and created campaigns that have drawn national attention. In addition
to grassroots and community-oriented feminist student organizations,
there are a number of national feminist organizations that recruit and
engage college students through on-campus student organizations—
these include the Feminist Majority Foundation, the National Organization for Women, Planned Parenthood, and even conservative national
organizations such as Feminists for Life.[18] We do know that student
organizations and activism are strongly related to the institutional and
campus context,[19] but there is no other research about feminist student
organizing.

Feminist organizations play an important role in maintaining movements, because the dedication of established members ensures persistence and continuity.[20] But do young feminists feel connected to
feminist organizations? How do student feminist organizations today
transform feminism, perpetuate the feminist movement, and form feminist communities?

University of Minnesota: Oppositionally Oriented Feminism

Collective identity is dependent on the boundaries between movement participants and opponents; this provides a sense of cohesion
among activists.[21] The blurry boundaries between feminists and nonfeminists,[22] especially among young activists,[23] means that there are a
number of questions remaining about their collectivity and solidarity.
The U of M can be effectively used to illustrate the process of feminist boundary construction because the feminists there had the least
hospitable environment for mobilization. They also had the strongest
sense of feminist collective identity among feminists in the study, as evidenced by students' devotion to their feminist student organizations.
Feminism at the U of M is *oppositionally oriented*. It was defined by
struggles with university administration over its conservative policies
and with conservative students who spearheaded campaigns to defund
progressive and feminist student organizations. During my participant
observation, students from several feminist organizations described how
organized conservative students had continually constructed barriers or

undermined their progress. Because of this opposition, they created a small, tight-knit circle of feminists, despite being at the largest university in this study.

The U of M students were the least politically engaged among the three sites, although they are involved in many student organizations, and they do protest, particularly around issues of war and reproductive rights. It is also the campus with the most right-wing student organizations, who have over the last ten years built groups with substantial funding. According to the feminist students I interviewed, their conservative peers argue that because feminist and progressive organizations serve a minority of the U of M population, their portion of student service fees should be less. Students expressed anger and perplexity over this reasoning, but were resigned to it. Mixed-race, lower-middle-class lesbian Zan said, "It always comes down to money, and conservative people have money, and they feel like minorities don't need a space because there aren't many of them. And it's not cost effective to give minorities spaces, because there are always going to be fewer of them, so they don't matter as much." Zan felt as though progressive organizers were dwarfed by conservative students and their supporters. Note her description of "space"—Zan and other students felt as though they were hard pressed to find a physical and metaphorical place in which they could build an activist community.

The struggle for funding at the U of M was mainly between the feminist student group and the student service fees committee. Every student enrolled for six or more credits pays several hundred dollars in student service fees that are divided among student organizations. The feminist students I interviewed spoke with great emotion about the uneven fee allocation among student groups, which some attributed to the overrepresentation of conservative students on the student service fees committee. For example, while the president of two right-wing student organizations served on the student fees committee, he allocated a fifty-five-thousand-dollar increase for the two primary conservative student organizations.[24] For the 2012–2013 academic year, the conservative student newspaper *Students for a Conservative Voice* was allocated $83,560, and the conservative student group Collegians for a Constructive Tomorrow was given $85,483.[25] These budgets were two to three times the amount most of the student "cultural centers" received (including the women's student organization, the disabled student organization, and the queer student organization), even though, unlike the conservative organizations, they have offices, resource centers, and staff. Students in these cultural centers argued that there are very few conservative students involved in each of the conservative organizations, and that their events draw small audiences and are limited in scope. Despite their objections and alliances with other cultural centers, feminist students felt relatively powerless in the face of the committee. This conflict reflects a new conservative tone in the state of Minnesota. In my interviews at the U of M, I encountered many more students who expressed conservative ideologies than at the other schools. According to my survey data, U of M students were most likely to agree that students of color, and women, LGBTQ, and low socioeconomic status students were greatly or somewhat disadvantaged on their campus.

The relative conservatism of the U of M was implicit in the name of the school's prominent feminist organization: the Women's Collective. Historically, it has kept the term "women" instead of "feminist," and has tried to maintain an inclusive and moderate image. This choice was made in order to ensure funding from the conservative-leaning student service fees committee, a common social movement strategy, as "movements juggle multiple public presentations for different audiences."[26] Students thought a group that served women would be more readily funded than a group that was conspicuously feminist. However, during my research at the U of M, I observed an impromptu conversation between five or six members of a relatively large feminist organization. During the conversation, they were brainstorming whether to change the name of their organization to include "feminism," while also having a noncumbersome acronym. Their motivation for including "feminism" in their group name was to be more inclusive (i.e., not just women) and more radical (i.e., "feminism" as a more radical term than "women"). They did not change their name at the time. I speculate that they hesitated because their organization may encounter more challenges operating as an openly feminist group instead of as a women's group. The feminists at the other two schools were not concerned about this, and freely used "feminist," "radical feminist," or "womyn" in their organization names.

For students at the U of M I interviewed, participation in feminist groups was a more indispensable ingredient of their feminism than at the other schools. U of M students used strong language to affirm the importance of being a member of a feminist organization. White, middle-class queer woman Sophia said that participation in her feminist organization was "hugely important" to her feminism. Many students felt that their feminist groups helped integrate them into a "feminist community" at the university. The term "feminist community" was not used as commonly by students at the other two campuses. Zan laughed when I asked her if participation in organizations was an important part of her feminism, as though her answer was obvious. She then said, "Yes, it's where I find my community." When I asked White, middle-class bisexual Brooke, "Would you say that your involvement in the Women's Collective is a valuable part of your feminism?" she said, "Oh yeah, it's huge. I think it's getting bigger especially because it taps me into a community of activists and feminists. The people I'm with shape the way I view feminism and so the Women's Collective is a huge part of that." For Brooke and Zan, their involvement in feminist groups was critical to their sense of belonging and community with other like-minded activists, particularly as they felt surrounded by conservative students. Lauren, a White, middle-class queer woman who is a member of two feminist organizations, spoke about the importance of a feminist community: "I think it gives you a grounding to have an organization behind you because it allows you to reinforce your identity, because other people are there supporting you. It's really nice to have that community of people who are just focused on activism and really want to work on this. I think that definitely 'boosts up' my feminism." Lauren gained a community of feminists through her participation in feminist organizations—which invigorated her activism. Although I would not go so far to say that students on the other campuses did not perceive their involvement in feminist organizations as important to their feminism, the phenomenon was clearer and stronger at the U of M. I attribute this to the context. At the U of M, there was more of a range of students from conservative to liberal, whereas at Smith and UCSB, progressive perspectives were the norm. U of M students also had the clearest adversaries or opposition in conservative student organizations, and according to some students, the administration as well. Because feminism is the least accepted at the U of M, feminists there experienced the clearest boundaries between who was feminist and who was not.

Smith College: Institutionally Oriented Feminism

Given that feminist collective identity is reliant on a distinction between feminists and nonfeminists, what does it mean to be a feminist within an institution that is, to many members, inherently feminist? The feminist collective identity at Smith was distinct from that of the other two institutions because of its all-women student body, feminist history, and women leaders in all aspects of school life. All of the presidents appointed since 1975 have been women. Research on graduates of women's colleges indicates that all-women institutions foster self-confidence, leadership skills, and egalitarian views on gender roles.[27] This, and the culture of "taking women seriously,"[28] undoubtedly produced a unique feminist culture at Smith. In my survey, Smith students, at much higher rates than other students, reported that they participated in any actions or events devoted to promoting gender equality. They also were more likely to identify as feminist than students at UCSB and the U of M. As feminism was commonly accepted among students, administration, and faculty, nonfeminists were difficult to find.

"Smithies" have a clear sense of feminist "we-ness," evidenced by the uniform ways in which students speak about their feminist culture. Since their feminism was deeply connected to and expressed through being students at Smith College, their collective identity was founded in an *institutionally oriented feminism*. Smith students' sense of feminist "we-ness" differed from that of other research sites on several levels. First, common terms used by Smith students included "hegemonic gender regime" and "cis gender," and the majority of the students discussed the presence of transgender students at Smith in a positive light. In my interviews, students' descriptions of feminism, with few exceptions, included comments about moving beyond the binary and/or inclusion of transgender people in feminism. Second, students reported that feminism and gender were spoken about frequently outside the classroom. This provided students the opportunity to practice and develop feminist perspectives and language, and for many students in this study, to hone a sense of feminist solidarity. Third, their fashion and style stood apart from that of students at the other two campuses, fashion and style being, along with language, important elements of collective identity.[29] Students wore very short hairstyles dyed different hues. They also sported unconventional ensembles, such as accessories adorned with spikes, ripped t-shirts and jeans, or eye-catching, unusual color combinations. One student reported with a laugh that it was common knowledge that the longer students are at Smith, the shorter their hairstyles become.

Bea illustrated this point, and reminded me of many other Smith students in her appearance and language. Her hair was short and dyed bright blonde in random pieces. She spoke with energy and exuberance. A fluorescent yellow bra showed underneath her ripped shirt emblazoned with "LOVE, PEACE, BEER." She identified as a queer, middle-class White woman, with a Study of Women and Gender and Psychology double major. Of Smith, Bea said,

> One of the reasons why I'm going to Smith as a woman is because it is a place where women are educated and, aside from the trans students, we have a really great trans community as well and I welcome them with open arms, but all our leaders are female. All of our organizations are led by women: our president's a woman. We have an equal distribution of male and female professors, which I think is hard to find.

To Bea, Smith was unique because it affirmed and acted upon its commitment to women's leadership and teaching. Perhaps because of this environment, many students said that even in classes that have no direct relationship to gender or feminism, these topics would be incorporated into readings and discussion. When I asked Liz about the contexts in which feminism arises, she said, "In classes. At Smith, it always comes up. In readings, class discussions . . . a lot of professors integrate feminism into course work, which I find interesting." Other students reported speaking about feminist issues in their college houses, with their friends, and at meals—issues related to women and feminism were entrenched in many aspects of campus life. In this way, Smith stood out as a distinctly feminist college that integrated feminism in a variety of institutional dimensions: in the classroom, in extracurricular activities, and in social settings.

Because of its institutionalized feminism, feminist reputation and history, and single-sex student body, those who matriculate at Smith College are likely to be predisposed to either embrace a feminist identity or be open to feminism. Christina R., a White woman who discussed at length the day-to-day difficulties of being poor at an elite school, discussed the campus as attracting particular students: "I feel like since it's a women's college, most people come to Smith already leaning towards feminism. I mean, the whole point of Smith, how they advertise the women's college is that it empowers women and it gives them confidence and it teaches them they can be just as capable as men." Many other students concurred, including Michele, an African American, heterosexual, working-class woman, who said, "Feminism is in the comfort zone at Smith, it's not foreign, it's not something you have to try hard to pitch." Smith was uniformly described by its students as "feminist." The survey data indicate that students at Smith are more likely to have stronger feminist identification than students at the other two schools. They are also more likely to indicate that they belong to a feminist student organization.

So how did Smith students, being "naturally feminist," form a collective identity? Being "naturally feminist" meant that although feminism was assumed to be part of the environment, participants in this study also felt that feminism was not on the forefront of their minds. For example, Bette, who had thought a lot about the position of feminism in her life, said,

> I think compared to the general population, I'm probably way more feminist than a lot of women, but I feel like being a feminist differs depending on the context. Because I feel like here [at Smith College], there's really not a need to be super feminist, because it's really a female empowered place already. When I need to wear the feminist cape, I do. I don't feel like I need to here.

Bette exemplified the institutional specificity of feminist collective identity, and spoke of a "situational feminism" that depends on location.[30] Many other Smith students reiterated what Bette expressed regarding the influence of Smith on their feminism. When I asked Sophia, a mixed-race, upper-middle-class heterosexual woman, if she thought of herself as a feminist, she responded, "[C]ompared to who? Do I think I'm a Smith feminist? No. Do I think I am a feminist compared to a normal woman, outside in the real world? Then, yes, yes [laughs]." While collective identity relies on a boundary between "us" and "them," at

Smith, the "them" is an abstract nonfeminist other with whom they do not have regular contact on campus. Smith students knew that antifeminists existed outside of Smith and that they would have to harden their feminist shell after graduation.

In Jo Reger's comparison of feminism in different environments, the participants where feminism was accepted were likely to be less focused on gender inequality in favor of other issues.[31] I propose that because of the feminist history, feminist tone, and all-women student body of Smith College, gender is a less salient identity for its students than other features of identity.[32] For example, Bea, the student with the larger-than-life persona quoted previously, said of Smith later in our interview, "[At Smith] women can succeed without having to worry about negative stereotypes and getting overshadowed by men who are traditionally the ones who have a voice that's held in more esteem. . . . *I don't have to feel stressed about my gender because I don't have to worry about it on Smith campus*" (emphasis added). Although they did not state this sentiment as directly, other students made references to not being troubled by or conscious of gender in a single-sex setting. Interestingly, although they may be relieved of some gender concerns while on campus, the student body is still highly motivated and politically aware. Students direct their attention to queer issues and transgender issues, and generally advocated "thinking beyond the binary." The transgender student group was large and very popular.

Feminist organizations at Smith were undoubtedly influenced by the institutionally oriented feminism at Smith—it influenced feminist activists' networks and support. White, middle-class, heterosexual Maddelena, a member of Radical Religious Feminists, said when I asked about using the word "feminist" in the title of her organization, given its negative connotation in some settings, "Here, I don't think it's a big deal at all. There are a lot of organizations at Smith that have women in the title or have the word 'feminism' in the title or loudly proclaim they have feminist tendencies. There probably doesn't exist a group like this at any other college. Here, feminism does not have that [negative] connotation." Maddelena's interpretation of the institutional feminist context of Smith meant that it "wasn't a big deal" to form a feminist organization, which she contrasted with other schools, where it probably would not have been as accepted. But Anna P., a White, middle-class queer woman who was a leader in a feminist body-acceptance organization, had a different interpretation. She said, "It's so funny, because people don't understand why there are feminist groups on campus, because, they consider all of Smith to be a feminist organization, in and of itself." Although Anna P.'s organization did not replicate any other campus offerings, she felt as though her feminist organization was perceived as redundant. Gabriella, a White, middle-class queer woman and leader of a feminist group that is doing "super activist" activities, agreed with Anna P. in some respects. When I asked about her campus activism, she said, "I also feel like we are preaching to the choir." Since feminism was an agreeable concept at Smith, participants at times felt that they were not introducing anything new to the activist conversations, or that their peers were lethargic about women's issues. Anne W. described her experiences in a pro-choice campus group: "I think people tend to be like, oh a pro-choice club 'yay!' [sarcastically], and then there's not much feeling about it. It's not like other campuses where there would be opposition per se, there's just ambivalence." According to students, some feminist organizations at Smith were seen as redundant at best and unnecessary at worst.

It is not remarkable if a feminist group dies out at Smith. Due to feminism's institutional embeddedness, feminists have a number of other outlets. When I asked Gabriella how she became the leader of a main feminist organization at Smith, she said, "I joined midway through last year, during my sophomore year, mostly because a friend said 'this organization has no one in it and you should join.'" Gabriella was frustrated with the lack of interest in feminist organizations, but she managed to resuscitate and expand the group.

Because feminism was all around them, feminist sentiments were easily applied to a range of student organizations. Smith student Anna C. reported that the connections among her organizations strengthened her personal understanding of feminism:

> [B]eing part of STAND [human rights organization] has furthered my understanding of women, and giving equality to women and how it can help society as a whole. And I think when you connect different things to feminism it just makes things more clear, because now you're not just talking about feminism as a movement, you're talking about people, peo-

ple everywhere. And when you can relate it to yourself and what you're involved in I think it impacts you more than it not being related.

Her participation in a feminist and human rights organization facilitated her realization that improving the status of women actually improved the society as a whole. Like Anna C., Sylvia, a White, bisexual, lower-middle-class woman, made connections between feminism and other struggles. Sylvia was in an organization of class activists at Smith, which she said was "completely" feminist: "I mean, working-class issues, they're also women's issues. Just historically . . . women do make up the majority of blue-collar workers, and they have ever since the industrial revolution. Women's issues have always been tied with lower-class issues."

Smith nourished an *institutionally oriented feminism.* Although boundaries between feminists and nonfeminists remain important elements of establishing collective identity, I did not find evidence of a strong oppositional feminist collective identity at Smith. Because of the campus environment and the college's history, Smith students did not describe borders between feminist insiders and outsiders. The strong sense of being a "Smithie" created and nurtured the collective consciousness that is integral to a feminist collective identity.[33] The feminist institutional embeddedness meant that feminist student organizations were not always seen as important outlets for feminist solidarity and community, but that feminist perspectives were incorporated in other groups.

University of California–Santa Barbara: Hybrid Feminism

How do feminist collective identities meld into an atmosphere that largely values social justice activism? The *hybrid feminism* at UCSB is identified by its support of progressive student organizations and its reputation as an activist campus. UCSB has a long student activist history, particularly evident in the 1960s and '70s. For example, in 1969, UCSB students organized a "wharf-in" at Santa Barbara's Stearns Wharf to protest offshore drilling. In 1970, UCSB students occupied the faculty club. Although the student paper at the time reported how student "demonstrators enjoyed the club's liquor, food, and swimming pool facilities, and sang songs together," students had a long list of grievances and demands of the administration.[34] The students spoke out for greater transparency in the university's decision-making processes. They expressed concerns about the "entire structure and function of the university."[35] The protests at the time culminated in the burning of the Bank of America in Isla Vista, for which several students were indicted.

The accomplishments of these UCSB activists were well documented and have become a campus legacy. In 2011, sociology professor Dick Flacks led a "history walk" around campus and Isla Vista as part of the all-campus reunion. In 2012, UCSB hosted a conference celebrating the history of the Students for a Democratic Society (SDS) and the 1962 Port Huron Statement, the document that inspired the New Left and student activists. The event was cosponsored by numerous campus organizations, including the student government. Although the protests reflected the political environment of the era, in comparison to the other two campuses, UCSB has the most active and colorful history of student organizing.

This progressive culture shaped the *hybrid feminism* at UCSB. A hybrid is "an organization where identity is comprised of two or more types that would not normally be expected to go together."[36] Women's movements have specifically benefited from hybrid organizations and ideologies, not only because of the movements' persistence over time but also because of the challenges of organizing such a broad and diverse identity category.[37] The hybrid perspective is useful in analyzing feminist collective identities, which, in the case of UCSB, included conceptions of feminism closely tied to social justice.

The tradition of UCSB student organizing and the left-leaning student government fostered a strong progressive community in which feminism was often integrated into organizations with diverse missions and goals. Although it did not have a baseline of feminist culture like that at Smith, UCSB student feminism was evidenced by involvement in feminist organizations and progressive activism more generally. In comparison to Smith and the U of M, UCSB had the most effectual environment for feminism and related student activism.

Students consistently elected a student government that supported student organizations and the advancement of their causes (often feminist). For example, in the spring of 2012, the student government voted to ban any campus advertisement for "crisis pregnancy centers."[38] These anti-abortion centers are found near many college campuses, and employees lure students with the promise of a pregnancy test and later reveal their anti-abortion stance. This ban was the result of organizing by a student group called "End Fake Clinics," formed in conjunction with a feminist studies course. The student government, in October 2012, also passed resolutions in which student senators promised to support the LGBTQ community and student organizations committed to ending gender-based and sexual violence at UCSB and in Isla Vista. The president of the student government "assured the Senate that their decision [to support the resolutions] will affect the student body, particularly women."[39] The support that the student government offers nurtures an environment in which organizations include a variety of progressive claims in their missions and goals.

In UCSB's hybrid environment, the multicultural sororities were likely to be feminist. Many Latina and African American students were involved in multicultural sororities that they called feminist. UCSB student Diana described her sorority as "a multicultural based organization committed to the empowerment of women. We don't say we're feminists empowering women. In a sense, it is understood within our organization." In contrast, UCSB student Miriam, a Latina, lower-middle-class heterosexual, and the social chair of a UCSB multicultural sorority, called her organization feminist. She talked about its goals to provide professional and social opportunities to its members, as well as to serve the community. Summer spoke to me about her African American sorority, which she considered feminist. After describing the founding of her sorority by a group of Black women in 1922 as a way to change their lives, she highlighted the activities they do to support and empower women in their community. These included programs that helped single mothers in Santa Barbara. The majority of the women I interviewed who were members of multicultural and Black sororities were first-generation college students. Their presence at UCSB in and of itself had more political meaning than for the students whose family members pursued higher education. Similarly, these multicultural sorority members uniformly chose their sorority "big sisters" or other sorority friends as role models, indicating the solidarity and importance of establishing a network of women of color at their university. They took seriously the edict that being in a feminist organization meant that they empowered themselves, their fellow sorority members, and women in the community.

An intersectional feminist perspective was critical to feminism at UCSB. Feminist students were involved in more than one student organization, and they spoke about how the processes, ideologies, and approaches of their organizations were feminist. UCSB student Camille spoke about how the numerous groups she is part of, both gender related and not, are feminist. "In my opinion, they are all feminist organizations. But no, they don't focus specifically on gender. The human rights group is about the human rights framework, which is essential to the feminist framework. The coalition [I am a member of] is mostly focused on income and your ability to afford a public education. Those are key components of feminism." Camille's feminism carried over to other groups; because her understanding of feminism was both gender focused and, more generally, social justice focused, her participation in organizations that concentrated on the accessibility of higher education and on human rights was inherently feminist. Many students spoke about their organizations' feminist character. At first I thought that these students were probably feminist studies majors and had become deft at using feminist language. It did not matter, however, whether the students were feminist studies majors or not. In fact, I received a few "no duh"–type looks when I asked whether and how their organizations were feminist. For example, Anselmo, a mixed-race, heterosexual man, active in a wide range of student organizations with environmental, religious, and human rights concerns, said,

> The idea of feminism intersects with almost every single effort that you do. Like environmentalism, that doesn't sound [like] feminism, but you can look at how Mother's Day is coming up, and Valentine's Day just happened, and you get those flowers, everybody buys them, a lot of people don't know that they come mostly from Colombia . . . and women pick flowers with pesticides, and it causes cancer and reproductive problems. Does it have to do with the environment? Yeah! But, it also has to do with feminism and racism and all these things intersect. *I suppose that's one of the goals of all the groups [I'm involved in], is to show how struggles intersect.* (emphasis added)

Anselmo's activism fundamentally joined issues of social conflict—including race, class, gender, and immigration status. His goal in activism was to show the interconnectedness of social justice issues.

The multicultural sororities at UCSB, too, were integrated into the network of feminist organizations on campus. Sorority members spoke with me about their numerous coalitions with other feminist organizations, an example being the womyn's board banquet (featured in the opening of this chapter). At UCSB, I attended a speak-out against abusive relationships, sponsored by the women's center and a multicultural sorority. The emcee was a woman I interviewed as president of her multicultural sorority. Most of the women in attendance appeared to be women of color from several multicultural sororities.

UCSB students stood out in their solid network of feminists who incorporated divergent progressive goals (including multicultural sororities and organizations affiliated with student government). The meaning of their feminism was strongly related to participation in a vibrant social movement community. Because of this, the "we-ness" of UCSB feminists was closely connected to the "we-ness" of general student organization participation. In many cases, feminists were in the same organizations, planned the same events, and were motivated by the same causes as the progressive students more generally. But unlike at Smith, feminists helped push gender-related initiatives in other progressive groups. Organizational hybridity at UCSB also fostered the strongest effects of social movement "spillover," such as feminist ideologies incorporated in Greek life, art, and cultural organizations, and student government.[40]

Movement Identity: A Third or Fourth Wave?

In the last fifteen years there has been a proliferation of popular writing on young women and third wave feminism, both domestically and globally, some using the label "third wave."[41] The emergence of such a body of literature is attributed to two related factors. First, in the early to mid-1990s, an older generation of feminists was concerned about who was going to ensure the continuation of feminism.[42] Second, and partially in response to a lack of recognition, young feminists took to writing productively about their identities and grievances.[43]

Third wave feminists were invested in identifying with a movement that emphasized diversity of participants, ideas, and tactics.[44] They also stressed intersectionality and the complex nature of identity. Many third wave feminists destabilized the notion that there is a unified "woman," rejected the gender binary and rigid gender roles, embraced sexuality, and sought to include men in the movement. Building on the perceptions that feminism was dead and that second wave feminists lacked energy and innovation, third wave feminists spoke to a new generation of young feminists.[45] To many people, young feminism has become synonymous with third wave feminism.

Did the women in this research identify with third wave feminism? It was surprising how few were interested in or even knew about third wave feminism. Out of the seventy-five interviews I conducted, three students identified as third wave feminists, one at each campus: a heterosexual Black woman at UCSB, a queer White man at the U of M, and a queer White woman at Smith. They did not have much conviction about it, however. Their interview comments were like those of Smith student Bea: "I would count myself within third wave because I don't think I'm in the fourth wave and there's a really active feminist movement going on"; her adoption of the third wave related more to wanting to be counted within current feminist mobilization than to any particular conviction about the third wave. U of M student Gilgamesh, who languidly identified as third wave because "I think [third wave] is better accounting for the problematic aspects of feminism from before it," confirmed that some third wavers' orientation is mainly a distancing from previous generations of feminists.

Smith student Eileen, a White, upper-middle-class heterosexual woman, was hesitant to align with third wave feminism. When I asked whether she would identify as a third wave feminist, she said,

> I feel like I'm supposed to. That's the impression that feminist scholarship has forced on me. So, like I'm a third wave feminist, but what will fourth wave feminists say about third wave feminists? And, are all of my ideas and philosophy totally aligned with third wave feminism? A lot of feminists, or women who you could categorize as third wave feminists, don't conceive of themselves or articulate themselves as third wave feminist though they may hold consistent beliefs with them.

Eileen did not like the waves, and found the framework confining. Unlike Eileen, those students who did identify with third wave feminism felt that it was something feminists ought to do. Smith student Anne W. said, "I think for me there are some things I like about third wave feminism, but I don't think it's really something I've attached myself to." Some Smith students knew about third wave feminism because they educated themselves about it on the Internet, but many of the other interview participants did not know about it.

Although none of the respondents were particularly thrilled about adopting a "wave" identity, some of them were more likely to embrace the fourth wave. Smith student Lily said, "I don't know, is the third wave even happening? What I've read is that we're transitioning into the fourth wave. I don't know if I identify with any wave per se." A few students were a little more excited about a fourth wave. Smith student Gabriella said, "I feel like we're in fourth wave. I feel like blogging and the Internet sort of community has become the fourth wave." Smith student Anne W. said, "There's part of me that thinks we're already onto the fourth wave." She continued,

> I started thinking about the fourth wave when Hillary [Clinton] lost [the presidential nomination]. I think it was a lot of emotion, it was very obvious that some type of unfairness had taken place, not in terms of who won and lost, but I think in terms of how people were portrayed and what was focused on. *I think it was in a time when everyone wanted to think we were postfeminism, we really weren't, and it was an indicator that third wave was failing. It either wasn't doing enough, or wasn't aware that there were still things that need to be done. I like to think of the fourth wave, if there is a fourth wave, as the anger that came out of the knowledge that maybe we weren't back to square one, but we weren't where we thought we were.* (emphasis added)

For many people, a unified feminist wave is a feminist vitality. That I didn't find this to be the case in my particular research does not indicate a lack of feminist vigor. Rather, these findings provide additional evidence that the wave framework is not reflective of the realities of feminist mobilization or identities. This resonates with the *waveless* feminist model and with previous research indicating that the wave framework is problematic because it diverts our attention from the development, continuity, and complexities of feminism.[46]

The sustaining of the wave model relies in part on divisions between participants active in different surges of mobilizing. Second wave feminists, for example, are assumed to share some characteristics of the time period in which they were most active, and are thought to be separate from the third wave. Third wave feminism, by its definition, cannot exist while second wave feminism is flourishing. Thus, expectations for the current state of feminism are focused on the efforts of third wave feminists (or fourth wave feminists). This vividly exposes the fault in the wave framework. Those activists who may generationally be most closely affiliated with the second wave are still mobilizing at the same time as those activists who may most closely resemble third or fourth wave feminists. As we can see from the participants' responses in this research, vibrant feminist activism occurs outside the confines of the wave identifications. The wave approach not only flattens complex activism, but it also creates unnecessary separations between feminists of different generations or backgrounds. This oversimplification manufactures generational divides—feminists from all political generations have dismissed each other, criticized each other, or questioned each other's motivations and accomplishments.[47] That these divisions are realistic reflections of feminism is doubtful.[48]

To ascertain participants' attitudes toward previous generations of feminists, I asked participants in interviews and the survey if they thought the feminism of the 1970s improved the status of women. I expected these answers to show some degree of hostility or ill will, given the generational dissent so commonly written of. Participants in this study, whether or not they identified as feminists, made many positive comments about how feminists have contributed to a more just world. Moreover, 83.3 percent of the survey respondents agreed with the statement, "Feminism of the 1970s advanced women's status in the U.S."

In the interviews, I was struck by the number and variety of affirming reflections about older generations of feminists. The most common response to the question was that feminism of the 1970s put women's issues on the national radar, and increased the cognizance of gender inequality in society at large. Gabriella, a Smith student and leader of a feminist organization, said, "Even though they get a bad rap, I think they opened a space for other people to raise their voices to what was going on and to be public about it . . . bringing women together in the community, that is vocal, is really important." Gabriella recognized that feminism of the 1970s had a negative reputation in some circles, but emphasized how important its contributions were in terms of solidarity. UCSB student Angelina said feminists succeeded by "saying it was a problem, and that they weren't going to stand up for it anymore. That allowed other women to have that same voice, so other women could speak up, having that movement gave people a voice." To Angelina, feminists gave strength to each other and momentum to the movement. U of M student Sophia said, "I think that time has definitely allowed us to generate more of a feminist consciousness, and bring things to the public and bring things to the front of people's minds, which we haven't always been able to do." She continued, "I think that the ideas of questioning what was going on and giving women space to question, that was really important and it led to other people raising their voices." Empowering others and finding a place for other oppressed individuals was critical to feminism. UCSB student Elsa said,

> I think that during that time there's a lot of representation of women in academic [arenas], speaking of their experiences. But, I think that it was advancement for, more women of color. Coming in and saying we're different from you but we have different struggles . . . this is what's going to be talked about. I think it was an advancement for women to open their circle and address those kinds of issues, and women just holding those higher positions as college graduates, or not as college graduates, as politicians, and giving voice to others who didn't have that agency.

From Elsa's perspective, the development of 1970s feminism gave women of color opportunities to share their experiences and injustices—to expand how we think about the category of women. As a result, women in positions of power were able to lift up other women.

Students noted how feminists of previous generations improved women's job opportunities and home lives. UCSB student Summer expressed positive sentiments towards feminists: "I feel like women are breaking through glass ceilings. I feel like they are all good examples of the product of the 1970s." Smith student Bea also spoke of the workplace, but from a legal perspective, "There were a lot of laws that came out of the 1960s and '70s that really helped women, especially in the work-place." Other students spoke about advances in the workplace benefiting women at home, and the feminist change that allowed more egalitar-ian family arrangements. Said Lindsay, from UCSB, "You can tell [its impact by] the way that men view a woman, there are lots of men out there who would say . . . a man can be a house father, or [a woman can] make as much or more money than a [man], whereas before the feminist movement you wouldn't have seen that." Smith student Margarite also remarked on women's employment and family, enthusiastically recalling previous generations of feminists:

> AUTHOR: Do you think feminism of the 1970s improved the status of women?
>
> MARGARITE: Yes! Just the mentality that women can hold a job, and can have a family at the same time. Or that women don't have to have four children, it's okay to have two. Just in the opportunities that women are allowed to have, and the mentality about what women are allowed to do.

Expanding women's prospects in the workplace and home was appreci-ated by young feminists. However, admiration for 1970s feminists was not reserved for feminist study participants. U of M student Morningstar, who was not a feminist and seemed to dislike the feminists she knew, brightened up when I asked her about feminists of the 1970s. She said,

> I think they made a lot of advances. Just as much as I support women who want to stay at home, not all women want to stay at home and it's really hard when you live in a culture that says, "If you're unmarried, you can be a teacher or a nurse, but as soon as you get married if you have to work, that means that your husband isn't a good husband. You should be home in your dress, showered, with the kids washed, and a martini for your [husband]"—so I think they made a lot of really big strides for us and they've helped out a lot with us being able to do whatever we want both in our personal lives and with our bodies.

Morningstar, despite her distaste for present-day feminists, tied feminism to the variety of fulfilling life choices men and women currently have.

The theme of bodies and reproductive rights was central to the advances of the 1970s feminist movement. Smith student Anna P. said, "As far as extending the right to make your own choices surrounding reproduction I think yes, I think definitely they were quite helpful and radical at the time." She continued, "[I]t did a lot to expand reproductive rights, and bring to the surface that these are important issues, the Hyde amendment and things like that." One of the most lasting successes of 1970s feminism, to Anna P., was reproductive rights. Fellow Smith student Charlotte spoke of reproductive rights and sexuality:

> You can have sexual intercourse without fearing pregnancy. It was such a stigma to be an unwed mother, so I think that, that really held us down when we're bound by our ability to pursue sexual experience and sexual pleasure with anyone that we wanted to, without feeling like we had to be bound to that person. I think that was significant. After that, birth control grew larger and now we have emergency contraception, and now we have STD screening and prevention. To have more ways that women can protect themselves or have more control over their bodies, whereas they used to be at the mercy of men, who did have control over their bodies.

Charlotte spoke spiritedly of how prior to 1970s feminist organizing, women were "at the mercy of men." She noted that feminism not only allowed women to have control over their bodies but also led to other medical advancements.

Students noted the founding of feminist organizations as an important component of improving the status of women. Smith respondent Bette said, "[T]here are still major women's organizations that operate because of the feminist movement of the '60s. In that sense, if it weren't for that move, we wouldn't have a lot of those organizations we have now." UCSB student Ninjabi spoke of organizations:

> I think there's more organizations that actually pay attention to struggles of women of color. . . . Didn't Loretta Ross found a group that focuses on reproductive justice? Not only the right to abort but the right to have chil-

dren, I mean, against forced sterilization and everything like that. I think [feminism] has come a long way in that more organizations are paying attention to struggles outside of the struggles of white middle-class women.

Fellow UCSB student Ayaliza said,

Yes, they're now more openly able to voice their opinions in the political spectrum, you know, voting rights, forming unions and organizations like NOW, that was a big deal, it was like BOOM! women are here and they're taking a stance and voicing their opinions. And now, it's not seen as so extreme as it was before. Now, you have women organizations and it's a mainstream thing. Like there's womyn's comm and a women of color group over there. It's not like, "whoa there's a woman's group," it's more accepted now.

I was surprised that students valued the organizational advancements of feminists, especially given the research about young women's lack of interest in previous generations of feminists.

In spite of the acknowledgment of such positive elements of feminism, participants' comments about previous forms of feminism were not all favorable. For example, U of M student Brooke said,

Since the status of women is a pretty complicated issue in the way that certain women's perspectives were privileged in the feminist movement, I think that maybe the way that some women's experiences were ignored did not help the status of women whatsoever. It, maybe, was even more of a dangerous thing because there was this illusion that women's lives were being improved while others' were being ignored. At the same time, I recognize that there have been huge differences since then such as bringing gender issues to the forefront of political and social discussions.

Anna P. from Smith was very concerned about reproductive rights, saying, "I don't think that [feminism] focused enough on women of color, I think that their voice was absent much of the time." Both Anna P. and Brooke were dedicated to and confident in their feminist identities, yet they also did not hesitate to point out previous generations' shortcomings.

It is thought that feminism may be passed down from generation to generation, that there are inevitable parallels between those who came of age in different political generations.[49] Although it is true that there are differences in feminism determined in large part by the political and cultural context in which an individual comes of age,[50] as Lee Ann Banaszak reminds us, "[D]ivisions in a movement can mask considerably continuity."[51] Because feminism has changed, there is an assumed hostility between generations.[52] This is flawed for a number of reasons— namely, because there are so many different types of feminism, it is impossible to ascertain whether there is one particular relationship among feminists. Conversations limiting feminism to intergenerational fighting or waves do not reflect the perspectives of my interview participants. They also obscure continuity in the movement.

Chapter 4 Conclusion

This chapter opened with a description of the womyn's banquet at UCSB. At the event, students celebrated unity among women and feminists by gathering community members and social justice organizers. A dedicated "herstorian" presented the history of women's organizing on campus, speaking about the continuity and change in campus feminism. This event reflected the cohesion among feminists and other activists on the UCSB campus, who, with their *hybrid feminism*, had support from a number of organizations and institutional entities. They were proud of their campus's history of activism, as it created extensive networks of activists who supported each other and were in many ways unified. In contrast, the feminists at the U of M had keen opposition to their organizing, reflected in their *oppositional feminism*. In this context, feminists felt a strong connection to their fellow feminists, and created a tight-knit community that was highly valued by participants. However, this did not mean that participants in this study did not coalition or focus on issues of intersectionality, as had been found in previous research about variations in feminism by community.[53] Rather, in addition to having a close-knit feminist community, participants also valued their peers who had progressive viewpoints, and they joined forces to combat conservatism on campus. Smith's *institutional feminism* meant that study participants assumed that everyone on campus was feminist;

students were unified in their agreement about the consequence and relevance of feminism. However, this assumption of feminism made their organizing lack vibrancy or urgency at times, because their opposition or necessity was not clear to some of their peers. The feminists shared their dedication to feminist ideologies in choosing to attend Smith and in applying their feminism to other organizational settings when necessary.

The collective identities of these campus feminists are inclusive and externally oriented.[54] Further, the collective identities supported and sustained by feminist organizations on each of the campuses were brought by activists to other movements, blurring the boundaries between which elements of feminist collective identity are internal and which are external to the movement.[55] Movement participants extended feminist frames to immigrant-rights movements, to antiwar movements, and to movements fighting for accessible public education.[56] This makes it difficult to distinguish between who is inside and who is outside the movement, reflecting recent perspectives on the intersectional nature of collective identity construction.[57] However, such a collective identity may also aid feminist mobilization as a result of inter- and intra-movement solidarity.[58] This chapter illustrates not only that collective identity is an ongoing process but that movement participants do not have singular or one-dimensional collective identities.[59] If we are wondering where young feminists have gone, we will find them only if we employ an expansive and contextually specific approach.

There was no indication of third wave solidarity—in fact, participants in this study were largely resistant to the third wave and the wave framework more generally. They did not like labels, nor were they comfortable with having a particular wave identity foisted upon them. The usefulness of the *waveless feminism* concept is stressed. However, despite resistance to the waves, there was no evidence of the "first-person-singular" feminism being employed by young women.[60] These feminists did have a collective orientation, albeit a dynamic and evolving one, and felt indebted to the feminists who came before them.

Respondents' feelings about the accomplishments of 1970s feminists shed light on generational differences between feminists. Despite some negativity, overall, the positivity of participants regarding their impressions of the advancements made by 1970s feminists was striking. This suggests that the divisions caused by the wave framework, and the fabricated cat fights between feminists, are neither helpful nor reflective of these feminists' experiences. Their loyalty and positivity demonstrate the ongoing nature of dedication to feminist change. Participants' reactions show how they are carrying the torch of feminists: they are still concerned with reproductive rights, feminist organizations, and gender inequality. At the same time, this highlights the relevance of the stalled gender revolution—the problems participants in this study identified as those that older generations have addressed are also the same problems that continue to plague us.

Collective identity is a property of groups and individuals, and of interrelated layers of "organizational, movement, and solidary" identities.[61] Despite variations in collective identity, feminists on each campus had three features in common that bound them together. First, they subscribed to an intersectional feminism that incorporated their grievances about gender, race, class, sexuality, and immigration-status inequalities. Their dedication to each of these issues was a critical part of their feminism, and the activists assumed that this was a primary principle of the feminist movement. Although a layperson might speculate that multiple-issue feminism dilutes the movement,[62] this is not the case. Rather, many feminists, and particularly women of color, have been dedicated to intersectional issues for generations, and these young feminists are perpetuating what many feminists have always been concerned about. Second, at each campus, feminist organizations were important sites in which to learn about feminism, to form solidarity with others, and to mobilize around the inequalities that students observed in the world around them and studied in classes. It is true that their allegiances to their feminist organizations were not uniform at each campus or between campuses, but the importance of these groups to their development as feminists and activists was considerable, particularly as feminist organizations are barometers of the feminist movement more generally.[63] The third point that provided cohesion among feminists was that, overall, participants in this study had positive feelings towards feminists of the 1970s. Several study participants acknowledged the shortcomings of previous generations of feminists. However, at the same time, they held appreciation for the advancements that previous generations had made—they believed that their lives were altered for the better by the accomplishments of the feminists who came before them. This feminist cohesion should not be underestimated. Because it connects young feminists to previous generations and situates them within a lineage of feminists, it is important evidence of continuity and persistence. When we step outside the traditional wave perspective, we can understand the movement with greater detail and precision.

5

Can Facebook Be Feminist?

Online, Coalitional, and Everyday Feminist Tactics

The popular website Everyday Feminism, using the tagline "intersectional feminism for your everyday life," provides information about feminism in short, easily digestible pieces. "At Everyday Feminism, feminism makes it the norm that all people are human beings and every person deserves the same rights and opportunity to determine their own lives regardless of their social status."[1] One day in 2015, Everyday Feminism blog headlines included "How queer relationships can get stuck in harmful gender norms (and why we really need to get unstuck)"; "The pro-choice movement has a white supremacy problem and anti-choice advocates are using it to their advantage"; and "White privilege, explained in one simple comic." The comprehensive site offers online courses, a speakers' bureau, and a mass of online content.

In contrast to Everyday Feminism, the unrelated Everyday Sexism project operates a website, a Tumblr account, and a Twitter account with 63,900 followers to date, on which individuals submit examples of daily incidents of sexism: "By sharing your story you're showing the world that sexism *does* exist, it is faced by women everyday and it *is* a valid problem to discuss."[2] Tweets on the Everyday Sexism Twitter feed empathetically expose the interactional nature of gender inequality:

Man sees my 3 year old Chinese-American daughter and says "I like Oriental women they don't talk back" shocked I was offended #everydaysexism

That cute moment one too many men shout at you in the street so you scream back the fire of a thousand female rages at them @everydaysexism

@EverydaySexism review at work was almost perfect except for one problem: too assertive, need to be more "nice," more "delicate" responses

@EverydaySexism talking tech stuff w/friends. Man steps in and asks if I actually know what I'm talking about and do I need help explaining.

The popularity of the Everyday Sexism and Everyday Feminism sites is a testimony to the urgency of the topics. They are sought-after venues for individuals to express their grievances and to create solidarity with others. The tweets and blog entries capture similar protests and tactics of participants in this research, who also were aggravated by everyday sexism, were interested in intersectional feminism, and learned about inequality and feminism online. In this chapter, I discuss the online, coalitional, and everyday tactics of feminists on each college campus: What tactics are employed by college feminists today? How do feminist tactical repertoires shift in different locations and in relationship to the varying collective identities found on each campus? How do students enact feminism in their everyday lives? How do their tactics reflect their intersectional approach to feminism?

Tactical Repertoires

"Tactical repertoires," or the amalgamation of tactics employed by a social movement organization, link social movement actors to each other, to opponents, and to authorities.[3] Verta Taylor and Nella Van Dyke established a conceptual framework for social movement tactics, emphasizing contestation, intentionality, and collective identity.[4] Many factors influence tactical repertoires, including external historical conditions as well as internal movement processes. Taylor and Van Dyke's framework also considers how tactical repertoires influence movement outcomes.[5] The powerful association between the women's movement and bra burning, in which case the fictional tactics were conflated with the movement itself, has had a lasting and meaningful impact on the women's movement.[6] Gender and social movement scholars have expanded theories of tactical repertoires and goals in order to understand the distinctively gendered forms of activism deployed by women's movements that have contributed to their endurance.[7]

Repertoires of contention change over time, and when a movement is not at the height of its mobilization, participants tend to focus on cultural events that ensure the maintenance of collective identity and promote movement continuity.[8] Through the highs and lows of movement activity, movements persevere by "promoting the survival of *activist networks*, sustaining a repertoire of *goals and tactics*, and promoting a *collective identity* that offers participants a sense of mission and moral purpose."[9] Tactical repertoires during periods of little mass support may change, however, because challenging groups typically face a reduction in numbers and resources.[10]

Online Feminism: Facebook and Blogs

Online feminism, or what I call Facebook Feminism, has exploded as a driving force of feminism.[11] The implications of Internet feminism remain undertheorized, and some are hesitant to overstate the influence of the Internet on social movement communities.[12] However, vivid examples of strong online feminist communities abound, running the gamut from feminist blogs to multinational feminist organizations circulating feminist news. They suggest that Internet activity significantly upheld women's feminist communities.

Because online feminism remains, for the most part, unanalyzed, there is a perception that feminist organizing may not be happening on the web. The widespread belief that young women are disinterested in feminism is driven by the lack of understanding of the changes in feminist tactics. This phenomenon was featured in an online article: "Young Feminists to Older Feminists: If You Can't Find Us, It's Because We're Online."[13] This article was one of many written in response to remarks made in *Newsweek* by Nancy Keenan, executive director of NARAL (National Abortion Rights Action League), questioning the devotion of young women to issues of reproductive freedom. The author of "Young Feminists to Older Feminists," Stephanie Herold, argues that young feminists are using the Internet to advance feminist claims. Herold writes, "Whether we tweet feminism or blog about it, young feminists use the Internet to expand and explore what it means to be involved in the feminist movement. We usually do it in addition to other feminist work, using the Internet to launch campaigns, reach new audiences with our message, and create a sense of feminist community."[14] Just as online feminism can only be fully understood within the larger context of face-to-face feminism, contemporary offline feminism can only be fully understood with a consideration of the Internet.

Facebook was utilized by nearly all the feminists in this research, and they were not hesitant to extoll its virtues. UCSB student Camille said, "I think it's important to recognize that Facebook can be the best feminist resource in the world." Study participants used Facebook for multiple reasons. Organization members used the site to advertise events, create community, and further their feminist campaigns. Individual feminists used the site to set up boundaries between feminists and nonfeminists, to facilitate social justice conversations, and to disseminate feminist news articles and blog posts.

All of the organizations cited in this study used Facebook to advertise events. On Facebook, any subscriber can produce an event page and send invitations to individuals, organizations, or networks. The opportunities for event dissemination are far-reaching, and Facebook has rapidly replaced more traditional venues for advertising. During an "Activist 101" workshop at the U of M, a local community organizer said that paper posters were nearly obsolete because of online advertising.

Feminist organization members faced funding shortages that impeded their abilities to organize. Facebook is free. The Smith feminist group that was allocated only seventeen dollars for one semester could not afford to copy fliers, make posters, or even chalk campus sidewalks with notices of an upcoming event. Instead, members relied on a Facebook event page, underscoring the use of the Internet to counteract limited resources. UCSB student Bridget told me about the importance of Facebook when she found out that a program instrumental to her success at UCSB was being cut—the program assists UCSB students from underprivileged backgrounds in transition to the university. She used Facebook to plan a fundraiser to keep the program running: "I found out on Tuesday what was going on [about the program cut], Wednesday we had a meeting, Monday we had a fundraiser, it was fast!" She said, "It was perfect! I got people moving, that's how I contacted people, that's how I got ahold of a lot of people, that's how the fire started. I was able to do it through Facebook." When Smith student Anne W. sends Facebook invitations for an upcoming meeting of her pro-choice organization, "at least an additional eight people show up." If she forgot to send the invite, attendance was more apt to be sparse.

Organization members used Facebook to communicate issues and promote projects. During sexual assault awareness month, the UCSB antirape organization devoted one meeting to the topic of Facebook and text-message stalking. Student leaders encouraged participants to post Facebook status updates describing the seriousness of stalking ("It's not a joke, it's not okay"). Lisa, a member of the organization, told me that she posted a number of these status updates. She reported receiving mostly positive feedback, which she attributed to the activist-friendly nature of UCSB. Many of her Facebook friends inquired further about the stalking and sexual assault awareness months:

> A lot of them were positive reactions but I do definitely remember a few reactions where it was not intentionally offensive, but very dismissive. At least those few said something so it gave me a chance to respond back, which was, I think, effective. I'm glad sometimes to have a negative reaction just because I take that as an opportunity to educate them.

Other students reported that they managed their feminist organizations' Facebook pages and disseminated news articles, feminist blog posts, and relevant current events to their membership and friends of the organization. On a site in which individuals have hundreds, even thousands of friends, it is an effective means of communication. In this respect, it is a particularly useful tool for feminist campaigns whose goals are to educate and spread awareness.

Facebook also helped establish boundaries between feminists and nonfeminists. It was a site for boundary contestation, and many students told me about arguments on the site. In interviews, student descriptions of Facebook confrontations were often accompanied by knowing eye-rolls and sighs, indicating just how common they were. At Smith, a Saturday afternoon event I attended included at least fifteen minutes of discussion about a Facebook conflict. The discord concerned another Smith group that invited a speaker to campus who was thought to be antiwelfare. At the Saturday event, leaders of that organization passed out hard copies of the Facebook dispute and planned how to protest the speaker. Mostly, though, Smith students clashed with their off-campus nonfeminist Facebook friends. Also at Smith, Iowan Anna P. told me about a conversation that unfolded on her Facebook page:

> I posted something about immigration in Iowa, which I view as a feminist issue. And there was a dialogue on my Facebook page between a peer in high school and my history professor at Smith. So we have this ignorant Iowan and this Smith professor going back and forth about immigration. . . . and they went at it [laughs].

Smith student Vivica said that she was repeatedly compelled to confront friends about sexist Facebook posts. One male friend posted something offensive about a woman's body size, and in response Vivica's post relayed a theory from a sociology text called "Behind the Mask of a Strong Black Woman" linking individual experiences to structural racism. Another friend posted a positive comment about lingerie retailer Victoria's Secret. In response, Vivica posted how "Victoria's Secret uses prison labor to make their bras." She continued, "[P]eople never want to see how their privilege affects other people negatively. I just have to deliver it." (Vivica now has the reputation for killing threads, i.e., abruptly ending conversations, on Facebook.) Many students shared stories about sexist and racist posts on the social media site, predominantly with friends from their former high schools. Although one student said that she resorted to "unfriending" these individuals, the other students viewed these interactions as opportunities for education. What they accomplished in these endeavors is not known. However, given the students' regard for the importance of feminist education, Facebook discussion plays a role in their organizational and everyday feminism. Or, as UCSB student Mary Ann said when telling a story about a feminist interchange on Facebook, "[I]t all starts with conversations."

Feminist blogs served as a valuable means of disseminating feminist information, educating about feminist movements, and creating feminist community.[15] Many students reported that they talked about what they read on feminist blogs with roommates and friends and forwarded links via Facebook, demonstrating the potential for blogs to reach wide audiences. Although Smith students were the most interested in femi-

nist blogs, students at all three campuses listed similar blogs they visited in order to learn about the feminist movement and to read feminist
commentary. These included Feministing, Feministe, Racialicious, and
Jezebel.

Smith student Gabrielle said feminists of her generation were mobilizing with different tactics than previous generations of feminists. She
cited feminist blogs as a key transformation in the movement. Smith
student Anne W. rattled off a number of feminist blogs that she read
daily, and said,

> I think in general [reading blogs is] a good way to get your feminism on,
> and to keep up to date and informed. Being educated is the best possible
> way to have, for lack of a better word, weapons on your side. I think a
> lot of them are very much preaching to the choir, like a feminist blog for
> feminists, but it is nice to remind yourself that there are other people who
> think what you think.

Smith student Lily said, "Feminist bloggers definitely set a tone for
things. Not only do they make people who use the Internet aware of
gender inequality, but they give their own perspective and alert people
to different protests or activist things that are happening."

The power of feminist blogs also resides in initiating dialogue on-
and offline. Participants in this study told me about posting links to
their favorite blogs on their Facebook pages, and about the resulting
conversations. One Smith student said she did not have to visit all the
feminist blogs she follows, because her friends posted the best articles
on Facebook. Christine R., also a Smith student, told me that she talks
with her friends about what she reads on Feministing and Jezebel, an
activity many other students shared, especially at Smith, where students
speak effortlessly about feminism in social settings.

Blogs also foster online feminist communities that are more expansive than those offline. Smith student Liz said, "[Blogs are] good because
they also connect you with a group of people who generally have the
same interest as you do, and you get a lot of meaningful and insightful
information from them." Gabrielle, also at Smith, told me that she considers the six–seven feminist blogs she follows a "feminist community."
U of M student Gilgamesh said that feminist usage of the Internet en-

larged the feminist community. He said, "Before, [community] was who you went to school with or who was in your geographical community, but [online feminism] expands who is in the community."

While feminism online may seem starkly different from feminism offline, it reconfigures elements of traditional feminist modes such as self-help and consciousness-raising groups.[16] Although it occurs in very different settings, the process of politicization may be similar. For example, feminist websites develop communities of readers who get to know each other by posting comments regularly or by talking offline about blog entries. Feminists may become aware of the connections between their individual lives and broader social inequalities through sharing knowledge, experiences, and news. While consciousness-raising groups required face-to-face meetings between individuals in the same geographical area, online communities may be established across a variety of boundaries and are open to those individuals who may not know any feminists in their day-to-day, offline lives. Common issues are discussed in online and offline feminist communities, including experiences of and reactions to sexism in everyday life and ways to support each other through difficult life experiences.

The accessibility of computers and the ease of blogging and using social media augment existing social movement organizations and allow participants to communicate their messages and create communities when other resources are unavailable.[17] The Internet pushes feminism in new directions. It speeds up the processes of organizing and network building, creates and nourishes communities across geographic divides, and introduces new tactics and strategies. However, because online feminism is less visible than offline feminism, this type of mobilization has been undervalued.[18]

Everyday Feminism

Everyday feminism is the "politicization of everyday life, embodied in symbols and actions that connect the members of the group and link their everyday experiences to larger social injustices."[19] Everyday feminism involves expressing movement ideologies and goals through actions and behaviors in the realm of appearance, dress, consumption habits, and social relationships. Women's movement scholars have analyzed how the incorporation of feminist principles in everyday life and interaction nurtures movements during inhospitable time periods.[20] Everyday feminism remains an important tactic of contemporary feminist culture. Because it does not involve the same kind of conscious coordination that organized actions do, everyday feminism is often provoked by the emotion of the moment.[21] Social movement activity also includes "millions" of daily actions by countless individuals, some of whom never belong to a social movement organization.[22] Extending the "personal is political" ideology so central to the women's movement, a study by Jane Mansbridge and Katherine Flaster found that women who reported having called someone a "male chauvinist pig" were motivated, in most cases, by feminist identity and solidarity.[23] Although day-to-day action of individuals has been found to be important in the establishment and maintenance of social movements,[24] the connections between everyday activism and the sustaining of a movement as a whole are not completely understood. Furthermore, as intersectionality is a key component to feminism, it is not clear how everyday feminism incorporates concerns with other power structures and inequalities.

The students in this research spoke with ease and in great detail about the role of feminism in their daily lives. Because feminism is commonly described as "everywhere or nowhere" or "in the water,"[25] the assumption may follow that feminism is difficult to detect or articulate. I found quite the opposite, as research participants straightforwardly related how feminism permeated their lives. Consistent with participants' emphasis on intersectionality, they incorporated more than gender in their everyday feminism. I introduce a typology of everyday feminism, addressing how feminism shapes participants' *perspectives, personalities, interactions, language, relationships, understanding of their own privilege, beauty norms,* and *consumption habits.*

Feminism was an important *perspective* on participants' everyday lives. Anne W., a Smith student, reported having "a mental framework that is engrained with [feminism]" and said, "I put my feminism on when I wake up in the morning." U of M student Sophia: "[Feminism] really is very much about the lens with which I look at the world. . . . [I]t impacts my daily life just in the ways that I see things and the ways that I problematize the things that I see." For Sophia, who spoke a lot about intersectionality and the interconnectedness of inequalities, her everyday feminism was far-reaching. Like Sophia, UCSB student Janet also mentioned the critical eye she gained from feminism: "I think about power structures. . . . I'm more observant about things that other people take for granted. With regards to feminism, I really try to understand people's belief systems, and that affects how women treat women, treat men, the way my girlfriends treat their boyfriends, that kind of thing." Camille hoped that the lens of feminism through which she viewed her life would be used for social change: "There's always this extra voice in my mind, how is this tied to identity, how is this affecting me or other people around me, and how can I be part of a positive change?" Like Camille, Smith student Elizabeth considered social change and intersectionality: "[Everyday feminism] means addressing other forms of oppression that go along with the patriarchy, whether that is racism, or capitalism and neoliberal forces. . . . I definitely don't see feminism as an issue only related to female-identified people."

Participants claimed that this feminist perspective was "always" with them. UCSB student Camille said, "[Feminism] probably defines most of the things I do. It's always [there]." UCSB student Janet repeated this sentiment: "I think about it all the time. It's constantly in the back of my head." Lauren, from the U of M, said she cannot get away from feminism now that she has joined the Women's Collective and learned about feminism in her classes: "I just cannot think of anything else—my mind automatically goes towards feminism." Participants in this study were passionate about feminism. At times, it required effort for them to consider where their individuality ended and their devotion to feminism began.

A frequent reply to the everyday feminism question concerned participants' *personalities*. UCSB student Alaina said quickly "Well I know [feminism] affects my personality. It is my personality." Smith student Anne S. said that feminism is "just a part of me now . . . how I hold myself and how I live my life." Others described how feminism instilled in them a sense of self-assurance and self-respect. Smith student Christina R. said, "I think feminism helps me maintain my confidence and my composure." Smith student Anna C. said, "I would say feminism makes me proud to be a woman. I think it impacts my daily life in trying to show other people the strength of women." Smith research participants expressed pride in being women as a central element of their enactment of everyday feminism. Study participants at UCSB and the U of M did not make that point. For the most part, however, students' experiences with everyday feminism was similar across campuses, and they enacted everyday feminism in similar ways.

The feminist lens was employed *interactionally*. U of M student Shane said feminism influenced her position as chair of the queer student collective: "I notice, where are the women in the room? Do they have a voice? Does something about their identity, either self-identified or perceived, influence how they experience these spaces?" Shane reported that she was vigilant about creating an inclusive space. UCSB student Alaina deployed interactional feminism in social situations: "If I'm at a party, and I feel a guy is being overly grabby, I'll be like 'get off me,' I'll be very assertive. I can't separate it from myself, it's just me, it's how I act." Smith student Liz said that she corrected her peers when they expressed sexist views, saying that feminism made her "more aware of things that happen, like interactions. I'm taking a class at U Mass [Amherst], so I feel the need to say, 'no, a woman is not supposed to be a stay-at-home mom, and your wife is not supposed to cook for you, you can cook for her,' and things like that." Liz later talked about another interactional scenario when she spoke up in a history class at Vassar. African American women's role in the civil rights movement was ignored: "I think there's a problem in mainstream education, leaving women out."

Social movement scholar Charles Tilly writes that language "plays an important role in the construction, the endurance, and the diffusion of contentious politics. . . . [T]he effects of the collective word making go well beyond its immediate outcomes to become part of the culture of contention."[26] Interview participants reported that everyday feminism shaped their *language* or how they reacted to others' language.[27] Smith student Anne S. said that feminism was exhibited in her speech and how she held herself. Likewise, U of M collective member Gilgamesh said that when he was younger he used sexist language, but when he embraced feminism and became involved in the Women's Collective, he realized the importance of using nonsexist language and confronting those who spoke in sexist ways. Ninjabi, a UCSB student, provided numerous examples of this in her everyday life on campus and at her part-time job serving ice cream. She said, "Language is a big part of it, like you're such a pussy, or douche bag. Those terms really bother me.

And it affects my daily life because when I hear things like that . . . I go off on this feminist rant. So when I hear sexist terminology or see sexist behavior, I try to call it out." UCSB student Chelsea pointed out her professor's choice of words: "[T]oday, during one of my lectures my professor had one slide of a woman, and he said 'she was killed on this date' and then showed a slide of a man and said 'he was assassinated on this date' and it was peculiar, I noticed in other [class] readings, women are killed but men are assassinated." Chelsea's everyday feminism made her cognizant of language that devalues women.

Objecting to sexist language was commonly described by participants in this study as an act of everyday feminism. UCSB student Elsa said her feminism was exhibited by "standing up for myself. By me being independent, by me pointing out gender inequality within my work place, amongst my circle of friends, womanizing, degrading of women, I do speak up about it." Elsa hoped that this would influence her peers to think in a similar way, and to create change in the world. Anne W. discovered a lot of teachable feminist moments as she went about her daily activities, even at "feminist" Smith College. She reported confronting her Smith peers about their sexism, particularly when they spoke about women's bodies in a sexualized fashion. UCSB student Isabela said that feminism encouraged her to be socially inclusive and to speak out against sexism, but that it often felt like a burden to her. She told me about confronting a group of fraternity friends for not attending the sexual assault awareness event she had planned with her feminist organization. The interaction did not seem to go well. Laughing, Isabela said, "Sometimes I wish I wasn't so conscious all the time! I am very willing to speak up." When women point out chauvinist or sexist behavior, they are part of a larger landscape of interactions in which women assert their rights.

Participants also emphasized that their feminism motivated them to be critical of traditional gender expectations in their *relationships*. Heterosexual Smith student Maddelena said that her everyday feminism was most clearly exhibited in frequent arguments with her long-term boyfriend about paying for dinner. He insisted on paying and "sees it as his role," but Maddelena strongly believed she should contribute. When I asked Bea, who identified as queer, about everyday feminism, she immediately spoke about her relationships with men. "It's very difficult to date men and be a feminist. It's hard to find guys who are so comfortable with themselves that they let me do my own thing. I don't budge: I refuse to let men pay for me." Later she said, "I've dated guys where it's been a huge issue: they have refused to let me pay and they will sneak the waiter and pay for me and it's uncomfortable and I'm like, 'Don't pay for me, I don't want you to.'" Smith student Lily said that feminist ideologies influenced her dating relationships. "I remember being single, and dating, and I remember being with men, and thinking I'm saying too many things, and I'm probably sounding too smart, and I should probably dumb it down a little. But I don't. And I think that's how feminism has affected me." Christina R., a Smith student, talked about how feminism influenced her everyday life:

> I was younger and a man would make a comment about my body, I would have thought that all I'm worth is my body . . . like in order to get a guy to love me, I had to be sexual, and I had to dress sexy, and I had to wear makeup, and now I understand that I don't need to do that. Feminism has really helped me do that. It's helped me understand that for a man to love me, he needs to respect me for who I am.

Smith College study participants also connected their everyday feminism to queer or lesbian issues. Transgender man Rueben thinks of everyday feminism mainly as "everyday gay rights and everyday trans rights." For Elizabeth, "We live in a hetero patriarchy that is incredibly oppressive. For me, being a radical feminist means questioning all of that and addressing it on a daily basis, everyday." Because of the incorporation of feminism in her everyday life, Anne S. said she did "not feel obligated to be in a heterosexual relationship to feel better about myself." Anna C. associated her everyday feminism with her preference to be in relationships with women. She said, "The relationship I'm in now, we're both very honest with each other. I'm just myself, and I've been in relationship with guys and I feel very much more comfortable [now]. And I think about it all the time." More than being comfortable with women, Anna P. said that everyday feminism made her "proud to be a woman, to be in an intimate relationship with a woman." In contrast to their heterosexual peers, women interview participants who were in relationships with women or transgender men spoke about how their feminism was supported in their relationships. This was exhibited by their speaking about feminist issues as a couple, having open and honest communication, and feeling completely comfortable being themselves. It is not surprising that participants reported sexist interactions occurring more often within heterosexual relationships than within same-sex relationships. It is possible that the difficulties feminists experience as they try to build egalitarian heterosexual relationships may help to explain why lesbians have historically been the bearers of feminist culture.[28]

Feminism informed study participants' *understanding of their own privilege*. Gilgamesh, at the U of M, said that his knowledge of feminism made him very sensitive to male privilege in his everyday life. He recounted a recent Women's Collective meeting when the membership discussed whether to change the name of the collective to include the word "feminism." Much to the displeasure of the rest of the meeting attendees, a male student took over, interrupted, and "man-splained" the negative connotations of feminism to the group. Gilgamesh said that "man-splained" is a derivative of "explained," as when "a man takes it upon himself to tell it like it is."[29] This consciousness of men "taking over" influenced the way Gilgamesh interacted in his everyday life. Similarly, when I asked Sammy, a male Women's Collective member at the U of M, about his everyday feminism, he said, "If I get off the bus at 11:35 at night with a woman at the same bus stop, I won't walk behind her. I'll allow her to start walking, and I will take my time gathering my stuff up, just in [case] this person feels uncomfortable." Smith student Elizabeth talked about her gender privilege: "Because I am a cis gender person, I can often forget about it. I think I'm way more aware of my gender, and am made more aware of my gender than cis gender males are. I think in comparison to trans people, I have the privilege of forgetting about it."

Everyday feminism has typically emphasized resistance to gendered *beauty norms*.[30] Although this was not at the forefront of their minds, participants in this study spoke about resisting prevalent beauty culture. U of M student Zan had a very short haircut and wore a t-shirt that said "Kinsey 6," referring to the level on the Kinsey scale that is exclusively homosexual. As a nursing student, she laughed at how much she stuck out among her peers, who mostly chose traditional feminine styles. The most important element of Zan's everyday feminism was her clothes. She said, "I feel almost defiant in almost anything I wear . . . [I]t doesn't matter what I wear, I am defiant . . . I'm going to piss someone off." UCSB student Mary Ann spoke of an inverse relationship between her increasing feminist development and decreasing effort at her appearance:

[Feminism] made me start to not really put on makeup a lot. In high school, I would wake up at 5:45, blow dry my hair, straighten my hair, pick out my outfit . . . and that's not even as bad as most people. And look now, I'm in sweats. It's very empowering to know that all these things that I know and I am learning, that I can see a perspective of the world that some people can't. That helps me realize that it's okay, these things are just distractions.

Smith student Margarite held a similar view: "[W]hen I'm getting ready and getting dressed, I think 'oh I'm not getting dressed for someone, I'm getting dressed for myself, for what I think I like, what I feel comfortable in.' Not like, I'm going to impress so-and-so today." Smith student Anna C. did not subscribe to feminine beauty norms herself, and tried to persuade her friends as well: "[I] show other people they should be proud not just to be a woman, but who they are as an identity. And I think I try to impact people to love who they are. I've had so many arguments with my neighbor about putting on makeup everyday, 'why do you need to do that?'"

Many of the women whom I interviewed for this study did not appear to embrace feminine beauty and appearance norms, and relatively few counted such standards as important features of everyday feminism. This suggests that interactional aspects of everyday feminism trumped previous formulations of everyday feminism that found women's beauty norms a focal point.

Participants in this study also linked their *consumption habits* to their everyday feminism. Smith student Gabriella, for example, was conscious of the global inequalities behind clothing purchases:

While I still may shop at places where I know that sweatshops went into making those clothes, I also know I'd have to spend three times as much to shop sweat free and I know I can't afford that right now. So it is being aware and also questioning those things, and also realizing that I'm not in a place where I can live a completely feminist life.

Although for financial reasons Gabriella could not avoid patronizing businesses that sold sweatshop-produced clothes, she identified her consideration as an important component of everyday feminism. Like Gabriella, Smith respondent Anna P. acknowledged the financial requirements of living a completely feminist life: "I prefer to shop locally, supporting local farmers, local goods, but then of course that stuff is so expensive, so you leave out an entire class of people because they can't shop there." Bea extended consumption to include both clothing and the media's representation of women and heterosexuality:

> Disney movies have been ruined forever, I don't think I could let my children watch Disney movies now. I can't shop at Forever 21 because of the exploitation of workers. Not that other shops don't exploit their workers too, but I watched a specific video about Forever 21, so educating myself about those issues has certainly opened my eyes to things, and it's shaped the way I will raise my children.

It is a mark of the success of the feminist movement that attention to consumption is so engrained in students' lives. Everyday feminism also confirms the continued relevance of the "personal is political." In fact, for student feminists, their everyday feminism *was* political and motivated by feminist allegiance. Their incorporation of feminism in their everyday lives was not planned in advance, and it was sometimes spontaneous, or "on the fly,"[31] yet it is critical to advancing a movement over many decades.

Feminist Coalitions

Broadly defined, coalitions are alliances between two or more organizations within the same movement or across different movements.[32] Coalitions are an essential tool of many mobilized participants' activism—they may form for a single event[33] or be more long-lasting.[34] Prior research suggests that single-event coalitions may be the most effective and least divisive[35]—minimizing occasions for ideological and personal conflicts.[36] What promotes coalitions? External to a movement, coalitions are the result of threat or opportunity between a movement organization and an authority, or between social movement organizations.[37] Internal to a movement, coalitions are formed by organizations that share beliefs or goals,[38] or by leaders who possess ties to more than one social movement organization.[39]

Historically, U.S. feminists have been marginally successful at building coalitions among themselves and between feminist and nonfeminist organizations. In their study of the U.S. women's movement from 1945 to the 1960s, Leila J. Rupp and Verta Taylor found that the Woman's Party did not establish coalitions with feminists or other movements: "[T]he women's rights movement attempted to use the issues and activities associated with other social movements for its own purposes, but did not attempt to mobilize groups of women or forge alliances with other movements."[40]

Participants were focused on protecting and nurturing their own community during this time, not only because the movement was in a downturn but also because the political environment for feminists was tenuous due to resistance to the ERA. There are, nonetheless, cases of very effective feminist coalitions. For example, a powerful coalition of seventy women's organizations successfully lobbied to include women's issues in South Africa's new constitution during its democratic transition.[41]

Feminists of the 1970s were more accomplished at coalitioning than previous generations, although obstacles still remained.[42] Benita Roth underscored the common grievances between feminists of different backgrounds, such as the demand for affordable childcare, freedom from domestic violence, and a need for education and employment opportunities.[43] Women of color particularly created strong coalitions "because they belong to multiple oppressed communities"; however, coalitional power asymmetries generate tensions that can be exhausting to group members.[44] Elsewhere, Roth argues that the desire to "organize one's own," or to mobilize within culturally homogenous communities, meant that building coalitions ranked low on some participants' list of priorities.[45] Such challenges are not insurmountable, as coalitions of feminists from different backgrounds eventually flourished.[46]

New generations of feminists are more likely to unite in coalitions than previous generations, as a result of their intersectional grievances and opposition to a monolithic women's solidarity. Nancy Whittier writes that third wave feminists are "less inclined to organize a 'women's movement' per se, and more inclined to build coalitions among women and men of different groups."[47]

College students' social networks span residence halls, classes, extracurricular activities, sports, and student groups. In relatively small communities such as college campuses, these networks are crucial: "[E]mbeddedness within primary groups and social networks in small communities is a strong predictor of individual participation."[48] Student organizations have historically collaborated within and across movements, as documented in detail by Nella Van Dyke in a study of a sixty-year period of student mobilization. She found that student organizations with bountiful resources *and* opposition led to coalitions within movements, while multi-issue organizations sustained all types of coalitions.[49] Social movement scholars have recently directed significant attention to coalitions in general;[50] however, we know little about feminist coalitions today.[51]

Smith: Spreading Feminism at the Cupcake Social

By New England standards it was a balmy spring day, and the Smith feminist cupcake social was geared up in a large room in the campus center. Floor-to-ceiling windows overlooked the large lawn at the center of campus. Upon entering the room, students were given plain, undecorated cupcakes. Representatives from nine feminist student organizations sat at tables around the room, each stocked with frosting and toppings. Attendees moved from table to table, where they had opportunities to decorate and eat their cupcakes while speaking to members of the feminist organization at each place. Members of the group who planned the event sold "this is what a feminist looks like" t-shirts. Despite arriving towards the beginning of the event, I found they were nearly sold out, although a helpful student mailed a shirt to me in Santa Barbara when they received another shipment.

Organizer Gabrielle said the purpose of the cupcake social was to "show [students] that feminism is broader than the issues they think it includes" and to create feminist community. Participants in a number of Smith groups considered their organizations feminist. While in the past the organizers have been frustrated at the lack of connection between organizations, this event was a success.

The event organizers invited all feminist organizations to participate (table 5.1).

Table 5.1: Participating Organizations in Smith Feminist Cupcake Social

FEMINIST ORGANIZATION	ISSUE/TACTICS
Beyond Gender Binary	transgender organization/workshops about trans issues
National Organization for Women, Smith Chapter	new organization, no events yet; emphasis on feminist history
Radical Catholic Feminists of Smith	liberal Catholics who advocate for women to have a more active role in the church
Afternoon Tea	a "feminine and feminist" social group
Smith Republicans	Republican party student group
Smith Democrats	Democratic party student group
STAND, Smith Chapter	human rights organization, fighting for Smith to be a "conflict mineral–free" campus
Body Talk	body acceptance organization
Feminists of Smith	primary organizing group/feminist education and direct action

As I moved around the tables, I spoke to all student representatives about why their organizations were feminist. Rueben, a transgender student involved in Beyond Gender Binary (BGB), told me that, although some feminists do not consider transgender men as feminist ("you know, because they are changing from women to men"), he did. He had a handwritten poster taped to their table that said "feminists are concerned with all people" and handed out a flier with phrases such as, "For every girl who threw away her easy bake oven, there is a boy who wishes to find one." In our interview a few days later, Rueben elaborated on how BGB was a feminist organization: "[BGB] is about increasing trans visibility on campus, increasing education and rights, which all leads inevitably to hopefully being able to live as we see fit in our bodies. *We do a lot with education, which is a form of working with equal access, giving people equal access to education, which is feminist*" (emphasis added). For Rueben and many other students, their feminism was bound to their activism in pursuit of general progressive social change. Few students at any institution disentangled their desire for a more just world generally from being a feminist specifically.

Some organizations were clearer about the role of women in feminism, however. Back at the cupcake social, a student with a pixie haircut and rhinestone-encrusted cat-eye glasses at the STAND organization table spoke to me in depth about her campaign to make Smith a conflict mineral–free campus. She told me that Stanford and Cornell universities were already conflict mineral–free, and they are hoping Smith will follow suit. When I asked her in what ways her organization was feminist, she said that she considered genocide and their conflict mineral–free campaigns to be feminist issues because both forms of social injustice affect women disproportionately. Similarly, the student at the Smith Democrats table spoke with me about all the connections between feminists and Democrats, and easily rattled off a list of the pro-women legislation that Democrats had recently passed.

Coalitioning was not only an expression of their intersectional feminism, however. Smith student Anna C. spoke about how she was consciously hoping to "spread feminism" through coalitions: "That's definitely a big goal, [to] touch people in different ways, if they could see these other orgs, and how they relate to feminism in some way, they could really make that connection." This resonates with many students' approaches to feminist mobilization. Students incorporated feminism in a variety of coalitions that had both women-centered grievances and more general social justice approaches to feminism. These three things were promoted because of the feminist sensibility at Smith.

The cupcake social was an achievement, but it is unclear whether a sustained coalition would function. Smith students were not always in agreement over different approaches to the movement, perhaps because of their extensive knowledge about and passion for feminism. Not all of them, for example, were keen about the existence of a campus chapter of a national feminist organization. Elizabeth's discussion of feminist and social justice groups was evidence of this tension:

> I think a lot of Smith's extracurricular groups are very normative and completely within the bounds of the system. There's a lot of people here who just want to save women in Africa or save women in India, and I think this tends to be really ignoring institutional problems, ignoring the

forces of neoliberalism and imperialism, ignoring the problems with U.S. democratizing and the U.S. going in and the IMF and the World Bank and basically colonizing them.

Although Elizabeth was on the more opinionated end of the spectrum, I heard enough remarks about the divergences in feminist ideology that I suspected long-term feminist coalitions would not survive. Moreover, there was little incentive. None of the feminist groups had much funding, rendering meaningless resource sharing, the main benefit of coalitions.

U of M: Whose U?

Whose University? (or Whose U?) was an ongoing coalition involving many members of the U of M Women's Collective. According to collective member Gilgamesh, "[T]he better part of our active membership is involved in Whose U?" The seeds of the project were sown by objections to the 2005 closing of the General College by then U of M president Robert Brunicks. The General College served Minnesota students who were not ready for the university, and prepared them for admittance to one of the main colleges. Students were typically from impoverished backgrounds and underfunded school districts. Although at the time, President Brunicks insisted it was more of a restructuring than a shuttering, numbers of minority and low-income admissions to the university declined in the wake of the decision. In response, Whose U?'s website said, "The Whose University? Campaign is organizing students, educators, workers, and community members to challenge the U of M's priorities in equal access and resources for underrepresented groups."[52] The coalition focused on three areas, specifically targeting the incoming university president, who would be responsible for creating a ten-year plan:

1. Admissions: Who has access to the University of Minnesota?
2. Student Cultural Centers: Who is supported by the University of Minnesota?
3. Ethnic Studies: Whose knowledge is valued by the University of Minnesota?[53]

The "Student Cultural Centers" focus is most relevant to this research, because the Women's Collective is considered a "cultural center," as are the queer, disabled, international, Latina/o, Black, American Indian, and Muslim student groups. Each of these organizations had significant membership bodies and occupied large office and lounge spaces on the second floor of the student union at the center of campus. As addressed in chapters 3 and 4, many of these cultural centers lost funding while right-wing student organizations gained funding at unprecedented rates. Moreover, university administrators were considering arguments from conservative students who pointed out that their organizations did not have ample space in the student union, and that liberal student organizations were favored in the space-allocation process. The threat of losing their space spurred Women's Collective members to become involved in Whose University? However, their participation was also intertwined with the Women's Collective's dedication to intersectionality, social justice, and educational accessibility.

Many collective members were so committed to the Whose University? campaign that they reportedly slept only a few hours a night in preparation for their day of action, when the coalition activists chartered buses and arranged for substitute teachers and chaperones, so that hundreds of low-income high school students could visit the U of M campus. The activists hoped the high school students would learn about the university and consider the U of M as a post–high school option. The day included a speak-out about the need for educational accessibility and inclusivity, performances by music groups from the high schools, and educational events for the high school students in each of the cultural centers. Because I was conducting my research during the month in which the coalition was at its peak planning stages, the offices of the Women's Collective were frequently crowded with Whose U? coalition members in a commotion of last-minute planning.

Interviews with the collective members often turned to the subject of the Whose U? coalition. Sam, a member of the collective, described the event and its feminist approach: "Whose University? is important to me because it is addressing institutional problems that minorities must deal with. We ask: Who has access? Who is supported? . . . Whose knowledge is valued? These are all questions that relate to issues that [the Women's

Collective] directly and indirectly addresses." Students described the importance of the campaign to their feminist mobilization, and spoke about the interconnected nature of feminism and social justice. In fact, their involvement in Whose U? was not especially notable to them as *feminist*; to many it was an assumed part of their allegiance to social justice and equity.

Interviewees did not disclose any problems within their collaboration, nor did I observe any interpersonal concerns in their mobilization: their sustained organizing was impressive and their day of action went off without any visible hitch. In many ways the coalition worked at the U of M because of the presence of administrative and student opposition. There was agreement among feminists and social justice activists that the shuttering of the general college was damaging, and they shared a goal to hold the university, a public land-grant institution, accountable. Second, progressive students cultivated a strong sense of solidarity to counteract mobilized conservative student groups who organized to reduce the funding of progressive groups. Although there were differences in the funding level of each organization in the coalition, they shared their resources, and a strong dedication to the coalition.

UCSB: Plentiful Coalitions

UCSB students formed a myriad of coalitions, and their presence was ubiquitous in respondents' descriptions of their activism and in my observations of their campus feminism. This was due to the pride that students had in the institution's activist history. Many Latina feminist activists worked in collaboration to empower their fellow Latinas. A UCSB sorority member, for example, told me about a coalition to encourage underrepresented Latina youth in Santa Barbara to matriculate at UCSB. She said, "[F]all quarter we put on the Latina youth leadership conference, we recruited ladies from local high schools, and we had a day for them here, with workshops and guest speakers, and wanting them to pursue higher education." UCSB feminist organizations coalitioned with other organizations to put on events that sounded similar to the Whose U? Day of Action. Summer said, "We work with quite a few Latino sororities and fraternities, and other Black sororities and fraternities. We work with other chapters of our sorority. Mostly we work with other Greek organizations. Next year, we hopefully will branch out . . . but also keep our connections, because we've had some really good collaborations with those organizations."

Bridget belonged to an organization that "targets first-generation, low-income students, and it allows them to stay for two weeks in the dorms and meet other student like themselves, to basically help them transition from high school to college." Unfortunately, because of University of California budget cuts, she had to fight to keep the program alive. She was grateful to the members of multicultural Greek organizations who supported her efforts, but reported a racial divide in support. Speaking of her campaign to keep the program running, she said,

> BRIDGET: You reach out to the non-ethnic Greeks and they never show face.
> AUTHOR: Non-ethnic Greeks are all White?
> BRIDGET: It's drastically split here. The multicultural and ethnic Greeks are growing, but when I first got here, it was really small.

Bridget's experiences suggest that progressive students are supported by and coalition with other like-minded people, who are often students of color. They were unproductive at harnessing the energies of other (White, Greek) students. Latina students like Bridget benefited from programs that aided them in their transition to college. They were consequently brought into activist networks that advocated for these programs and communities. Although students uniformly described UCSB as an excellent place to be an activist, Bridget's comments suggest that part of the positivity could be due to activist students collaborating with other students of similar backgrounds who were concerned with similar social justice grievances.

Camille, illustrating this point, was involved in at least six student organizations, from the women of color spoken word group to the human rights group. When I asked her whether she cosponsored events between organizations, she responded enthusiastically:

> All the time. Honestly my time is extremely limited, and all the things I do intersect. Even if they are focused on different identities, they really are fundamentally all human rights focused. And, I think that is essential to all of them. And, you have to understand it's also the networking

abilities that you create here. And kind of getting involved in the activism community here, and building trust, and I've realized that cosponsorships on a flier may mean something, *but it's also meaning that I've got their backs and the other people's backs. We're constantly cosponsoring and working on each other's campaigns.* (emphasis added)

While it was clear from their achievements and visibility that these coalitions were effective due to strong networks ties,[54] Bridget's and Camille's comments made me wonder whether opposition in some parts of the student body was offset by enough activist networks to negate the lack of support.

One of the largest coalitions of student organizations protested University of California budget cuts in 2011. It garnered campus and media attention. Camille said, "I am one of the organizers and facilitators of the UCSB coalition . . . students and workers who activate the students against the budget cuts. We've been at the forefront of the statewide objection to the privatization of higher education." Although many of the members of the feminist organizations were also members of the coalition, the feminist organizations themselves were not publicly involved in the coalition as the feminist organizations at the U of M were with the protest over closing the General College there. I suspect that two of the main feminist organizations did not advertise their coalition participation because of restrictions related to their university funding.

The continued threat of budget cuts motivated students at the U of M and UCSB, confirming that threat is an important stimulus for coalitions. Budget cuts and higher education issues were viewed as having relevance for women, and their challenges to fight for social equality. There was no similar institutional threat to Smith students in this respect. As Jo Reger found in a study of feminists in college and community organizations, students at a small liberal arts college were unlikely to mobilize unless there was a specific threat or grievance.[55] Although students at Smith mobilized to educate their peers about pressing social issues, they were not mobilized in coalitions to the same degree as students at the public universities.

Of the three campuses, UCSB had the highest population of students of color, and its feminist groups had the most participants of color. Consequently, their coalitions were racially and ethnically diverse. At the other two campuses, the feminist organizations were not exclusively

White, but they had considerably less racial diversity. At Smith, the feminists of color I interviewed were more likely to be involved in a feminist and ethnically based organization (such as Nosotras, a Latina group) than in a solely feminist organization. The U of M had the most racially homogenous student body of the three research sites; as a result the Women's Collective members were nearly all White. Collective members expressed frustration with this situation. It may also have motivated their involvement in the racially diverse Whose University? coalition.

Chapter 5 Conclusion

Tactics provide opportunities for activists to target elites and authorities who control institutional policies and practices.[56] They also communicate and transmit information to activists, and build solidarity and community. My analysis demonstrates how tactical repertoires remain consistent over time in some respects, but also shift according to changes in communication technology, the availability of resources, and societal support for a movement's claims. As theories of movement continuity suggest, expanded repertoires of contention benefit subsequent mobilization.[57]

Student organizations used both long-standing and innovative feminist tactics. Following the traditions of many feminists, students did speak about sexual assault and sexual harassment, hosted discussions about feminism, and sponsored educational events. However, they also expanded tactical repertoires by focusing on intersectional grievances, following in the tradition of many feminists of color. Feminists often relied on a broad frame of social justice. Their conviction that feminism was connected to interrelated inequalities such as classism, racism, and homophobia was exhibited in the events they planned and in their concern with educational accessibility.

With respect to technological advancements, research participants used Facebook to create feminist communities, establish boundaries between feminists, share feminist news, and further their feminist organizational goals. Because very few groups had abundant resources, Facebook also allowed students to advertise events and communicate with members at no cost. Feminist blogs provided solidarity among feminists, and research participants also learned about feminism from these blogs. The role of the Internet in feminist mobilization was striking, and the significant extent to which students immediately named Facebook and blogs as influential to their feminist mobilization took me by surprise. Internet tactics expand the way we think of feminism and its incorporation in everyday life.

Coalitions influenced the tactics of feminist organizations on all three campuses. Successful collaborations occurred within a wide swath of student groups. Their tactical emphasis on working across movements and organizations was consistent with activists' intersectional grievances and expansive collective identities. These feminists were more successful in coalition building than their counterparts in previous generations. Their decisions to form coalitions were based on their goals. For example, at Smith their goal was to bring feminist groups together through the cupcake social to show the breadth of feminism at Smith. At UCSB and the U of M, activists' concerns were broader than gender, and they had visions of mobilizing a massive number of students to pressure administrators to make the university more accessible. However, because of their common student status, close social networks, and institutional mandates to cosponsor events, coalition building was probably less of a feat for the students in this study than for feminists in community organizations who lacked such strong networks. Coalitions spoke to the wide acceptance of feminism as part of the master frame of social justice.

Everyday feminism was a significant feminist tactic used by all of the feminists in this study. Participants reported that feminism shaped their interactions and motivated them to speak out against sexist language. Moreover, feminism was a lens that focused on how participants viewed their world, interpreted their surroundings, and understood their personalities. These features of everyday feminism propel the ideologies of the movement, motivating participants to mobilize and to resist everyday sexism.[58] There can be little question that for the women in this study, everyday interactions are political in and of themselves, and are pivotal to social change.

Feminism perseveres and is tactically consistent with earlier cycles of feminist activism, incorporating movement activity in everyday life and emphasizing coalition formation. As feminism evolves, there are fewer demarcations and separations than the wave framework allows for or predicts. Furthermore, activists' use of online tactics promotes other features critical to a lasting movement: innovation and creativity.

6

Conclusion

Not all men harass #womyn, but all #womyn have been
harassed #YesAllWomen #feminism #patriarchy
@Tara_Leigh27

@Stanford survivors have rally today at 12pm to hold school
accountable #rape #YesAllWomen #StandwithLeigh
@BraveMissWorld

Because wanting to have sex but also wanting to be respected is seen as contradictory #YesAllWomen
@KateBoudet

That's why the #YesAllWomen movement is important, it
takes us all, men and women, to end rape culture
@Kate_Kae_

This book opened with a description of the tragic murders in Isla
Vista, California, that spurred international attention to gender
inequality with #YesAllWomen. Such surges of hashtag activism
reflect what social movement scholars know to be the familiar rhythm
of social change. These actions, and other, similar campaigns such as
#BlackLivesMatter and #SayHerName, have their origins in preexist-
ing mobilizing structures, or in networks of activists poised to work
collectively.[1] These individuals are likely to be practicing movement
politics in their everyday lives and interactions, in their organizations
and institutions, on- and offline. This established sense of solidarity
and motivation to create change is already in place when a specific
event causes mass mobilization. As #YesAllWomen and other similar campaigns generate widespread discussion of feminism, they offer
critical opportunities to ask, Where did these feminists come from?

How did they learn about the movement? How are they "doing" feminism in their everyday lives?

This book reveals how college campuses are generative environments for feminism, and valuable sites for the perpetuation of the movement. Although not in the places or forms we might expect, I found feminism in multicultural sororities, student governments, college organizations, and online. Antifeminists shaped campus activism and energized tight-knit feminist communities. My research demonstrates that feminism cannot be understood either in waves or as flourishing or as dead.[2] Instead I argue that young feminists are carrying the torch of the movement, important in propelling feminism into a new era. *Finding Feminism* reveals the tactics, practices, and identities of young feminists who are part of an energetic and innovative movement. Because "[f]eminism necessarily changes as the world women inhabit changes," we need to look for feminist activism and solidarity in places not previously examined in order to comprehend its persistence.[3]

Continuity and Change

At the April 7 meeting of the University of Minnesota Women's Collective, students gathered in the comfortable resource center in the bustling student union at the center of campus. Both men and women were in attendance. The meeting began with members introducing themselves and stating whether they would like to be referred to with female or male gender pronouns. During the hour-long meeting, members debriefed about their Hip Hop Against Homophobia event the previous week; decided which member of the collective would speak at the Take Back the Night rally; agreed to contribute money to the disabled student group's event Igniting the Power in Disability and to the Whose U? campaign; discussed a possible coalition with the campus atheist organization; and agreed to give the proceeds of an upcoming concert to a shelter for Minneapolis women and girls exploited in sex trafficking.

The topics of this meeting agenda, and the many others discussed throughout the book, reveal continuity and change in feminism over time. Previous generations of feminists may be surprised by the Women's Collective having active male members, announcing their preferred gender pronouns at the start of a meeting, or planning feminist events around educational accessibility. But feminists of the 1960s and '70s probably attended Take Back the Night rallies, donated funds to women's shelters, and organized concerts. As historian Leila J. Rupp wrote, the first wave of the international women's movement was based on "a recognition of women's universal economic disadvantage and the multifaceted manifestations of violence against women—the notion of commonality across differences of class, ethnicity, religion, and other fundamental cleavages lives on."[4] The movement has endured not only because gender inequality persists and because solidarity bridges differences but also because participants have adapted their strategies and tactics in order to accommodate the evolving challenges facing feminists today.

In some ways, the feminism presented in this book is comparable to that of previous generations of feminists. Nearly one hundred years later and in different parts of the world, similar issues galvanize feminists today: relationship violence, sexual assault, reproductive justice, the wage gap, rape culture, and the gender binary. As did feminists of the past, my participants focused on intersectional issues—they were largely concerned with interlocking inequalities of gender, race, sexuality, immigration status, ability, and socioeconomic status. They continued to use tactics historically employed by feminist groups, emphasizing community, coalitions, cultural change, and everyday expressions of movement politics.

In other ways, the feminism practiced by the participants in this study was different from previous modes of feminism. Some of these divergences are due to the successes of the feminist movement—that is, feminists of the 1970s were able to integrate into institutions of higher education and create women's and feminist studies programs/departments. This incorporation allowed feminists described in this research to study feminism and enact feminist ideologies in the classroom and in extracurricular activities. Because of these historical successes, I found feminists active in sororities, in student government, and in a broad range of student campaigns, in addition to women's centers and women's studies programs. Building on the past, these opportunities undoubtedly perpetuated the movement and were of integral importance.

Other divergences were related to grievances and tactics. Although the problematic nature of the gender binary has remained a consistent grievance, the focus on transgender rights among some students was more at the forefront of their minds than in previous generations. Even though past feminists have similarly relied on coalitions, some of the issues that motivated the activists in my study were particular to the time and institutional context, focusing on contemporary issues such as immigration reform and the steep cost of public higher education. Participants' coalition work in these areas shines a light on the broad spectrum of feminist repertoires of contention. Analysis of their coalition work illustrates the tactical dimensions of intersectionality. Moreover, as feminism was infused into many organizations, events were arranged that specifically convened these groups, highlighting the feminist nature of a wide array of organizations. The online tactics so popular among feminists in this study diverge from previous modes of feminism. Not only do feminists organize face-to-face activism using the Internet, but they rely on blogs and social media to learn about feminism and feminist critiques of current events.

Participants in this study, whether or not they identified as feminists, had positive views of the ways previous generations of feminists have contributed to a more just world. Moreover, 83.3 percent of the survey respondents agreed with the statement "feminism of the 1970s advanced women's status in the U.S." In interviews, too, I was struck by the number and variety of positive comments about feminists: feminists put women's issues on the national radar and increased the cognizance of gender inequality. Participants affirmed that feminists improved women's job and career opportunities, including workplace laws that protect women. They were effusive about how feminists allowed them to, as one respondent said, no longer "be at the mercy of men" when it came to feminist advancements in terms of reproductive justice and expression of sexuality. A number of students noted the founding of feminist organizations as an important component in improving the status of women—and in paving the road for other feminist organizations. Students reported that the advances made by feminist movements in the educational fields were significant—in access to higher education and resources for women students, and in validating women's experiences and conducting research by and for women in the academy. The study also demonstrates how the institutional context of higher education teaches the histories of feminists and successes of feminism, thus perpetuating knowledge about the movement and, it seems, goodwill towards feminists.

Abeyance Structures

Throughout *Finding Feminism*, I have shown how the feminism movement continues and persists in a variety of different contexts and with a number of tactics. Using these findings, I extend Taylor's abeyance theory,[5] which refuted the widespread belief that the U.S. women's movement mobilized through two concentrated waves of protest (in the early 1900s and in the 1960s) and died in between.[6] Through the ebbs and flows of movement activity, movements persevere by "promoting the survival of *activist networks*, sustaining a repertoire of *goals and tactics*, and promoting a *collective identity* that offers participants a sense of mission and moral purpose."[7] During abeyance, or times in which social movement participants struggle to find support for their claims, social movement participants rely on internally oriented activities, often of a cultural nature, to maintain their identity and political vision.[8] Although the modern U.S. women's movement arose at the height of the 1960s cycle of protest, women had been organizing around many social and political issues for at least a century. These predecessors contributed important organizational, ideological, and tactical resources to the emerging mass feminist mobilization.[9] At the same time, women's movements influenced those of the New Left with a critique of male dominance that connected sexism with racism, capitalism, and militarism.[10] The lasting impact of the abeyance framework is the uncovering of previously unrecognized social movement activity.[11] Rather than viewing political conflict as occurring in street protest or mass mobilization only, a theory of abeyance encourages us to see political conflict all around us and pay attention to the number of ways in which movements persist over time.[12] It is difficult to determine whether a movement is in abeyance until we have some hindsight, although Michael Messner and his coauthors call today's grassroots women's movements "largely in abeyance."[13] Engaging the concept is useful as a foundation for understanding the dynamics of any long-lasting social movement.

Abeyance theory has been applied to numerous social movements, and it has also been extended to account for changes in movement participation, dynamics, and tactics in other ongoing movements.[14] The initial abeyance formulation was based on the context of 1950s feminist organizing. It has not been systematically updated to reflect the changes in movements over the past twenty years. A revised abeyance framework allows for greater precision in analyses of any long-lasting social movement. *Finding Feminism* extends our current understandings of abeyance and movement persistence to include three new structures critical to movement endurance: *institutional abeyance structures, everyday abeyance structures*, and *online abeyance structures*.

Institutional Abeyance Structures

Colleges and universities are essential to the persistence of the feminist movement. Through academic programs/departments, classes, student organizations, and institutional histories, the research sites in my study supported and ensured movement continuity, albeit to varying degrees. By expanding upon the notions that institutions can be friendly habitats[15] or "free spaces"[16] for feminist mobilization, I highlight the unexpected opportunities for feminism in higher education.[17]

Movement ideologies became very familiar to participants through student networks and academic courses. Whether or not they had taken feminist studies classes, three-fourths of all survey respondents in my research agreed that feminists are still working hard to ensure gender equality. The inclusion of feminism in students' college and university experiences may have combated the feminist stereotypes that participants inevitably encountered.

Both women's studies departments and women's centers feature in *institutional abeyance*. They have historically shaped receptivity to feminist claims-making and have permanently altered the context of campus feminism. However, their roles in *institutional abeyance* are not the same. Women's studies courses provided frameworks for students to understand the intersectional and structural natures of inequalities they experienced in their everyday lives, and frequently led to student activism and engagement in gender-based protest. Women's studies courses were but one dimension of campus feminism. Study participants also learned about feminism in non–women's studies classes. This is a testimony to the wide-reaching cultural influence of women's studies practitioners and women's movement participants. (We also know that the staff and faculty of women's studies programs are targets of attack by the Right and particularly vulnerable to budget cuts.) In contrast to women's studies departments, women's centers were largely separate from campus feminist organizing. This is not a criticism of women's centers but more of an acknowledgment that they were not, in my research, central to *institutional abeyance structures*. Women's centers are probably more related to other aspects of campus feminism, such as providing programming for faculty and staff, and advocating for women on campus.

Many participants in this study found important feminist communities in their student organizations. Although the numbers of explicitly feminist organizations varied by campus, feminism informed student mobilization in multicultural sororities, queer student groups, student government, and organizations affiliated with national women's organizations. In garnering important leadership and organizational skills, students transformed their institutions through their activism. *Institutional abeyance structures* function as springboards that supply activist networks, collective identities, tactics, and feminist ideas that promote advocacy for gender equality on campus.

In the past, social movements were explicitly understood as extra-institutional. Scholars have only recently begun to analyze the dynamics of social movements inside institutions, such as higher education.[18] *Finding Feminism* underscores the need to examine not only "institutional activists"[19] but also the role of institutionally sponsored activities in movement organizing. Although student protest will always be an important form of contentious politics, we must not overlook other forms of student organizing that counteract the tradition that overemphasizes street-centered protest. This view opens the door for analysis of all types and elements of student mobilization beyond protest events, including the cultural dimensions of student organizing, community building, and feminist consciousness development. With a more expansive view of social movements, and one that includes what is happening inside institutions of higher education, we can understand the number of ways in which feminists are continuing to mobilize to make change. From this perspective, we can see how the institutional setting effectively prolongs the feminist movement, and in essence sustains a waveless, continuous feminism.

Everyday Abeyance Structures

The evidence in this book demonstrates the significance of the everyday practices of activists, and how *everyday abeyance structures* sustain a movement over time.[20] Although incorporation of movement principles in everyday life has been found to be an important component of driving a movement forward over long periods of time, the relationship between everyday feminism and feminist continuity demands greater clarity. I found that individual interaction and incorporation of feminist principles in participants' daily lives was critical in feminists' expressions of movement identities and ideologies. Despite these actions being spontaneous, or "on the fly,"[21] they were critical to women's enactments of feminism.

The everyday feminism that drove participants in this research was related to both individual-level and movement-level feminism. Participants expressed their understandings of the principles of feminist ideology and their allegiance to the movement when describing how feminism was incorporated into their everyday lives. The typology of everyday feminism presented in this book highlights the incorporation of feminism in participants' *perspectives, personalities, interactions, language, relationships, understanding of their own privilege, beauty norms,* and *consumption habits.* This underscores how the movement shaped not only participants' understandings of the world and their perceptions of inequality but also the way they understood themselves and their own position in society. In addition to this individual-level focus, participants in this study told me detailed stories about feminism driving their interactions with others, including boyfriends and girlfriends, family members, and strangers. Interactionally, their dedication to feminism motivated participants to speak out when others violated their feminist sensibilities in school, at work, and in social settings. Participants who reported the importance of feminism in their everyday lives very easily described connections between their everyday lives and the movement. Although *everyday abeyance structures* can be purely solo endeavors, they are not always so. For many of these feminists, *everyday feminism* was connected to their participation in feminist organizations, insofar as students learned about feminist perspectives and found a community of solidarity to support them as they encountered situations that challenged their feminist worldviews. Far from being solely an individual-level perspective, this daily feminism is reliant upon knowledge about movement ideology and feminist approaches to the world. While participants in a social movement during abeyance are typically centered on maintenance rather than expansion of a movement, I found that participants' use of *everyday abeyance structures* fueled movement vitality and expanded the reach of feminism.

The ways in which participants in this study expressed everyday feminism were related to gender inequality and reflected the multiple inequalities they experienced in daily life. Some participants' everyday feminism was exhibited in their discomfort with heteronormativity or unequal gender expectations in heterosexual dating relationships. One respondent in a relationship with another woman felt that she could more easily practice feminism in her day-to-day life because of her same-sex relationship. Other participants noted the importance of feminist principles in terms of consumption practices. They acknowledged that socioeconomic privilege affords individuals "feminist" buying power, such as in purchasing relatively expensive non-sweatshop-produced clothing or organic produce. Feminist participants' interactional everyday feminism drove their astute observance of power dynamics, for example, when those from marginalized communities were given opportunities to contribute to a student group meeting, or when a professor devoted more time to the subject and research of White men in contrast to women or communities of color.

Scholars of the women's movement have found that the incorporation of movement principles in everyday life nourished participants during abeyance or down times.[22] During abeyance, social movements largely rely upon internally oriented activities, often of a cultural nature, to maintain their identity and political vision.[23] Even if a movement does not achieve its intended goals, its discourses and frames, collective identity, and tactics can be highly influential through its impact on subsequent movements. Consider the phrase "the personal is political," which emerged out of the women's consciousness-raising movement as a way of linking private experiences to gender domination. The expression "male chauvinist," initially coined by feminists and still used today, not only demonstrates the everyday interactional nature of feminism but is also evidence of the lasting impact of social movement discourse.[24]

Everyday feminism is also equated with an individualist feminism. The popularity of the topic is used to support the argument that young feminists have shifted from a collective to a self-centered focus.[25] This approach to everyday feminism is exemplified by the "first-person-singular" third wave feminist,[26] who is engrossed in her own personal life without a sense of the importance of collective organizing. Although everyday feminism could indeed be divorced from any other form of feminism and potentially could be a self-serving neoliberal feminism, this is not what my research suggests.[27] Some scholars have acknowledged that this type of feminism does not necessarily spell the downfall to the collectivity of feminism. In her examination of the everyday and cultural feminism of zine culture, Alison Piepmeier writes,

> These grrrl zines *are* deeply invested in personal reflection, but this is not mere navel gazing. . . . To a certain extent, the focus on the personal operates like second wave consciousness-raising, allowing individual girls and women to recognize inequalities in their own lives and then begin to articulate them to others so that outrage—and then activism—can emerge.[28]

Piepmeier complicates the notion that an individualist feminism is necessarily antithetical to a collective alignment. Instead, depending on how it is practiced, the everyday feminism approach may be intimately connected to the continuity of the feminist movement at large.

Everyday abeyance structures demonstrate the importance of quotidian activities in perpetuating a movement. The concept disrupts the notion that individual incorporation of movements must come at the expense of collective organizing. Rather, we should focus on how individual activity sustains and relates to larger feminist organizing. An understanding of exactly what everyday feminism looks like and how it influences social change clarifies the continuity and relevance of the feminism movement today.

Online Abeyance Structures

Compared to activists in male-dominated movements, feminists have historically employed less visible tactics: community change and solidarity, everyday feminism, consciousness-raising, and other strategies of a cultural nature. While feminists have at times employed hyper-visible and disruptive actions, most of their activity have been overlooked or underestimated because of its comparative invisibility. My research showed that the tactical repertoires of previous generations of feminists remain relevant, especially cultural tactics and community building, which have been key features of sustaining a long-lasting movement. However, participants are now engaging in many of these activities online, evidence of young feminists' tactical innovation.[29] Jennifer Earl and Alan Schussman suggested that the Internet is a generative abeyance structure and may be a cost-effective means of propelling mobilization during periods of dwindling resources and support.[30] Respondents' use of Internet and communication technologies pushed feminism forward, creating *online abeyance structures.*

The students in this research used the Internet to sustain and build solidarity with their feminist communities; to interact with adversaries; to express feminist knowledge and language; and to learn about feminism.[31] Their curiosity about feminism was satiated online. The Internet provided information about the feminist movement that they would not have otherwise gained. Participants in this study learned about the feminist movement and its history and tactics through feminist blogs, social media, and organizational websites. Online information imparted a complex and multidimensional understanding of feminism. Although it is possible that individuals would garner similar information by reading feminist books or enrolling in feminist studies classes, the ease of information retrieval online meant that study participants sifted through substantial information and found online content that resonated with their experiences. Participants in this study reported regularly reading feminist critiques of current events. This encouraged feminist camaraderie and conversation, which would not necessarily have resulted from reading a book or participating in a class. Their classroom experiences reinforced or complemented the feminist knowledge gained outside the classroom.

Online abeyance structures were especially useful to feminist groups, whose maintenance was critical to the ongoing movement. Online technology, such as Facebook and feminist blogs, allowed organizations to reach wider audiences. Online social networks were used for similar goals as offline networks—such as recruiting new members, disseminating information about upcoming events and meetings, and creating solidarity through the circulation of feminist information.[32]

Online abeyance structures can be more egalitarian than many offline networks. Women of color, young women, and individuals without formal education have voices on the Internet. Thus, online feminism most accurately reflects the range of feminism practiced today. We know that women have less access to the mainstream media and that feminists in particular are especially villainized by the media. Online work and tactics allow women without advanced degrees, without fame or notoriety, to share their experiences and thoughts about feminism. This ultimately diversifies conversations about the movement and ensures its continued relevance.

Similar to previous conceptions of feminism, online feminism relies on friendship networks, and communities are critical to sustaining and advancing the movement.[33] The preexisting networks that sustain the feminist movement of the present are not the offline women's clubs or consciousness-raising groups of the past, but rather online networks engaging feminists and adversaries. Facebook and blogs facilitate networks in which to challenge dominant perspectives and nourish an oppositional culture, just as letter-writing campaigns did in the past.[34] That blogs and Facebook challenge mainstream media and highlight feminist perspectives closely resembles Whittier's findings regarding offline 1980s radical feminist organizing: "[B]ecause cultural hegemony triumphs by making nondominant points of view invisible or unthinkable, the establishment of a visible, institutionalized culture that promotes an oppositional reality is certainly a form of social change."[35] Blogs made feminist perspectives and commentaries easily accessible to a large audience, and Facebook enabled feminist campaigns and conversation with antagonists, both heightening the visibility of feminism. Online feminism perpetuates the tradition of feminists challenging hegemonic culture by promulgating feminist ideology, generating community, and injecting feminist language into nonfeminist spaces.[36]

Feminist Identities and the Wave Framework

As individuals adopt feminist identities or proclaim allegiance to the movement, feminism is advanced. How have feminist identities changed over time? Do young people today embrace individual feminist identities? Do they have a sense of solidarity with other feminists? Does third wave feminism resonate with them, as has been much touted by popular and academic scholarship alike?

Third Wave Feminism and Waveless Feminism

In my research, most feminists lacked interest in and knowledge of third wave feminism. They were either uninformed about the third wave or they disliked feeling that the identity was foisted upon them. This contradicts the widespread assumption that many young feminists embrace third wave feminism. During the late 1990s and 2000s, young feminism was synonymous with third wave feminism.[37] This lack of interest in third wave feminism among participants was surprising given the literature, but perhaps not surprising given that the wave framework does not accurately depict the nuances and complexities in feminism. Also, participants in this research would not fit neatly into a surge of mobilization.

Perhaps it is positive that these millennial participants were not enamored with the wave framework. The misunderstandings and oversimplifications of the feminist movement that are in large part due to an allegiance to the feminist waves reduced a complex and multifaceted movement to something (too) easily illustrated and digested. Joining in other feminist critiques of the wave framework, I argue that loosening our grip on the wave framework as shorthand for feminist generations or different surges of mobilization will help us think more broadly about feminism. *Waveless* feminism powerfully disrupts and makes us question this framework. Language is important. Using nonreductionist language will help us rethink and open up different avenues to explain feminism. *Sans* waves, we are forced to think about persistence, continuity, and continued mobilization. "Waveless" does not mean lack of momentum or complete harmony. It allows us to think carefully about movement continuity—and how and where movements persist over time.

The benefits of expanded views of feminism are not insignificant. Feminism of the 1970s has been "white-washed," ahistorically labeled as the province of White women. Benita Roth wrote, "When the second wave of feminism is seen as feminisms, the audacity of all feminists who challenged the status quo from wherever they were situated is recaptured and highlighted, and we are forced to recognize the power of feminist visions."[38] Speaking against the wave framework, Roth showed how Black, Chicana, and White women all were important to the development of modern feminism in the "pluralistic reality of feminist organizing."[39] The framework affects how we remember and retell the feminist movement. Participants in this study were not impervious to these perspectives, and their emphasis on intersectionality in part arose from their wishing to distance themselves from a movement they understood as not accurately reflecting the true diversity of organizing. We may challenge one-dimensional analyses of the women's movement by accenting the diversity and dynamic nature of the women's movement. Not only is an expanded view of feminism important for the sake of historical accuracy and analytical and theoretical precision,[40] but it also ensures that accurate understandings of feminism help inform the future of the movement.

Individual Feminist Identities and the Feminist Spectrum

The multiple understandings and applications of feminism drive confusion about what feminism is, and create difficulties in measuring it. The fence-sitters in this study, as Pamela Aronson calls them,[41] would neither completely adopt nor reject feminism. Reasons for fence-sitting varied by individual and campus. One reason was the feeling participants had that in order to embrace feminism it was necessary to have a higher level of dedication to the movement than they had. Other participants felt that some of their habits and practices were not in alignment with feminism (listening to music with sexist lyrics), or that their feminist peers had a greater feminist understanding and devotion than they did. Others disliked the term "feminist" because of its negative connotation. They said that they were not feminist, but were avid supporters of gender equality.

Even those who were very feminist did not always align in their descriptions of feminism. There were also nuances among those who were strongly feminist. Although rates of feminist self-identification were similar by race and ethnicity, in interviews I found that women of color were more likely than any other group to modify their feminist identity with an additional descriptor such as "Chicana" or "Third World." Others modified by using such terms as "radical feminist."

In order to understand the full range of feminist identities and practices, scholars have previously suggested the utility of recognizing a spectrum of feminism rather than either a yes or no feminist identity.[42] These findings confirm that an expansive and contextually specific view of feminism is important to portray the array of feminist identities. Some would fall on the less feminist side of the spectrum despite their dedication to principles of feminism, and others would fall on the very feminist side of the spectrum, for example. Some participants felt so devoted to feminism that it was engrained in their personalities and perspectives on the world. Understanding the origins and motivations of these explanations tells us a lot about the movement, what it means to be a feminist, and what parts of a feminist identity resonate with some participants and not others. This approach is not only about how closely a person identifies with feminism or how she modifies her identity in reference to other feminists. It allows for individual variation along the spectrum of feminism. A person's age and life stage may shape her relationship to feminism, and her place on the spectrum and relationship to feminism may change over time.

Collective Identity

My research uncovered the significance of local and institutional contexts in generating the collective identities of movement participants and their organizations. Dissimilar institutional cultures generated varying types of collective identities. Smith College, the all-women's college steeped in feminist ideology, shaped an *institutionally oriented identity*, in which a level of feminism was assumed to exist at all times. Consequently, for some, feminist organizations or proclamations of feminist identities were thought of as redundant or unnecessary. In contrast, the antifeminist environment at the U of M created *oppositional identities*, in which feminists clung to each other for movement sustenance. As a result, they forged vibrant feminist networks and communities. The *hybrid identities* of UCSB were steeped in the institution's activist history, of which students were proud. This context meant that feminists were generally supported as they worked with mobilized networks on a variety of progressive causes. On each campus, their feminist organizations, communities, and solidarity depended on the position of feminism in the institution and its history, as well as the student activist culture. Their level of solidarity was also related to how they experienced their gender. At Smith College, gender was not that important to participants; students reported not even thinking about being women. This probably was related to the fact that feminism was not at the front of their minds. When we understand why, even despite some similarities in field sites, movement identities and cultures can vary so much, we can see how critical community-level analyses are in the understanding of social movements.[43]

When I speak about my research to public audiences and to individuals, occasionally someone will say that feminist mobilization would never fly at their conservative and/or religious school. Nonetheless, possibilities for feminist mobilization and solidarity exist even in antifeminist environments. Although these possibilities are certainly place dependent, the circumstances of the U of M show us that feminists can find pockets of support and invaluable community networks despite study participants' reporting that the institution itself was not particularly feminist. Moreover, the engagement in online feminism and the power of the Internet to educate students in disparate communities about the history of feminism and to offer feminist perspectives on current events provide important contexts in which to develop feminist collective identities and feminist solidarity, regardless of the receptivity of the institution.

While the boundaries between feminists and nonfeminists were place and institution dependent, the grievances that motivated them, as well as some of their tactics, were consistent across campuses. There were cross-campus points of feminist collective identity. What bonded feminist students at all three campuses was a commitment to intersectionality, dedication to feminist organizations, and positive views of previous generations of feminism. Feminists across campuses were outraged about the persistence of sexual assault and rape culture, for example. They also shared a dedication to online feminism and learned about much of feminism from feminist blogs and Facebook feeds. Feminists across campuses joined coalitions of feminist and other progressive activists. Although I would not go so far as to say that we can point to a broader or cross-campus collective identity, these similarities were striking.

The Gender Revolution, Uneven and Stalled

The continuity of the feminist movement is based in part on the recognition of gender inequality and the relevance of feminism, which is why so much writing has been devoted to unpacking a new generation's understandings of and experiences with gender inequality. This book provides evidence that runs contrary to the assertions promoting the idea that young women do not understand inequalities and have no need for feminist organizing in their lives. Research participants noted that they often see representations of women in the media as much stronger and more powerful than they actually are in real life. Perhaps echoing these media messages, older feminist activists have said that young women are ignorant of the inequalities they are facing and will continue to face, that they are clueless about the importance of feminism, that they have been wearing "rose-colored glasses."[44] We should remember that skeptical attitudes toward young feminists are nothing new. In what may have a familiar ring, in the 1940s a National Women's Party member commented that young women were "not interested in anything but cosmetics, T.V. and modern amusements."[45] This type of discourse perpetuates inaccurate perspectives on young women's lives and, as a result, their relationships with feminism. It can also be ageist and sexist shorthand for dismissing young women's life experiences.

On the whole I found that the women in this study recognized an abundance of evidence of interactional, structural, and cultural inequalities. Regardless of the school they attended and their demographic background, feminist and fence-sitter participants were aware and observant of the inequalities that molded their young lives at home, at school, and in relationships. Far from seeing the world with "rose-colored glasses," many participants noted inequalities in every facet of their lives, which led them to adopt feminist identities and join feminist organizations. From a young age they reported noticing variations in their families' expectations of them compared to expectations of their brothers: their fathers' emphasis on the importance of marriage, or their mothers' subtle preparation of their daughters for a life tethered to domestic duties. One participant animatedly reported to me her mother's wistful descriptions of how much she loved raising children, yet at the same time she could not mask her sadness about not having the opportunity to develop her own passions. Several participants reported conversations they had with their boyfriends and platonic male friends, in which they palpably felt that they were expected to minimize their talents and dull their effervescence so as not to outshine their male counterparts. In many college classrooms, too, participants noted that their male peers felt comfortable dominating classroom airtime in a way they and their women classmates did not. In forecasting their future personal and professional lives, some participants expected inequalities of gender, race, and class to shape their opportunities. In a matter-of-fact tone, participants in this study related how the wage gap would affect them: they knew they would probably make less than their male coworkers and would take longer to pay off debts. As a result, feminist participants in my study organized around affordable education, higher educational accessibility for low-income students, as well as other, more gender-specific issues. Although, to my knowledge, none of my participants were planning on bearing children in the immediate future and they were not altering their plans because of possible future family obligations, they spoke of the challenges they anticipated in balancing family obligations and professional goals.[46]

Participants' vivid recollections of experiencing inequalities were often deeply emotional. The cadences in their voices revealed their anger and frustration. Yet these recollections did not seem raw, or fresh. There was a matter-of-factness about their descriptors. Participants in this study did not seem to have only recently come to the realization that the world is shaped by inequality. It was an expected and understood part of their everyday lives.

I did, however, find some evidence of denial of gender inequality—expressed in the "I haven't experienced gender inequality, but" phenomenon. These participants stated that they had not experienced gender inequality but in the same breath listed numerous examples of gender inequality. Even some nonfeminists had no difficulty recalling examples, such as one respondent who casually said her boyfriend's roommates would demand, "woman, go make me a sandwich" or rolled her eyes when she told me how she would inevitably be harassed when passing a fraternity house on a run. Some of this unwillingness to admit the existence of inequality did seem to be driven by the postfeminist logic that feminism had already accomplished what needed to be accomplished.

It is true that young women today live in a world in which they will not face some of the inequalities that have impacted the lives of older generations, or at least not to the same degree. Research participants did not have first-hand experiences with the many mobilizing grievances that once spurred feminist and other social justice organizing. It is also true that participants will face additional inequalities as they age.[47] However, by and large, they were not ignorant of the racism, classism, sexism, and homophobia that shape our communities and of the challenges they will face as individuals.

The gender revolution is unfinished. Whereas there once seemed to be promising momentum for massive changes in the gender order, scholars have found that advancements have stagnated.[48] Research has documented that these participants are correct in feeling inequalities all around them. Women do have a more difficult time fitting in with rigid and inflexible workplace structures; women in heterosexual partnerships will be responsible for the bulk of the domestic duties; young women do begin to downscale their dreams and professional passions in anticipation of these challenges.[49] Some reproach young women's individualist notions of feminism or lack of involvement in a nationwide feminist movement agitating for further changes.[50] It is important that we add greater depth to these narratives, as I have done in this book, building on the long, complex, and multifaceted history of feminism.

It is not only for accuracy that we must take a closer look at younger generations' engagement with feminism and employ a wider feminist lens to discover the varieties of feminist mobilization. There are also concrete ramifications for the life of the movement. First, if a movement is deemed irrelevant, it will not attract participants. Although the movement is not a PR campaign, to paraphrase Gloria Steinem, it is necessary to appeal to some degree to potentially mobilized participants. Second, in order for a movement to succeed, it needs not only human capital in the form of activists and agitators but also resources and agents of support. Feminist publishing houses, feminist organizations, feminist businesses, and feminist principles within institutions are all important resources that allow a movement to go forward. If feminism is seen as narrow and outdated, these will no longer flourish. Third, a movement needs allies, those people who will aid the mobilization of others and add to the momentum of a movement.

The impact of feminism has been felt far and wide in other social movements, too, effectively prolonging the feminist movement. Feminist participants, tactics, and networks spill over to bring feminism to other progressive social movements, and have done so for generations of feminism, even from the time of suffrage.[51] Particularly in mixed-gender movements with gender conflict, feminist spillover has been valuable for creating feminist spaces that have allowed women to participate in these movements. Of Occupy Wall Street, Heather McKee Hurwitz and Verta Taylor write, "Benefiting from second wave and contemporary feminist personnel, OCCUPY developed a variety of feminist organizations and networks to mobilize women's participation in the movement to respond to gender conflict with the goal of strengthening OCCUPY by building a larger base of support inclusive of women and their interests."[52] Thus, movements such as Occupy Wall Street, #BlackLivesMatter, and #SayHerName are evidence of the impact of feminist abeyance structures on other movements.[53]

When we consider avenues that help feminists in reinvigorating the uneven and stalled gender revolution, it is important to recognize and also uplift the young activists mobilizing on and off college campuses across the country. Recognizing the ways in which they are confronting inequalities in committing to the movement on- and offline, inside and outside feminist organizations, and in individual and collective ways will encourage the perpetuation of one of the longest-lasting social movements in modern history. Acknowledging and understanding a complex and vigorous movement of more than one hundred years demands a recognition of what feminists have accomplished and continue to accomplish. In order for feminists to be supported and encouraged, and to inspire other feminists to join the fray, a full picture of who feminists are and what they do is required.

Finding Feminism argues that there are many signs of a reinvigorated gender revolution among college students. Institutional integration of feminism and innovative feminist activism on campuses show that we can be certain feminists are still mobilizing and agitating for change.

Even as this is the case, this research shows that there is great potential for feminists to continue the momentum of the movement through online research, student groups, and everyday action.

Because gender inequality is still present in manifold ways, it is crucial that we perceive the way feminism has been transformed over time and identify how individuals and groups are working to change society. This is not only important as an intellectual exercise. When we truly understand where and how feminism is happening (in all its variations), we may join and support feminists in their goals. In order to perpetuate a movement, it is critical that new feminists carry the torch with the support of those on the sidelines. This is only feasible if feminism is visible and feminists are well understood. Only nuanced and contextually specific analyses of feminists, including a consideration of their similarities and differences, will effectively capture how feminists are organizing to change their communities and the world.

APPENDIX

The Research

A number of years ago I had the opportunity to work with a vivacious, imaginative, and funny group of college feminists. This group identified as radical—in their approaches to feminism, consumption, politics, and sexuality. They organized a zine library, feminist music acts, sex worker art shows, clothing swaps, protests supporting reproductive freedoms, and teach-ins ranging from transgender rights to alternatives to mainstream menstrual products. Although it was a student group sponsored by their university, their events were open to anyone, and they often involved community organizations and community members. They identified as feminist, but were not hung up on it. They never talked about waves.

One cool spring day, two prominent third wave feminists arranged a visit to the office of the feminist group. The third wave feminists were on a national book tour. Members of another campus organization hosted them, and generously offered a meeting between the third wave feminists and the student group, thinking it would be a perfect connection.

At the appointed time, the third wave feminists energetically pushed their enormous, expensive-looking baby carriages into the office, each holding a large paper cup of coffee. Some of the students exchanged glances with each other, others shifted uncomfortably on the sofas. The first words of one of the third wave feminists were, "We're so excited for you! You have a Starbucks just one flight below your office!" The two women did not know that this was a sensitive topic. The students had been involved in an unsuccessful campaign to keep Starbucks out of the student union, in order to support a local coffee shop. Starbucks won, and there were some lingering bitter feelings. For the students, this Starbucks moment was a symbol of the continual involvement of big corporations in their university, which was, to them, antifeminist. The meeting began with an uncomfortable tone, and it continued awkwardly. The university feminists peered at the third wave feminists as if to say, "You are the traveling feminists? You write books and lecture on young women and feminism?" The third wave feminists must have sensed an uncomfortable dynamic, but did not let on.

The meeting was short and uninspiring, at best. The two groups did not share a feminist language, and they did not have a common understanding of feminist goals. My only regret is that neither the university feminists nor the third wave feminists addressed the source of the tension, because it would have been an excellent learning opportunity. This interaction, although brief, has been etched in my memory even though it took place many years ago. The scenario highlights salient themes in feminism such as the tensions between feminists and divergences in feminist targets, tactics, and goals. This motivated my interest in research about continuity and change in feminism.

Methods

Feminist scholars frequently look to college students and young women to understand whether feminist mobilizations continue.[1] Historically, college students have been the prime participants in movements for social change. However, to date there has been very little research on social justice organizing among college women.

Using interviews, surveys, and participant observation, I collected individual- and organizational-level data in 2011 at three different institutions of higher education: the University of California–Santa Barbara, the University of Minnesota–Twin Cities, and Smith College. I chose these three institutions because they are different from each other in respect to type of institution, geographic region, student demographics, and student activist and feminist culture—I also had some degree of entrée at these institutions, which is not inconsequential. I acknowledge that these three specific schools may color my results. Because of this, I include considerations of how the institutional specificities have shaped my results. These schools are not generalizable to all schools, and readers will find similarities to or differences from the schools or institutions with which they are familiar. A goal of *Finding Feminism* is to examine feminism in different contexts, and to paint a broad picture of college student feminism. Since scholars of feminist movements have always found that there is not one cohesive feminism, a comparative study allows me to evaluate how contextual variation influences mobilization, dynamics, collective identity, and abeyance structures.[2]

Why College Students?

The application of gender and social movement theories to college students provides a fruitful examination of the processes of identity construction, movement dynamics, and mobilization within institutions. College students explore identities, friendship circles, classroom interests, and extracurricular activities. Many of them are living without their parents for the first time and are developing their own perspectives and attitudes. Attention to personal development and community building occurs in many colleges (depending on their resources), such as in programming by campus women's centers or university dorms.

College students have a long and rich history of social movement participation.[3] In her research on the civil rights movement, Francesca Polletta writes, "In the early part of the civil rights movement, activism was linked with—normatively required of—churchgoers; in 1960, *student* became linked to activist, became a 'prized social identity' that supplied the selective incentives to participation" (emphasis in original).[4] This tradition continues. For example, in the past few years, students in Chile, Quebec, the United States, and the UK organized massive protests to advocate for more affordable education. Those who were gathered in a critical mass were not just young people; their *student* identities were essential in the mobilization and framing of these movements. About the student protests in Chile, Eduardo Silva writes, "With respect to differences, university students consolidated an autonomous identity unconnected to political parties and developed a strong mobilization resource base. . . . That framing turned students into the fulcrum for a broader process of coalition-building that sustained mass demonstrations."[5] In this case, the success of student organizing rests in the student identities developed in the college context.[6] But not all students are organizing for progressive causes, of course. In their 2013 book *Becoming Right: How Campuses Shape Young Conservatives*, Amy Binder and Kate Wood find that college students on two very different types of campuses learn distinctive ways to enact their conservative politics and gain the support of national conservative organizations for their success.[7] Regardless of their grievances and targets, student identities and networks foster camaraderie, energetic mobilization, and tactical innovation unique to the student experience.

In large part, the persistence of student mobilization is attributed to biographical availability, or free time and flexible schedules.[8] In his study of student mobilization and processes of politicization in England, Nick Crossley found that it was the cohesive and active student networks that were critical in politicizing "novices."[9] Student networks also facilitate tactical diffusion across similar institutional types,[10] as in the case of the shantytowns that cropped up across the United States in the 1980s. To be sure, tactics and forms of mobilization vary by campus type. Some campuses are consistently "hotbeds of activism,"[11] while on other campuses, students are more likely to mobilize around specific grievances that directly influence the campus community.[12]

Social movement scholars have analyzed the personal and biographical consequences of organizing, and have found that movement participation matters in a variety of dimensions.[13] Participation in a movement changes participants because of the adoption of the values and goals of a movement.[14] Mobilized participants do not simply return to their regularly scheduled lives when their involvement in a movement subsides.[15] Instead, participants incorporate the values of a movement in their careers, relationships, and everyday lives.[16] Although the outcomes and biographical impact of student organizing is beyond the scope of this study, for many students their activism is part of a larger trajectory of a lifetime of movement activity, not merely a flash in the pan.[17]

Interviews

I conducted in-depth, semistructured interviews with seventy-five undergraduates (twenty-five at each institution). The information gathered in the interviews addressed questions at the individual level of analysis, and captured complex processes of feminist identification. The interview data also answered questions related to feminist practices and ideologies, motives for movement participation, and relationships between personal biography and feminist consciousness. I employed snowball methods to obtain interview participants: first, through students I met in the participant-observation portion of my research;

second, through announcements I made in undergraduate classes: and third, through posting and distributing fliers in high-traffic areas of each campus. The announcements stated that I was conducting research on college students, social inequalities, and feminism, and that all interested undergraduate students were welcome to participate. My aim was to interview student participants in feminist organizations as well as students who were not participants in feminist organizations, recognizing that many students cannot regularly take part in student organizations because of work and/or family commitments. Students were paid ten dollars in cash at the end of the interview, although five students would not accept the money. Some students acted as key informants about feminism and activism on their campus.[18]

Interview respondents were currently enrolled undergraduate college students, primarily between the ages of eighteen and twenty-one. Participants self-identified as White (n=42), Latina/o (n=8), mixed race/other (n=13); as Asian American (n=6), African American (n=5), American Indian (n=1); as heterosexual (n=46), queer (n=9), bisexual (n=9), gay/lesbian (n=7), queer and bisexual (n=1), and nonspecified sexuality (n=3); and as women (n=68) and men (n=7), including a transgender male. Many were first-generation college students. Twenty-seven self-identified as poor, working-class, or lower-middle-class, and forty-eight were in the middle-class range. The participants shared a degree of educational privilege. However, this sample diverges from a number of studies that focus on the experiences of White feminists: thirty-three of the seventy-five respondents identified as Latino, mixed race, Asian American, African American, or Native American. UCSB specifically has attracted a diverse undergraduate student body and has recently been granted "Hispanic degree-granting institution" status because of the high number of Latina and Latino students. Approximately a third of the interview participants belonged to feminist organizations and also served as key informants about their communities. The remaining participants were involved in social justice–oriented organizations or expressed interest in feminist, gender, and/or social justice issues.

The interviews lasted between sixty and ninety minutes. They were conducted in campus locations convenient for the students, such as the student center, a café, or in a few cases at Smith College, at students' on-campus houses. The interview schedule included general questions about the respondents' backgrounds, hopes for their futures, and experiences with social inequalities. Interview participants were asked about their perceptions of feminism, including whether they identify as feminist and their processes of coming to feminist consciousness or of resisting feminism. For those students who belonged to feminist organizations, I asked them details about their organizations, including successes and challenges, and strategies and tactics of the organization. The interview schedule included a section on the media, pertaining to whether the respondents recalled seeing feminism referenced on television or in the news, or if they had recently watched any television shows or films depicting feminist characters or strong women leads. I was hoping to follow the model sociologist Laura Carpenter established in order to evaluate representations and interpretations of feminism in the media, the way students spoke with each other about feminism in the media, and the way representations of feminism in the media contributed to a collective identity that potentially reached across campuses.[19] Unfortunately, with a few exceptions, this line of questioning was largely a failure because the overwhelming majority of students reported that they did not have time to watch television or films, nor had they throughout their undergraduate years. However, participants in this study did have a lot to say in response to questions about Facebook and blogs. Their comments suggest that, for many of them, their time spent relaxing is spent online.

All interviews were digitally recorded, transcribed, and coded for emergent themes. Themes included the importance of college classes and organizations in fostering feminist identities, respect and appreciation for previous generations of feminists, and a common perception of being underestimated in their everyday lives due to their gender and age. Additionally, there was notable variation among college campuses, as related to everyday feminism and acceptance or rejection of feminist identities.

Participant Observation

One unique feature of these findings is that the in-depth, semistructured interviews I conducted were supplemented with participant observation in feminist student organizations at each research site and at a national feminist conference. The unit of analysis in the participant-observation portion of data collection was predominantly campus organizations, and related to the tactics, grievances, collective identities, and strategies of campus feminist organizations. I spent ten weeks at UCSB, and three weeks each at Smith College and the University of Minnesota. I attended the meetings and events of campus organizations that included the words "gender equality," "feminism," or "women" in their title or mission. I chose the organizations on each campus that were well known for their feminist mobilization, and with the exception of UCSB, each campus had one primary feminist organization. At UCSB, I conducted research with two organizations; at the University of Minnesota, one primary organization and one related organization (a large coalition that included members of the primary organization); and at Smith College, one primary organization and a few related organizations (organizations with significant overlap with the primary organization). I had varying degrees of entrée into these organizations. I did not have entrée into organizations that require membership, such as the Latina sororities at UCSB, several of which are considered feminist by their members. To mitigate this situation, I interviewed individual members of these groups and attended some of their events.

I disclosed myself as a researcher to the members of each organization, who welcomed me. During the course of my participant observation, I attended regular meetings, lunch meetings, workshops, lectures, film nights, lunches, discussion groups, and a feminist cupcake social. I "tabled" for the UCSB antirape organization (sat at a table outside the campus library and handed out information), and I helped the members of the UCSB Womyn's Union plan a large banquet for students, faculty, and staff. For that event, I contacted possible speakers, publicized the event, helped with set-up and tear-down, and drove a group of members to a local art supply store for decorations.

In my field notes, I wrote down information about the actions, words, emotions, and interactions of participants. My initial field notes were hand written, but at the end of an event or a day of research, I immediately typed them on the computer and elaborated upon my experiences. Themes that emerged from my analysis of the data obtained through participant observation are the significance of institutional setting and context in shaping campus feminist cultures, similarities in grievances and tactics across campuses, and differences in the contours of collective identities among campuses.

Survey

The third source of data is an online survey conducted on all three campuses that is intended to add depth to the interviews and participant observation. The survey speaks to the individual level of analysis, and allows me to make claims regarding the climate on each campus, predominantly related to reported behavior and experiences as well as individual and collective identities. The survey augments the qualitative data by providing context,[20] supplying additional evidence to demonstrate how my findings diverge from other recent studies of contemporary feminism,[21] and allowing me to make stronger conclusions and connections across research sites.[22] Hosted by the UCSB Survey Research Center, I also received funding to give away an iPad, an enticement to increase the response rate.

I obtained 1,397 survey responses total (UCSB, n=793; Smith College, n=361; University of Minnesota, n=243). Although the schools are of varying sizes, the number of responses at each school was more lopsided than I had hoped. However, the results did confirm findings in the participant observation and interview portion of the data. I speculate that more UCSB students responded because the request was coming from a fellow UCSB student and UCSB was the most hospitable environment for progressive student organizing. Although there are relatively fewer Smith students, many of them responded to the survey because Smith students seem very interested in speaking about feminism and sharing their opinions and viewpoints. Finally, I speculate that the University of Minnesota garnered fewer responses because students are simply not as interested in inequality and student activism and would not necessarily be inclined to take a survey on the topic. Overall, the varying survey responses reflected the rest of my research: students enrolled at schools with strong traditions or models of activism and/or feminism are more inclined to be interested in the topic and to take the survey.

The different levels of responses may mean that the students who took the survey are much more likely to be interested in feminism and/or student activism than other students on their campus. Because of this, I focus my analysis on variations among those students who express an affinity towards feminism and "social justice" narratives, rather than comparing them with the smaller number of students who took the survey but were not interested in the issues. Also, the different responses at each campus make me less confident in some cross-campus comparisons; in particular, I fear that activists and feminists are overrepresented in the University of Minnesota survey. When I use the survey data throughout *Finding Feminism*, I make note of how the variation in responses may influence my analysis.

This research was open to all registered students. Thirty-four percent of my survey respondents identified as people of color. However, men were not particularly interested in an interview or in taking my survey. Women were disproportionately represented in both datasets. Sixty-eight out of seventy-five interview participants were women. Seventy-seven percent of the survey respondents were women, and the women were more likely to identify as feminist (33.5 percent) than the men were (11.1 percent).

I initially solicited respondents through advertisements on Facebook. They appeared on the sidebar of the pages of Facebook users who indicated in their profile that they attended one of the three schools. This yielded few results. Next, I disseminated the survey link over a range of undergraduate listserves on each campus, including student organization and department listserves. In order to solicit responses from students of a variety of academic majors, I contacted department administration in the sciences, humanities, and social sciences and requested that my announcement be forwarded to undergraduate majors. I targeted the same departments at each research site, to try to reach students of like academic dispositions, and followed up when necessary. Because I had to rely on administrators to forward my messages, in some instances I cannot be sure that all the intended students received the survey advertisement.

The survey consisted primarily of closed-ended questions. Questions asked about students' experiences with and perceptions of discrimination and social inequalities on their campus; whether they think that social inequality such as sexism, racism, classism, or homophobia will affect their personal or professional lives; their knowledge of and attitudes towards feminism and gender inequality; and their involvement in student organizations. I analyzed the survey data using SPSS along with an RA. The survey data address questions about perception and knowledge of the feminist movement, involvement in feminist organizations, and feminist identity. The survey also addresses larger questions about student experiences with inequality and how that influences participation in student organizations. Finally, the survey data illuminate themes related to the "uneven and stalled"[23] or "unfinished"[24] gender revolution, insofar as it solicits responses about students' perception of and experiences with gender inequality at school, home, and work.

College Campuses

Smith College

Smith College is a private women's liberal arts college in the town of Northampton, Massachusetts (approximately twenty-nine thousand residents), fondly called "Lesbianville, USA" by many residents because of its lesbian-friendly culture. It is located in western Massachusetts, about a two-hour drive from Boston, and is in a scenic area at the base of the Berkshire Mountains. Northampton has an average household income of $51,018, a median house value of $289,766, and a median age of 38.9 years.[25] It is also an intellectual community. The Pioneer Valley is home to a five-college consortium made up of Smith College, Amherst College, Hampshire College, Mount Holyoke, and the University of Massachusetts–Amherst.

Like many women's colleges, Smith College has a distinct culture that emphasizes empowering women. There are now only approximately sixty women's colleges remaining in the United States. East coast women's colleges, such as Smith and the others in the "Seven Sisters" consortium, initially educated women from elite families. The single-sex environment placated fathers who were nervous about sending their daughters away from home, but who wanted refined and learned children. A principle of "taking women seriously" dominates women's colleges, their administration, and student and campus cultures,[26] many of which were founded during time periods in which it was considered radical to educate women. Research on students and graduates of women's colleges indicates that all-women institutions foster self-confidence and leadership skills, as well as egalitarian views on gender roles.[27] Much of this research was driven by earlier studies that found women's college graduates more likely to be high achievers[28] and elected to U.S. Congress, despite the relatively small number of women in the United States who attend women's colleges.[29] Quantitative longitudinal studies have mixed conclusions related to the advantages of attending coeducational or women-only colleges.[30] A recent study[31] presents similar career and family outcomes in both co-ed and all-women's college students as a testimony to the improving climate for women at co-ed institutions. However, in a study comparing the two college types, Mikyong Kim found higher levels of "peer social activism and altruism" in women-only colleges than in co-ed colleges, and that faculty at women's colleges are more strongly oriented to diversity, "liberalism, social activism and community orientation, and student orientation" than their counterparts at co-ed colleges.[32] Smith is also noted to be a feminist-friendly campus, illustrated by its touting of its graduates Gloria Steinem (class of 1956) and Betty Friedan (class of 1942). This research sets the stage for the distinct culture and feminist context of Smith College, particularly in comparison to the two co-ed colleges in this study.

Table A.1: Smith College Undergraduate Demographics, 2011–2012

Total number of undergraduates	2,627
Women	2,625
Men	2
Percentage of undergraduates from out-of-state (excluding nonresident aliens and international students)	79%
Approximate yearly tuition, room, and board	$55,000
Race/Ethnicity	Number of undergraduate students; percent
Hispanic	204; 7.8%
Nonresident alien	281; 10.7%
Black or African American, non-Hispanic	128; 4.9%
White, non-Hispanic	1,157; 44%
American Indian or Alaska Native, non-Hispanic	7; .27%
Asian, non-Hispanic	320; 12.2%
Native Hawaiian or other Pacific Islander, non-Hispanic	4; .15%
Two or more races, non-Hispanic	108; 4.11%
Race and/or ethnicity unknown	418; 16%

Smith College Common Data Set, 2011–2012, http://www.smith.edu.

Smith College campus culture revolves around "house" life. Ninety-five percent of undergraduates live in "houses" on campus, many of which are beautifully converted Victorian homes. In 2011, Smith was featured on the *Princeton Review*'s top list of colleges with "dorms like palaces." Each house has a formal living room used for the tradition of the weekly house tea. On Friday afternoons, a tea service is delivered to every house living room by a college employee, usually including a selection of fresh fruit, cheese, and pastries baked in the house kitchen. Amidst the stately surroundings and with floral tea sets perched on the table, one could imagine a room of college students in the early 1900s, beautifully dressed and speaking softly about their poetry class or their fiancé at nearby Amherst College. Instead, although the surroundings look largely the same, today the living rooms are filled with rowdy students, many with piercings and tattoos and some still wearing pajamas, chattering excitedly about the weekend, or perhaps reliving last night's hookup with the woman who sits next to her in engineering class.

In many respects, the traditions of Smith College contrast with the lives of its current student body. In interviews, students expressed mutual admiration of the college and dismay at its largely homogenous and elite student population. However, an abundance of beloved rituals like Friday Tea contribute to the unique experience of being a "Smithie," of which its students are proud. As a result, it has a loyal and well-connected network of alumni. Its most recent quarterly alumni magazine featured thirty full pages of alumni updates sent in by women who graduated between 1932 and 2010.

There were many different types of feminist organizations featured in my study at Smith. The main feminist organization had been in existence for many years, although, as is common with student groups, their membership and energies had ebbed and flowed. At the time of my data collection, there were a handful of very dedicated members who focused on their own group events and on coalitioning with other organizations. This main group had no office or central space (none of the organizations at Smith in my study did—in contrast to the U of M and UCSB), and when I attended a meeting it was over lunch in the cafeteria of a member's house (dorm). A new feminist organization cropped up during the time I was conducting fieldwork, a group with a national feminist organization affiliation. There was some tension because of this, with the more established group flummoxed by why nobody from the new group reached out to the older group. There were also a number of organizations that were social justice focused—including a Latina group and a socioeconomic-inequality group. I attended open events when I could—as members of these organizations individually informed me that the groups were feminist.

University of Minnesota

Unlike Smith College, the University of Minnesota–Twin Cities is a Big Ten public research university located in the metropolitan area of Minneapolis/St. Paul, Minnesota (approximately 3.5 million residents). In Minneapolis, the median household income is approximately $43,369, the average age is 33.6, and the median home value is $230,300.[33] In St. Paul, the statistics are similar. The Twin Cities have a reputation for big business, and medical and economic innovation. Target Corporation, 3M, General Mills, Best Buy, Supervalu, and United Health Group are some of the Fortune 500 companies that have their headquarters in the Twin Cities.[34] There are numerous other colleges and universities in the Twin Cities, although the "U" is the largest, and one of the largest employers in the state. It has over eighteen thousand faculty and staff system-wide.[35]

Because of the large size, it is more difficult to categorize a distinct character in comparison to the other two research sites. However, one interview participant categorized the U of M as "very Minnesotan," and several others alluded to its Minnesotan nature. This was the only research site where interview participants mentioned the characteristics of the state when describing their campus. Indeed, many Minnesotans do possess unique personality attributes, in large part due to residents' identification with their Swedish and Norwegian heritage, which seems to have only moderately diminished over generations. Students referenced Minnesota's history of Scandinavian immigrants and industrious Lutherans, and the frigid weather that keeps residents indoors several months of the year. While both urban and rural residents of the state retain much of this strong cultural background, the demographics of the state have dramatically shifted in the last twenty years, and Minnesota is now home to the largest population of Hmong Americans in the country and a large Eritrean community. However, if you walk around the university, you may notice that it remains a racially homogenous student body, which many interviewees noted.

Table A.2: University of Minnesota–Twin Cities Undergraduate
Demographics, 2011–2012

Total number of undergraduates	29,061
Women	15,036/ 51.7%
Men	14,004/ 48.2%
Number of undergraduates from the Twin Cities Metro Area	15,429
Number of undergraduates from greater Minnesota	4,778
Number of undergraduates from Wisconsin, South Dakota, North Dakota	4,864
Approximate yearly in-state tuition and fees	$12,400
Race/Ethnicity	Number of undergraduate students; percent
American Indian	347; 1.2%
Asian	2,691; 9.3%
Black	1,454; 5.0%
Hawaiian	78; .3%
Hispanic	714; 2.5%
International	1,988; 6.8%
White	21,305; 73.3%
Race and/or ethnicity unknown	484; 1.7%

"All Enrollment Data for Spring 2011," Office of Institutional Research, University of Minnesota, http://www.oir. umn.edu.

The large, metropolitan campus, located on both sides of the Mississippi River, consists of the East bank, West bank, and St. Paul campus. A free shuttle ferries students to the various parts of campus. Because of the icy-cold Minnesota weather, underground tunnels called "The Gopher Way" (named after U of M's Goldy Gopher mascot) conveniently connect many buildings. A large double-decker bridge spans the Mississippi River and connects East and West banks. The bridge's bottom level is for vehicles, and the top level is enclosed to lessen the harsh wind and snow for those who are walking. At the beginning of each school year, student groups are allowed to paint one interior segment of the pedestrian level of the bridge to advertise their groups, often showcasing artistic creativity. Next to the bridge near the student union is perhaps the most architecturally striking feature of the campus—the stunning Frank Gehry–designed Weisman Art Museum. With Gehry's signature twisted aluminum and geometric façade, the museum sits perched on the West bank of the Mississippi River. It spectacularly reflects the sunsets over Minneapolis.

The university has schools for undergraduates, graduates, and researchers, and includes several highly ranked graduate and professional schools—medical school, law school, school of public affairs, and school of management. Many medical innovations began at the U of M, including the world's first heart transplant, and Minnesota continues to be a leader in medical-device innovation. Located on the sprawling St. Paul campus, the school of food, agricultural, and natural-resource sciences trains students and researchers in a number of animal and agricultural fields. In fact, the honey crisp apple was developed by food scientists there.

As a Division One school, the University of Minnesota has especially popular athletic teams. Socially, fraternities and sororities dominate the school, with some of the oldest fraternities in the country sitting on "frat row." Because of the size of the university, there are many student organizations, mostly supported by the student service fees paid by every student. There are a growing number of conservative or right-wing student organizations and publications at the university, which have been very vocal about feeling that their views are marginalized. This has caused some tensions among student groups and between student groups and student affairs administration.

There was one principal feminist organization at the University of Minnesota. This organization has existed for many years, with copious archives housed in its office. This organization has an office and lounge in the student union that is open and staffed during most business hours and serves as a resource center and social space for any interested students. With a part-time staff member who oversees operations and serves as a mentor, the organization has a large membership and support base, although it is not without its outspoken detractors. The organization has close ties with the queer student organization and many other social justice organizations, including socioeconomic and ethnicity-based organizations.

University of California–Santa Barbara

The University of California–Santa Barbara is a public research university with approximately twenty-one thousand undergraduate and graduate students in the coastal city of Santa Barbara, California (approximately ninety-three thousand residents). Santa Barbara has a median family income of $76,706 and a 2009 median home price of $876,292. Its median age is 36.8.[36] Dubbed "the American Riviera" because of its natural beauty and high cost of living, Santa Barbara has the reputation for being home to wealthy White residents. Nevertheless, UCSB has attracted a diverse undergraduate student body. UCSB has garnered "Hispanic degree-granting institution" status because of the high number of Latina and Latino students. The majority of UCSB students hail from Southern California (particularly Los Angeles and Orange Counties). UCSB has a colorful history of student activism that continues today as students organize for the Dream Act and against tuition hikes.

Table A.3: University of California–Santa Barbara, Undergraduate Demographics, 2011–2012

Total number of undergraduates	18,620
Women	9,762
Men	8,858
Approximate yearly in-state tuition and fees	$13,600
Undergraduates from Northern California Counties	5,785; 31%
Undergraduates from Southern California Counties	9,579; 51%
Undergraduates from UCSB Service Area (SB, Ventura, SLO, Kern Counties)	2,218; 12%
Undergraduates from other U.S. states	684; 4%
Ethnicity	Number of undergraduate students; percent
American Indian/Alaskan	174; 1%
Black/African American	677; 4%
Chicano/Latino	4,376; 24%
Asian/Pacific Islander, Filipino, East Indian/Pakistani	3,799; 21%
Other	109; 1%
White	8,333; 46%
International	354; 2%
Race and/or ethnicity unknown	798; 4%

University of California–Santa Barbara, Institutional Research and Planning, "2011–2012 Campus Profile," Jan. 11, 2012. http://bap.ucsb.edu.

UCSB overlooks the beach and has stunning natural scenery, and the beachside vibe permeates the campus culture. The majority of undergraduate students live either in on-campus dorms (many with ocean views and pools) or in off-campus housing in Isla Vista, a beachside neighborhood immediately adjacent to the UCSB campus. Because the campus is relatively small with so many students living nearby, the main modes of transportation are skateboards and beach cruiser bicycles. Skateboard lanes and a busy bike thoroughfare span the campus to accommodate the traffic. Interview respondents spoke often about the laid-back attitude of the undergraduate student body. During my research, many students looked forward to the annual "floatopia," an enormous floating party in which up to twelve thousand students tie hundreds of rafts and floats together and launch into the Pacific Ocean. In the spring of 2012, university administration and the Santa Barbara Sheriff's Office closed the beaches in Isla Vista to prevent another "floatopia" due to the danger to student safety and the litter that inevitably washes up on nearby beaches. In 2013 and 2014, the beaches were again closed the weekend the party was planned, and the party was moved to land. The university was plagued with problems in 2014, including a highly publicized meningitis outbreak, a gang rape, the tragic murder of six UCSB students, and a feminist studies professor charged with several misdemeanors after an on-campus scuffle with an antichoice protestor. The university administration is working to deflect attention away from these episodes, by emphasizing its highly ranked graduate programs, Nobel laureates, and strong sense of community.

Of the three institutions, UCSB had the greatest number of feminist organizations and affiliated organizations. Two main feminist organizations were affiliated with the women's center and student government, with the women's center group focusing on anti–sexual assault efforts. Both of these groups had extensive membership bases, robust and consistent attendance, and a full schedule of events. There were also a number of multicultural sororities whose members agreed were feminist.

As is evident from the descriptions, these three campuses are notably dissimilar, not only in their geographic locations and landscapes but also in their institutional and student cultures. Each school attracts students from different regions of the country and of diverse social, racial, and ethnic backgrounds. Once enrolled, they also have varying student experiences. As will emerge in my analysis, the campuses have distinctive student organizations and forms of feminist socialization. By employing a multicampus, comparative study, I am able to evaluate the nuances of feminist identity and feminist mobilizing structures in different contexts.

NOTES

CHAPTER 1. WHERE HAVE ALL THE FEMINISTS GONE?

1 "2014 Isla Visa Killings."
2 Medina, "Campus Killings.
3 Hess, "Why It's So Hard for Men to See Misogyny."
4 Lemon, "Hollywood and Violence."
5 "Rachel Sklar Explains 'Yes All Women,'" *CNN*, May 27, 2014, http://www.cnn.com.
6 Snow and Soule, *A Primer on Social Movements.*
7 Hawkesworth, "The Semiotics of a Premature Burial."
8 Zeisler, "On our Radar."
9 Rosin, "Marissa Mayer Thinks Feminists Are a Drag."
10 Baumgardner and Richards, *Manifesta*; see Reger, *Everywhere and Nowhere.*
11 England, "The Gender Revolution"; Kathleen Gerson, *The Unfinished Revolution.*
12 Reskin, "Bringing Men Back In."
13 American Association of University Women, *The Simple Truth about the Gender Pay Gap*; Maatz, "The Awful Truth behind the Gender Pay Gap."
14 Williams, *Still a Man's World.*
15 Danielle Paquette, "At This Rate, American Women Won't See Equal Pay Until 2058," *Washington Post*, March 16, 2015, http://www.washingtonpost.com.
16 Reger, *Everywhere and Nowhere.*
17 Aronowitz and Bernstein, *Girldrive*; Baumgardner and Richards, *Manifesta.*
18 See Reger, *Everywhere and Nowhere.*
19 Gilmore, ed., *Feminist Coalitions*; Reger, *Everywhere and Nowhere*; Staggenborg and Taylor, "Whatever Happened to the Women's Movement?"
20 Hawkesworth, "The Semiotics of a Premature Burial."
21 England, "The Gender Revolution," 149–66; Gerson, *The Unfinished Revolution, 2011*; Gerson, "Why Are Young Women More Ambitious Than Men?"
22 Franklin, *After the Rebellion*; Clay, *The Hip-Hop Generation Fights Back*; Soule, "The Student Divestment Movement"; Taft, *Rebel Girls*; Van Dyke, "Hotbeds of Activism."
23 Bruce, *Faithful Revolution*; Katzenstein, *Faithful and Fearless*; Raeburn, *Changing Corporate America from Inside Out*; Rojas, *From Black Power to Black Studies.*
24 Almeida, *Waves of Protest*; Fonow, *Union Women*; Maddison and Martin, "Introduction to 'Surviving Neoliberalism'"; Rupp and Taylor, *Survival in the Doldrums*; Weigand, *Red Feminism.*

25 Guenther, *Making Their Place*; Reger, *Everywhere and Nowhere*; Taft, *Rebel Girls*; Rupp and Taylor, *Drag Queens at the 801 Cabaret*; Taylor and Van Dyke, "Get Up, Stand Up"; Whittier, *The Politics of Child Sexual Abuse.*

26 Crossley and Taylor, "Abeyance Cycles in Social Movements."

27 Roth, *Separate Roads to Feminism.*

28 Cobble, Gordon, and Henry, *Feminism Unfinished*, xv.

29 Crossley et al., "Forever Feminism."

30 Crossley et al., "Forever Feminism"; Ferree and Hess, *Controversy and Coalition.*

31 Raeburn, *Changing Corporate America from Inside Out*; Taft, *Rebel Girls*; Taylor and Van Dyke "Get Up, Stand Up."

32 Piepmeier, *Girl Zines*; Taylor, "Social Movement Continuity"; Whittier, *Feminist Generations.*

33 Katzenstein, "Stepsisters."

34 Crossley, "Women's Activism in Educational Institutions"; Reger and Story, "Talking about My Vagina."

35 Taylor and Rupp, "Women's Culture and Lesbian Feminist Activism."

36 Staggenborg, "Social Movement Communities and Cycles of Protest."

37 Whittier, *Feminist Generations.*

38 Sulik, *Pink Ribbon Blues.*

39 Hurtado, "Relating to Privilege."

40 Ferree and Hess, *Controversy and Coalition*, 71.

41 Quoted in Freedman, "Tools of the Movement."

42 Springer, *Living for the Revolution*, 60.

43 Cassell, *A Group Called Women.*

44 Crossley, "Facebook Feminism."

45 Mansbridge, *Why We Lost the ERA.*

46 Luker, *Abortion and the Politics of Motherhood.*

47 Farmer, "Black Women March on Washington."

48 Crossley et al., "Forever Feminism."

49 Pino and Clark, *The Hunting Ground.*

50 Pino and Clark, *The Hunting Ground.*

51 Crossley and Taylor, "Abeyance Cycles in Social Movements"; Raeburn, *Changing Corporate America from Inside Out.*

52 Van Dyke, Soule, and Taylor, "The Targets of Social Movements."

53 Taylor and Rupp, "Women's Culture and Lesbian Feminist Activism."

54 Enke, *Finding the Movement*, 109.

55 Taylor, *Rock-a-by Baby*, 13.

56 Hess, "Why Women Aren't Welcome on the Internet."

57 Citron, *Hate Crimes in Cyberspace.*

58 Duggan, "Online Harassment,"

59 Blee, *Democracy in the Making*, 139.

60 Rohlinger, *Abortion Politics.*

61 Crossley, "'When It Suits Me, I'm a Feminist.'"

62 Rupp and Taylor, *Survival in the Doldrums*, 22.

63 Crossley, "'When It Suits Me, I'm a Feminist'"; Crossley, "Young Women's Feminist Identities."

64 Rosen, *The World Split Open.*

65 Pelak, "Contesting Collective Memory."

66 Polletta, "'It Was like a Fever.'"

67 Lind and Salo, "The Framing of Feminists."

68 Crossley, "'When It Suits Me, I'm a Feminist,'" 224.

69 Liss, Crawford, and Popp, "Predictors and Correlates of Collective Action"; Myaskovsky and Wittig, "Predictors of Feminist Social Identity among College Women."

70 Sandberg, *Lean In.*

71 Sandberg, *Lean In for Graduates.*

72 Williams and Dempsey, *What Works for Women at Work.*

73 Spar, *Wonder Women.*

74 Roth, *Separate Roads to Feminism.*

75 Crossley, "Facebook Feminism."

76 Kirsten West Savali, "Change Agents of 2014: Black Women on Social Media," *Root*, December 29, 2014, http://www.theroot.com.

77 Ferree and Mueller, "Feminism and the Women's Movement"; Reger, *Everywhere and Nowhere*; Staggenborg and Taylor, "Whatever Happened to the Women's Movement?"; Taylor, *Rock-a-by Baby.*

78 Gerson, *The Unfinished Revolution*; Gerson, "Why Are Young Women More Ambitious Than Men?"

79 England, "The Gender Revolution," 149–66.

80 England, "The Gender Revolution," 149–66.

81 Cotter, Hermsen, and Vanneman, "The End of the Gender Revolution?"

82 England, "The Gender Revolution," 149–66; Gerson, *The Unfinished Revolution*; Hondagneu-Sotelo, *Domestica.*

83 Cooper, *Cut Adrift.*

84 Bianchi et al., "Housework"; England, "The Gender Revolution."

85 England, Budig, and Folbre, "Wages of Virtue."

86 Reskin, "Bringing Men Back In."

87 Blair-Loy, "Cultural Constructions of Family Schemas."

88 See Gerson, *The Unfinished Revolution.*

89 Bass, "Preparing for Parenthood?" 380.

90 Ely, Stone, and Ammerman, "Rethink What You 'Know' about High-Achieving Women."

91 Stone, *Opting Out?*

92 England, "The Gender Revolution," 149–66.

93 Eileen Patten, "Racial, Gender Wage Gaps Persist in U.S. Despite Some Progress," Pew Research Center Fact Tank, July 1, 2016. http://www.pewresearch.org.

94 Correll, Benard, and Paik. "Getting a Job."

95 Pudrovska, and Karrake, "Gender, Job Authority, and Depression."

96 Rudman et al., "Status Incongruity and Backlash Effects."

97 Wolf, "What Really Lies behind the 'War on Women.'"

98 Staggenborg and Taylor, "Whatever Happened to the Women's Movement?" 41.

99 Taylor, "Social Movement Continuity."

100 Chafetz, Dworkin, and Swanson, *Female Revolt*.

101 Crossley and Taylor, "Abeyance Cycles in Social Movements."

102 Walker, *To Be Real*; Whittier, "From the Second to the Third Wave."

103 Drake, "Third Wave Feminisms"; Duncan, "Searching for a Home Place"; Henry, *Not My Mother's Sister*; Henry, "Solitary Sisterhood"; Reger, ed., *Different Wavelengths*; Springer, "Third Wave Black Feminism."

104 Whittier, "From the Second to the Third Wave," 60; see also Reger, "Organizational Dynamics and the Construction of Multiple Feminist Identities in the National Organization for Women."

105 Cochrane, "The Fourth Wave of Feminism."

106 Polletta, "'Free Spaces' in Collective Action."

107 Katzenstein, "Stepsisters."

108 Staggenborg, "Social Movement Communities and Cycles of Protest."

109 Taylor, "Social Movement Continuity."

110 Ghaziani and Baldassarri, "Cultural Anchors and the Organization of Differences."

111 Polletta, "'Free Spaces' in Collective Action."

112 Crossley and Taylor, "Abeyance Cycles in Social Movements."

113 Taylor, "Social Movement Continuity."

114 Rupp and Taylor, *Survival in the Doldrums*.

115 Crossley and Taylor, "Abeyance Cycles in Social Movements"; Gusfield, "Social Movements and Social Change," 324.

116 Cobble, Gordon, and Henry, *Feminism Unfinished*; Hawkesworth, "The Semiotics of a Premature Burial"; Laughlin et al., "Is It Time to Jump Ship? Historians Rethink the Wave Metaphor."

117 Thompson, "Multiracial Feminism," 344.

118 Rupp and Taylor, *Survival in the Doldrums*; Taylor, "Social Movement Continuity."

119 Cobble, Gordon, and Henry, *Feminism Unfinished*.

120 Taylor, "Social Movement Continuity."

121 Andrew and Maddison, "Damaged but Determined"; Bagguley, "Contemporary British Feminism"; Grey and Sawer, eds., *Women's Movements*.

CHAPTER 2. WHO NEEDS FEMINISM?

1 *Who Needs Feminism?* website, accessed May 16, 2016, http://www.whoneedsfeminism.com.

2 Rachel S. Seidman, "After Todd Akin Comments: Why Women—and Men—Still Need Feminism," *Christian Science Monitor*, August 23, 2012, http://www.csmonitor.com.

3   *Who Needs Feminism?* Tumblr post, http://whoneedsfeminism.tumblr.com.

4   *Who Needs Feminism?* Tumblr post, http://whoneedsfeminism.tumblr.com.

5   *Who Needs Feminism?* Tumblr post, http://whoneedsfeminism.tumblr.com.

6   Seidman, "After Todd Akin Comments."

7   Whittier, "From the Second to the Third Wave," 64.

8   Foster, "Women of a Certain Age," 73.

9   Foster, "Women of a Certain Age," 74.

10   Rivers and Barnett, *The New Soft War on Women*, 60.

11   McRobbie, "Post-Feminism and Popular Culture."

12   Foster, "Women of a Certain Age"; Rivers and Barnett, *The New Soft War on Women*, 176.

13   Foster, "Women of a Certain Age"; see Rupp, "Is Feminism the Province of Old (Or Middle-Aged) Women?"

14   Rowe-Finkbeiner, *The F Word*.

15   Foster, "Women of a Certain Age"; Rivers and Barnett, *The New Soft War on Women*.

16   Aronson, "Feminists or 'Postfeminists'?"

17   Rupp, "Is Feminism the Province of Old (Or Middle-Aged) Women?"; Whittier, *Feminist Generations*.

18   Harnois, "Different Paths to Different Feminisms?"

19   Ferree and Hess, *Controversy and Coalition*.

20   Schnittker, Freese, and Powell, "What Are Feminists and What Do They Believe?"; McCabe, "What's in a Label?"

21   Peltola, Milkie, and Presser, "The 'Feminist' Mystique."

22   *YouGov*, "Omnibus Poll."

23   Aronson, "Feminists or 'Postfeminists'?"

24   Whittier, "Political Generations," 770.

25   Schnittker, Freese, and Powell, "What Are Feminists and What Do They Believe?" 619.

26   Buschman and Lenart, "'I Am Not a Feminist, but . . .'"; Williams and Wittig, "'I'm Not a Feminist, but . . .'"

27   Dill, "Qualified Feminism and Its Influence on College Women's Identification with the Women's Movement."

28   Crossley, "'When It Suits Me, I'm a Feminist.'"

29   Hercus, *Stepping out of Line*.

30   Harnois, "Different Paths to Different Feminisms?"; Martin and Sullivan, *Click*; Reger, *Everywhere and Nowhere*.

31   Harnois, "Different Paths to Different Feminisms?"; Hurtado, "Relating to Privilege."

32   Hunter and Sellers, "Feminist Attitudes among African American Women and Men," 81.

33   Kane, "Racial and Ethnic Variations in Gender-Related Attitudes"; see Hunter and Sellers, "Feminist Attitudes among African American Women and Men."

34 Anderson, Kanner, and Elsayegh, "Are Feminists Man Haters?"; Flores, Carrubba, and Good, "Feminism and Mexican American Adolescent Women."

35 Whittier, *Feminist Generations*, 101–2.

36 Ray, *Fields of Protest*; Taylor, *Rock-a-by Baby*; Schnittker, Freese, and Powell, "What Are Feminists and What Do They Believe?" See also Aronson, "Feminists or 'Postfeminists'?"

37 Roth, *Separate Roads to Feminism*; Whittier, *Feminist Generations*.

38 Hercus, *Stepping out of Line*; Taylor, *Rock-a-by Baby*.

39 Aronowitz and Bernstein, *Girldrive*; Hernández and Rehman, eds., *Colonize This!*; Findlen, *Listen Up*.

40 Baird, Burge, and Reynolds, "Absurdly Ambitious?"

41 Correll, "Gender and the Career Choice Process."

42 Charles and Bradley, "Indulging Our Gendered Selves."

43 Rupp, "Is Feminism the Province or Old (Or Middle-Aged) Women?" 164, 170.

44 Foster, "Women of a Certain Age."

45 Peltola, Milkie, and Presser, "The 'Feminist' Mystique."

46 Rupp, "Is Feminism the Province of Old (Or Middle-Aged) Women?"

47 Foster, "Women of a Certain Age."

48 Harnois, "Different Paths to Different Feminisms?"

49 Rivers and Barnett, *The New Soft War on Women*, 160.

50 Foster, "Women of a Certain Age"; Rowe-Finkbeiner, *The F Word*.

51 Aronson, "Feminists or 'Postfeminists'?"

52 Reger, *Everywhere and Nowhere*.

53 Bass, "Preparing for Parenthood?"

54 Whittier, "From the Second to the Third Wave."

55 Hercus, *Stepping out of Line*.

56 Stein, *Sex and Sensibility*; Taylor and Rupp, "Women's Culture and Lesbian Feminist Activism"; Taylor and Whittier, "Collective Identity in Social Movement Communities," 104–29.

57 Green, "Queer Theory and Sociology"; Rupp et al., "Queer Women in the Hookup Scene": Taylor and Rupp, "Women's Culture and Lesbian Feminist Activism."

58 Gamson, "Must Identity Movements Self-Destruct?"; Harr and Kane, "Intersectionality and Queer Student Support for Queer Politics"; Valocchi, "The Class-Inflected Nature of Gay Identity."

59 Messner, Greenberg, and Peretz, *Some Men*.

60 Aronson, "Feminists or 'Postfeminists'?"

61 Bobel, "'I'm Not an Activist, though I've Done a Lot of It.'"

62 Ridgeway and Correll, "Unpacking the Gender System."

63 Breines, *The Trouble between Us*; Hunter and Sellers, "Feminist Attitudes among African American Women and Men"; Hurtado, "Relating to Privilege"; Roth, *Separate Roads to Feminism*.

64 Whittier, "From the Second to the Third Wave," 61.

65 Harnois, "Different Paths to Different Feminisms?"

66 Roth, *Separate Roads to Feminism*, 215.

67 Whittier, *Feminist Generations*.

68 Schnittker, Freese, and Powell, "What Are Feminists and What Do They Believe?"

69 Rivers and Barnett, *The New Soft War on Women*.

70 Whittier, "Political Generations."

CHAPTER 3. MULTICULTURAL SORORITIES, WOMEN'S CENTERS, AND THE INSTITUTIONAL FIELDS OF FEMINIST ACTIVISM

1 Katzenstein, "Stepsisters."

2 McAdam, Tarrow, and Tilly, *Dynamics of Contention*.

3 Taylor and Zald, "Conclusion"; Van Dyke, Soule, and Taylor, "The Targets of Social Movements."

4 Crossley and Taylor, "Abeyance Cycles in Social Movements."

5 Banaszak-Holl, Levitsky, and Zald, *Social Movements and the Transformation of American Health Care*; Katzenstein, *Faithful and Fearless*; Raeburn, *Changing Corporate America from Inside Out*; Rojas, *From Black Power to Black Studies*.

6 Armstrong and Bernstein, "Culture, Power, and Institutions."

7 Crossley, "Women's Activism in Educational Institutions"; Crossley and Taylor, "Abeyance Cycles in Social Movements."

8 Nick Crossley, "Social Networks and Student Activism."

9 Nick Crossley, "Student Protest."

10 McAdam, "The Biographical Consequences of Activism"; McCarthy and Zald, "Resource Mobilization and Social Movements"; White, "Structural Identity Theory and the Post-Recruitment Activism of Irish Republicans."

11 Soule, "The Student Divestment Movement in the United States and Tactical Diffusion"; Van Dyke, "Hotbeds of Activism."

12 Katzenstein, "Stepsisters."

13 Flacks, *Making History*; Soule, "The Student Divestment Movement in the United States and Tactical Diffusion"; Van Dyke, "Hotbeds of Activism"; Van Dyke, "Crossing Movement Boundaries."

14 Rojas, *From Black Power to Black Studies*.

15 Crossley, "Women's Activism in Educational Institutions."

16 Franklin, "Hidden in Plain View"; Rosen, ed., *Women's Studies in the Academy*.

17 Bart et al., "Women's Studies and Activism"; Boxer, "For and about Women."

18 Reynolds, Shagle, and Venkataraman, "A National Census of Women's and Gender Studies Programs in U.S. Institutions of Higher Education."

19 Levin, "Questions for a New Century."

20 Garcia, "Voices of Women of Color."

21 Hull, Scott, and Smith, eds., *All the Women Are White, All the Blacks Are Men, But Some of Us Are Brave*, xx.

22 Franklin, "Hidden in Plain View," 436.

23 Crossley, "Women's Activism in Educational Institutions"; Orr, "Tellings of Our Activist Pasts"; Ruby, "Workshop," 8; Taylor and de Laat, "Feminist Internships and the Depression of Political Imagination"; Crowley, "Women's Studies."

24 Levin, "Questions for a New Century."

25 Lovejoy, "'You Can't Go Home Again.'"

26 Stake and Hoffman, "Changes in Student Social Attitudes, Activism, and Personal Confidence in Higher Education."

27 Berger and Radeloff, *Transforming Scholarship*, 180.

28 See Institution Directory of National Women's Studies Association, http://nwsa.org.

29 McCaughey and Warren, "Responding to Right-Wing Attacks on Women's Studies."

30 McCaughey, *Women's Studies Program Administrators' Handbook*.

31 Aronson, "Feminists or 'Postfeminists'?"; Rupp and Taylor, "Forging Feminist Identity in an International Movement."

32 Reger, *Everywhere and Nowhere*.

33 Levin, "Questions for a New Century"; Lovejoy, "'You Can't Go Home Again'"; Stake and Hoffman, "Changes in Student Social Attitudes, Activism, and Personal Confidence in Higher Education."

34 Reger, *Everywhere and Nowhere*.

35 Parker and Freedman, "Women's Centers/Women's Studies Programs."

36 Kelli Zaytoun Byrne, "The Roles of Campus-Based Women's Centers," *Feminist Teacher* 13, no. 1 (2000): 48–60.

37 Katzenstein, "Stepsisters."

38 University of Minnesota, "Women's Center: About Us."

39 University of California–Santa Barbara, "Women, Gender, and Sexual Equity: About," accessed May 20, 2016, http://wgse.sa.ucsb.edu.

40 University of Minnesota, "Women's Center: Why a Women's Center."

41 Hamilton and Armstrong, "Gendered Sexuality in Young Adulthood."

42 Giddings, *In Search of Sisterhood*.

43 Giffort, "Show or Tell?"

44 Davalos, "Sin Verguenza."

45 Whittier, "From the Second to the Third Wave."

46 University of California–Santa Barbara, "Funding," UCSB A.S. Womyn's Commission, http://www.as.ucsb.edu.

47 Simon Benarroch, "Renovations in Motion for Coffman's Second Floor," *Minnesota Daily*, August 8, 2012, http://www.mndaily.com.

48 Katzenstein, "Stepsisters."

49 Smith College "Smith History."

50 Soule, "The Student Divestment Movement in the United States and Tactical Diffusion"; Van Dyke, "Hotbeds of Activism."

51 Buechler, *Women's Movements in the United States*; Rupp and Taylor, "Forging Feminist Identity in an International Movement"; Taylor and Whittier, "Collective Identity in Social Movement Communities"; Whittier, *Feminist Generations*.

52 Buechler, *Women's Movements in the United States*; Staggenborg and Taylor, "Whatever Happened to the Women's Movement?," 40.

53 Staggenborg, "Social Movement Communities and Cycles of Protest"; see also Rupp, "The Women's Community in the National Woman's Party, 1945 to the 1960s."

54 Rojas, *From Black Power to Black Studies*, 7.

55 Zald and Ash, "Social Movement Organizations."

56 Soule, "The Student Divestment Movement in the United States and Tactical Diffusion"; Van Dyke, "Hotbeds of Activism."

CHAPTER 4. THE BONDS OF FEMINISM

 1 Blee, *Inside Organized Racism*; Klandermans, "Transient Identities"; Taylor and Whittier, "Collective Identity in Social Movement Communities," 105.

 2 Melucci, *Nomads of the Present*.

 3 Taylor and Whittier, "Collective Identity in Social Movement Communities," 111.

 4 Rupp, *Worlds of Women*.

 5 Rupp and Taylor, "Forging Feminist Identity in an International Movement," 366.

 6 Rupp and Taylor, "Forging Feminist Identity in an International Movement."

 7 Aronson, "Feminists or 'Postfeminists'?"; Ray, *Fields of Protest*; Schnittker, Freese, and Powell, "What Are Feminists and What Do They Believe?"; Taylor, *Rock-a-by Baby*.

 8 Reger, *Everywhere and Nowhere*.

 9 Melucci, "The Process of Collective Identity," 47.

10 Henry, "*Fittism* Feminists and Third Wave Feminists," 667; see also Walker, *To Be Real*.

11 McRobbie, *The Aftermath of Feminism*; Piepmeier, *Girl Zines*.

12 Dicker and Piepmeier, eds., *Catching a Wave*.

13 Reger, "Organizational Dynamics and the Construction of Multiple Feminist Identities."

14 Ferree and Martin, eds., *Feminist Organizations*.

15 Taylor, "Watching for Vibes."

16 Gilmore, "Bridging the Waves"; Reger, "Organizational Dynamics and the Construction of Multiple Feminist Identities"; Taylor and Rupp, "Loving Internationalism"; Ferree and Martin, eds., *Feminist Organizations*.

17 Soule, "The Student Divestment Movement in the United States and Tactical Diffusion"; Van Dyke, "Hotbeds of Activism"; Van Dyke, "The Return of Student Protest."

18 Oaks, "What Are Pro-Life Feminists Doing on Campus?"

19 Reger and Story, "Talking about My Vagina."

20 Taylor, "Social Movement Continuity."

21 Taylor and Whittier, "Collective Identity in Social Movement Communities."

22 Whittier, *Feminist Generations*.

23 Henry, "*Fittism* Feminists and Third Wave Feminists."

24 Alex Zeman, "Student Service Fees Get Political," *Minnesota Daily*, March 7, 2010, http://www.mndaily.com.

25 University of Minnesota, "Student Service Fees Committee Recommendations for 2012–13 Funding," accessed May 20, 2016, http://www.studentservicesfees.umn.edu.

26 Currier, *Out in Africa*.

27 Kim and Alvarez, "Women-Only Colleges"; Riordan, "The Value of Attending a Women's College."

28 Tidball et al., *Taking Women Seriously*.

29 Gamson, "The Social Psychology of Collective Action."

30 Crossley, "'When It Suits Me, I'm a Feminist.'"

31 Reger, "Drawing Identity Boundaries."

32 Stryker, "Identity Salience and Role Performance."

33 Taylor, "Gender and Social Movements."

34 *El Gaucho*, February 4, 1970.

35 *El Gaucho*, February 4, 1970.

36 Heaney and Rojas, "Hybrid Activism"; Albert and Whetten, "Organizational Identity," 270.

37 Goss and Heaney, "Organizing Women *as Women*."

38 *Bottom Line* (student newspaper), May 2–8, 2012.

39 "LGBTQ Issues, Gender-Related Violence Call AS Senate to Action."

40 Meyer and Whittier, "Social Movement Spillover"; Rojas and Heaney, "Social Movement Mobilization in a Multi-Movement Environment."

41 Findlen, *Listen Up*; Hernández and Rehman, *Colonize This!*; Walker, *To Be Real*.

42 Gilmore, "Bridging the Waves," 97; Henry, "Solitary Sisterhood," 86.

43 Findlen, *Listen Up*; Hernández and Rehman, *Colonize This!*

44 Drake, "Third Wave Feminisms"; Duncan, "Searching for a Home Place"; Henry, *Not My Mother's Sister*; Henry, "Solitary Sisterhood"; Springer, "Third Wave Black Feminism"; Walker, *To Be Real*; Reger, *Different Wavelengths*.

45 Henry, "*Fittism* Feminists and Third Wave Feminists."

46 Rupp and Taylor, *Survival in the Doldrums*.

47 Foster, "Women of a Certain Age."

48 Aronowitz and Bernstein, *Girldrive*, 163.

49 Whittier, *Feminist Generations*.

50 Whittier, "From the Second to the Third Wave."

51 Banaszak, ed., *The US Women's Movement in Global Perspective*, 18.

52 Henry, "*Fittism* Feminists and Third Wave Feminists."

53 Reger, "Drawing Identity Boundaries."

54 Staggenborg and Taylor, "Whatever Happened to the Women's Movement?"

55 Meyer and Whittier, "Social Movement Spillover."

56 Benford and Snow, "Framing Processes and Social Movements"; Snow et al., "Frame Alignment Processes, Micromobilization, and Movement Participation."

57 Reger, Myers, and Einwohner, eds., *Identity Work in Social Movements*: Whittier, *Feminist Generations*.

58 Melucci, "The Process of Collective Identity"; Rupp and Taylor, "Forging Feminist Identity in an International Movement"; Taylor, "Social Movement Continuity."

59 Melucci, "The Process of Collective Identity."

60 Henry, "*Fittism* Feminists and Third Wave Feminists."

61 Rupp and Taylor, "Forging Feminist Identity in an International Movement," 366.

62 Henry, "*Fittism* Feminists and Third Wave Feminists."

63 Ferree and Martin, eds., *Feminist Organizations*.

CHAPTER 5. CAN FACEBOOK BE FEMINIST?

1 "Our Vision," *Everyday Feminism*, accessed May 25, 2016, http://everydayfeminism.com.

2 "Home Page," *Everyday Sexism Project*, accessed May 25, 2016, http://everydaysexism.com.

3 Taylor, Rupp, and Gamson, "Performing Protest"; Tilly, *From Mobilization to Revolution*; Tilly, *The Contentious French*; Charles Tilly, *Contentious Repertoires in Great Britain, 1758–1834*.

4 Taylor and Van Dyke "Get Up, Stand Up," 264.

5 Taylor and Van Dyke "Get Up, Stand Up," 278.

6 Crossley, "'When It Suits Me, I'm a Feminist.'"

7 Staggenborg and Lecomte, "Social Movement Campaigns"; Taft, *Rebel Girls*; Taylor, *Rock-a-by Baby*; Taylor and Van Dyke "Get Up, Stand Up," 278.

8 Staggenborg, "Social Movement Communities and Cycles of Protest"; Staggenborg and Lang, "Culture and Ritual in the Montreal Women's Movement"; Staggenborg and Taylor, "Whatever Happened to the Women's Movement?"; Taylor and Rupp, "Women's Culture and Lesbian Feminist Activism."

9 Taylor, "Social Movement Continuity," 762.

10 Taylor, "Social Movement Continuity."

11 Crossley, "Facebook Feminism"; Crossley et al., "Forever Feminism"; Duncan, "Searching for a Home Place"; Ferree, "On-line Identities and Organizational Connections"; McCaughey and Ayers, *Cyberactivism*; Rowe, "Cyberfeminism in Action"; Grey and Sawer, *Women's Movements*.

12 Earl and Kimport, *Digitally Enabled Social Change*.

13 Herold, "Young Feminists to Older Feminists."

14 Herold, "Young Feminists to Older Feminists."

15 Crossley et al., "Forever Feminism."

16 Cassell, *A Group Called Women*; Crossley, "Facebook Feminism"; Taylor, *Rock-a-by Baby*.

17 McCaughey and Ayers, *Cyberactivism*; Rowe, "Cyberfeminism in Action."

18 Crossley, "Facebook Feminism."

19 Rupp and Taylor, *Survival in the Doldrums*, 365.

20 Staggenborg, "The Survival of the Women's Movement"; Taylor and Whittier, "Collective Identity in Social Movement Communities"; Whittier, *Feminist Generations*.
21 Taylor, "Watching for Vibes"; Taylor, "Social Movement Participation in the Global Society."
22 Oliver, "Bringing the Crowd Back In"; Simi and Futrell, "Negotiating White Power Activist Stigma"; Taylor, "Social Movement Participation in the Global Society."
23 Mansbridge and Flaster, "'The Cultural Politics of Everyday Discourse."
24 Oliver, "Bringing the Crowd Back In."
25 Reger, *Everywhere and Nowhere*.
26 Tilly, *The Language of Contention*, 21.
27 Ferree and Hess, *Controversy and Coalition*.
28 Taylor and Rupp, "Women's Culture and Lesbian Feminist Activism."
29 Solnit, *Men Explain Things to Me*.
30 Whittier, *Feminist Generations*.
31 Snow and Moss, "Protest on the Fly."
32 Van Dyke and McCammon, eds., *Strategic Alliances*.
33 Van Dyke, "Crossing Movement Boundaries."
34 Staggenborg, "Coalition Work in the Pro-Choice Movement."
35 Cole and Luna, "Making Coalitions Work."
36 Arnold, "Dilemmas of Feminist Coalitions."
37 Roth, "'Organizing One's Own' as Good Politics"; Staggenborg, "Coalition Work in the Pro-Choice Movement"; Van Dyke, "Crossing Movement Boundaries."
38 McCammon and Campbell. "Allies on the Road to Victory"; Staggenborg, "Coalition Work in the Pro-Choice Movement."
39 Van Dyke, "Crossing Movement Boundaries."
40 Rupp and Taylor, *Survival in the Doldrums*, 165.
41 Seidman, "Gendered Citizenship."
42 Fonow, *Union Women*; Gilmore, *Feminist Coalitions*; Roth, *Building Movement Bridges*.
43 Roth, "'Organizing One's Own' as Good Politics."
44 Cole and Luna, "Making Coalitions Work," 74.
45 Roth, *Separate Roads to Feminism*.
46 Gilmore, *Feminist Coalitions*.
47 Whittier, "From the Second to the Third Wave," 60.
48 Taylor, "Social Movement Participation in the Global Society," 42.
49 Van Dyke, "Crossing Movement Boundaries," 244.
50 Van Dyke and McCammon, *Strategic Alliances*.
51 For a historical perspective, see Gilmore, *Feminist Coalitions*.
52 Whose University? Campaign, Film Project, and Event, "About the Project."
53 Whose University? Campaign, Film Project, and Event, "About the Project."
54 Taylor, "Social Movement Participation in the Global Society."

55 Reger, *Everywhere and Nowhere.*

56 Taylor and Van Dyke, "Get Up, Stand Up."

57 Taylor, "Social Movement Continuity."

58 Bates, *Everyday Sexism.*

CHAPTER 6. CONCLUSION

1 McAdam, *Political Process and the Development of Black Insurgency, 1930–1970.*

2 Grey and Sawer, *Women's Movements.*

3 Cobble, Gordon, and Henry, *Feminism Unfinished.*

4 Rupp, *Worlds of Women,* 226.

5 Taylor, "Social Movement Continuity."

6 Rupp and Taylor, *Survival in the Doldrums.*

7 Taylor, "Social Movement Continuity," 762.

8 Staggenborg and Lecomte, "Social Movement Campaigns"; Taylor and Rupp, "Women's Culture and Lesbian Feminist Activism."

9 Rupp and Taylor, *Survival in the Doldrums;* Weigand, *Red Feminism.*

10 Meyer and Whittier, "Social Movement Spillover"; Roth, *Separate Roads to Feminism;* Whittier, *Feminist Generations.*

11 Rupp and Taylor, *Survival in the Doldrums;* Weigand, *Red Feminism.*

12 Grey and Sawer, *Women's Movements;* Taylor, *Rock-a-by Baby.*

13 Messner, Greenberg, and Peretz, *Some Men,* 110.

14 Chang, *Protest Dialectics;* Edwards and Marullo, "Organizational Mortality in a Declining Social Movement"; Fillieule, *Devenirs Militants;* Holland and Cable, "Reconceptualizing Social Movement Abeyance"; Kendrick, "Swimming against the Tide"; Mooney and Majka, *Farmers' and Farm Workers' Movements;* Rupp, "The Persistence of Transnational Organizing"; Weigand, *Red Feminism.*

15 Katzenstein, "Stepsisters."

16 Polletta, "'Free Spaces' in Collective Action."

17 Polletta, "'Free Spaces' in Collective Action."

18 Armstrong and Bernstein, "Culture, Power, and Institutions"; Banaszak-Holl, Levitsky, and Zald, *Social Movements and the Transformation of American Health Care;* Katzenstein, *Faithful and Fearless;* Raeburn, *Changing Corporate America from Inside Out;* Rojas, *From Black Power to Black Studies.*

19 Santoro and McGuire, "Social Movement Insiders."

20 Reger, *Everywhere and Nowhere;* Rupp and Taylor, *Survival in the Doldrums;* Taylor, *Rock-a-by Baby;* Whittier, *Feminist Generations.*

21 Snow and Moss, "Protest on the Fly."

22 Corrigall-Brown, *Patterns of Protest;* Reger, *Everywhere and Nowhere;* Whittier, *Feminist Generations.*

23 Staggenborg and Lecomte, "Social Movement Campaigns"; Taylor and Rupp, "Women's Culture and Lesbian Feminist Activism."

24 Mansbridge and Flaster, "The Cultural Politics of Everyday Discourse."

25 Foster, "Women of a Certain Age."

26 Henry, *Not My Mother's Sister*.

27 Baumgardner and Richards, *Manifesta*; Henry, "*Fittism* Feminists and Third Wave Feminists."

28 Piepmeier, *Girl Zines*, 121.

29 Morris, "Black Southern Sit-in Movement"; Morris, "Birmingham Confrontation Reconsidered"; Taylor and Van Dyke, "Get Up, Stand Up."

30 Earl and Schussman, "The New Site of Activism"; see also Myers, "Communication Technology and Social Movements."

31 Crossley, "Facebook Feminism."

32 Ferree and Hess, *Controversy and Coalition*; Hirsch, "Sacrifice for the Cause."

33 Freeman, *The Politics of Women's Liberation*; Rosenthal et al., "Social Movements and Network Analysis."

34 Rupp and Taylor, *Survival in the Doldrums*.

35 Whittier, *Feminist Generations*, 53.

36 Crossley, "Facebook Feminism"; Keller, "Virtual Feminisms"; Shaw, "'HOTTEST 100 WOMEN.'"

37 Bobel, *New Blood*; Drake, "Third Wave Feminisms"; Reger, ed., *Different Wavelengths*; Springer, "Third Wave Black Feminism"; Whittier, "From the Second to the Third Wave."

38 Roth, *Separate Roads to Feminism*, 215.

39 Roth, *Separate Roads to Feminism*, 215.

40 Rupp and Taylor, *Survival in the Doldrums*.

41 Aronson, "Feminists or 'Postfeminists'?"

42 Taylor, "Gender and Social Movements."

43 Brown-Saracino, "How Places Shape Identity," 52; see also Guenther, *Making Their Place*, and Reger, *Everywhere and Nowhere*.

44 Foster, "Women of a Certain Age."

45 Rupp and Taylor, *Survival in the Doldrums*, 81.

46 Bass, "Preparing for Parenthood?"; Cech, "Mechanism or Myth?"

47 Rupp, "Is Feminism the Province of Old (Or Middle-Aged) Women?"

48 England, "The Gender Revolution," 149–66; Gerson, *The Unfinished Revolution*.

49 Bass, "Preparing for Parenthood?"

50 Foster, "Women of a Certain Age."

51 Meyer and Whittier, "Social Movement Spillover"; Whittier, 2004; Banaszak, 1996.

52 Hurwitz and Taylor, "Women Occupying Wall Street," 11.

53 Hurwitz and Taylor, "Women Occupying Wall Street."

APPENDIX

1 Foster, "Women of a Certain Age."

2 Klandermans, "Legacies from the Past"; Salime, *Between Feminism and Islam*.

3 McAdam, *Freedom Summer*.

4 Francesca Polletta, "'It Was like a Fever,'" 143.

5 Eduardo Silva, "The Winter Chilean Students Said, Enough!"

6 Soule, "The Student Divestment Movement in the United States and Tactical Diffusion"; Van Dyke, "Hotbeds of Activism."

7 See also Oaks, "What Are Pro-Life Feminists Doing on Campus?"

8 McAdam, *Freedom Summer*; Snow, Zurcher, and Ekland-Olson, "Social Networks and Social Movements."

9 Nick Crossley, "Social Networks and Student Activism," 33.

10 Soule, "The Student Divestment Movement in the United States and Tactical Diffusion."

11 Van Dyke, "Hotbeds of Activism"; Van Dyke, "Crossing Movement Boundaries."

12 Reger, *Everywhere and Nowhere*.

13 Giugni, "Personal and Biographical Consequences."

14 McAdam, "The Biographical Consequences of Activism"; Sherkat and Blocker, "Explaining the Political and Personal Consequences of Protest"; Taylor, *Rock-a-by Baby*.

15 Flacks, *Making History*; Taylor et al., "Culture and Mobilization."

16 Hasso, "Feminist Generations?"; Taylor and Raeburn, "Identity Politics as High-Risk Activism"; Whittier, *Feminist Generations*.

17 Corrigall-Brown, "From the Balconies to the Barricades, and Back?"; Corrigall-Brown, *Patterns of Protest*.

18 Blee and Taylor, "Semi-Structured Interviewing in Social Movement Research."

19 Carpenter, "Virginity Loss in Reel/Real Life." See Taylor, *Rock-a-by Baby*; Taylor, "Gender and Social Movements."

20 Roscigno and Danaher, *The Voice of Southern Labor*.

21 Almeida, *Waves of Protest*.

22 Andrews, *Freedom Is a Constant Struggle*.

23 England, "The Gender Revolution," 149–66.

24 Gerson, *The Unfinished Revolution*.

25 Northampton, Massachusetts, accessed May 20, 2016, http://www.city-data.com.

26 Tidball et al., *Taking Women Seriously*; Riordan, "The Value of Attending a Women's College."

27 Kim and Alvarez, "Women-Only Colleges."

28 Tidball, "Perspectives on Academic Women and Affirmative Action."

29 Harwarth, Debra, and Maline, *Women's Colleges in the United States*; Kim, "Institutional Effectiveness of Women-Only Colleges."

30 Stoecker and Pascarella, "Women's Colleges and Women's Career Attainments Revisited"; Tidball, "Baccalaureate Origins of Entrants into American Medical Schools"; Tidball, "Baccalaureate Origins of Recent Natural Science Doctorates."

31 Hoffnung, "Career and Family Outcomes for Women Graduates of Single-Sex versus Coed Colleges."

32 Kim, "Institutional Effectiveness of Women-Only Colleges," 302.

33 "Community Data Profile," *Minneapolis Plan*, accessed May 25, 2016, http://www.minneapolismn.gov.

34 http://www.positivelyminnesota.com.

35 "Find a Job," Office of Human Resources, University of Minnesota, accessed May 25, 2016, http://www1.umn.edu.

36 Santa Barbara Community Profile, 2012. http://www.cosb.county.

REFERENCES

Albert, Stuart, and David A. Whetten. "Organizational Identity." *Research in Organizational Behavior* 7 (1985): 263–95.

Almeida, Paul D. *Waves of Protest: Popular Struggle in El Salvador, 1925–2005*. Minneapolis: University of Minnesota Press, 2008.

American Association of University Women. *The Simple Truth about the Gender Pay Gap*. Spring 2016 ed. http://www.aauw.org.

Anderson, Kristin J., Melinda Kanner, and Nisreen Elsayegh. "Are Feminists Man Haters? Feminists' and Nonfeminists' Attitudes toward Men." *Psychology of Women Quarterly* 33, no. 2 (2009): 216–24.

Andrew, Merrindahl, and Sarah Maddison. 2010. "Damaged but Determined: The Australian Women's Movement, 1996–2007." *Social Movement Studies* 9, no. 2 (2010): 171–85.

Andrews, Kenneth. *Freedom Is a Constant Struggle: The Mississippi Civil Rights Protest and Its Legacy*. Minneapolis: University of Minnesota Press, 2004.

Armstrong, Elizabeth A., and Mary Bernstein. "Culture, Power, and Institutions: A Multi-Institutional Politics Approach to Social Movements." *Sociological Theory* 26 (2008): 74–99.

Arnold, Gretchen. "Dilemmas of Feminist Coalitions: Collective Identity and Strategic Effectiveness in the Battered Women's Movement." *Feminist Organizations: Harvest of the New Women's Movement*. Philadelphia: Temple University Press, 1995.

Arnold, Gretchen. "The Impact of Social Ties on Coalition Strength and Effectiveness: The Case of the Battered Women's Movement in St. Louis." *Social Movement Studies* 10, no. 2 (2011): 131–50.

Aronowitz, Nona Willis, and Emma Bee Bernstein. *Girldrive: Criss-Crossing America, Redefining Feminism*. Berkeley, CA: Seal Press, 2009.

Aronson, Pamela. "Feminists or 'Postfeminists'? Young Women's Attitudes toward Feminism and Gender Relations." *Gender and Society* 17, no. 6 (2003): 903–22.

Aronson, Pamela. "The Markers and Meanings of Growing Up: Contemporary Young Women's Transition from Adolescence to Adulthood." *Gender and Society* 22, no. 1 (2008): 56–82.

Bagguley, Paul. "Contemporary British Feminism: A Social Movement in Abeyance?" *Social Movement Studies* 1, no. 2 (2002): 169–85.

Baird, Chardie L., Stephanie W. Burge, and John R. Reynolds. "Absurdly Ambitious? Teenagers' Expectations for the Future and the Realities of Social Structure." *Sociology Compass* 2, no. 3 (2008): 944–62.

Banaszak, Lee Ann. *Why Movements Succeed or Fail: Opportunity, Culture, and the Struggle for Woman Suffrage*. Princeton, NJ: Princeton University Press, 1996.

Banaszak, Lee Ann, ed. *The US Women's Movement in Global Perspective*. Lanham, MD: Rowman & Littlefield, 2006.

Banaszak-Holl, Jane C., Sandra R. Levitsky, and Mayer N. Zald. *Social Movements and the Transformation of American Health Care*. Oxford: Oxford University Press, 2010.

Bart, Pauline B., Lynn Bentz, Jan Clausen, LeeRay Costa, Ann Froines, Galia Golan, Jaime M. Grant, Anne S. Orwin, Barbara Ryan, and Sonita Sarker. "Women's Studies and Activism." *Women's Studies Quarterly* 27, nos. 3/4 (1999): 257–67.

Bass, Brooke Conroy. "Preparing for Parenthood? Gender, Aspirations, and the Reproduction of Labor Market Inequality." *Gender and Society* 29, no. 3 (2015): 362–85.

Bates, Dawn, and Maureen C. McHugh. "Zines: Voices of Third Wave Feminists." In *Different Wavelengths: Studies of the Contemporary Women's Movement*, edited by Jo Reger, 179–94. New York: Routledge, 2005.

Bates, Laura. *Everyday Sexism*. New York: Simon & Schuster, 2014.

Baumgardner, Jennifer, and Amy Richards. *Manifesta: Young Women, Feminism, and the Future*. New York: Farrar, Straus, and Giroux, 2000.

Belkin, Lisa. "The Opt-Out Revolution." *New York Times Magazine*, October 26, 2003.

Benford, Robert D., and David A. Snow. "Framing Processes and Social Movements: An Overview and Assessment." *Annual Review of Sociology* 26 (2000): 611–39.

Berger, Michele Tracy, and Cheryl Radeloff. *Transforming Scholarship: Why Women's and Gender Studies Students Are Changing Themselves and the World*. New York: Routledge, 2011.

Bernstein, Mary. "Celebration and Suppression: The Strategic Uses of Identity by the Lesbian and Gay Movement." *American Journal of Sociology* 10, no. 3 (1997): 531–65.

Bianchi, Suzanne M., Liana C. Sayer, Melissa A. Milkie, and John P. Robinson, "Housework: Who Did, Does, or Will Do It, and How Much Does It Matter?" *Social Forces* 91, no. 1 (2012): 55–63.

Binder, Amy J., and Kate Wood. *Becoming Right: How Campuses Shape Young Conservatives*. Princeton, NJ: Princeton University Press, 2012.

Blair-Loy, Mary. "Cultural Constructions of Family Schemas: The Case of Women Finance Executives." *Gender and Society* 15, no. 5 (2001): 687–709.

Blee, Kathleen. *Inside Organized Racism: Women in the Hate Movement*. Berkeley: University of California Press, 2003.

Blee, Kathleen. *Democracy in the Making: How Activist Groups Form*. Oxford: Oxford University Press, 2012.

Blee, Kathleen, and Verta Taylor. "Semi-Structured Interviewing in Social Movement Research." In *Methods of Social Movement Research*, edited by Bert Klandermans and Suzanne Staggenborg, 92–117. Minneapolis: University of Minnesota Press, 2002.

Bobel, Chris. "'I'm Not an Activist, Though I've Done a Lot of It': Doing Activism, Being Activist, and the 'Perfect Standard' in a Contemporary Movement." *Social Movement Studies* 6, no. 2 (2007): 147–59.

Bobel, Chris. *New Blood: Third-Wave Feminism and the Politics of Menstruation* Piscat-away, NJ: Rutgers University Press, 2010.

Boxer, Marilyn J., "For and about Women: The Theory and Practice of Women's Stud-ies." *Signs* 7, no. 3 (1982): 661–95.

Breines, Winifred. *The Trouble between Us: An Uneasy History of White and Black Women in the Feminist Movement.* Oxford: Oxford University Press, 2006.

Brickman Bhutta, Christine. "Not by the Book: Facebook as Sampling Frame." *Socio-logical Methods & Research* 41, no. 1 (2012): 57–88.

Brown, Phil. *Toxic Exposures: Contested Illnesses and the Environmental Health Move-ment.* New York: Columbia University Press, 2007.

Brown-Saracino, Japonica. "How Places Shape Identity: The Origins of Distinctive LBQ Identities in Four Small U.S. Cities." *American Journal of Sociology* 121, no. 1 (2015): 1–66.

Bruce, Tricia. *Faithful Revolution: How Voice of the Faithful Is Changing the Church.* New York: Oxford University Press, 2011.

Buechler, Steven M. *Women's Movements in the United States: Woman Suffrage, Equal Rights, and Beyond.* Piscataway, NJ: Rutgers University Press, 1990.

Buschman, Joan K., and Silvo Lenart. "'I Am Not a Feminist, but . . .': College Women, Feminism, and Negative Experiences." *Political Psychology* 17, no. 1 (1996): 59–75.

Carpenter, Laura M. "Virginity Loss in Reel/Real Life: Using Popular Movies to Navi-gate Sexual Initiation." *Sociological Forum* 24, no. 4 (2009): 804–27.

Cassell, Joan. *A Group Called Women: Sisterhood and Symbolism in the Feminist Move-ment.* New York: David McKay, 1977.

Cech, Erin. "Mechanism or Myth? Family Plans and the Reproduction of Occupational Gender Segregation." *Gender and Society* 30, no. 2 (April 2016): 265–88.

Chafetz, Janet Saltzman, Anthony Gary Dworkin, and Stephanie Swanson. *Female Re-volt: Women's Movements in World and Historical Perspective.* Totowa, NJ: Rowman & Allanheld, 1986.

Chang, Paul Y. *Protest Dialectics: State Repression and South Korea's Democracy Move-ment.* Palo Alto, CA: Stanford University Press, 2015.

Charles, Maria, and Karen Bradley. "Equal but Separate? A Cross-National Study of Sex Segregation in Higher Education." *American Sociological Review* 67, no. 4 (2002): 73–99.

Charles, Maria, and Karen Bradley. "Indulging Our Gendered Selves: Sex Segregation by Field of Study in 44 Countries." *American Journal of Sociology* 114, no. 4 (2009): 924–76.

Charles, Maria, and David Grusky. *Occupational Ghettos: The Worldwide Segregation of Women and Men.* Stanford, CA: Stanford University Press, 2004.

Childress, C. Clayton, and Noah E. Friedkin. "Cultural Reception and Production: The Social Construction of Meaning in Book Clubs." *American Sociological Review* 77, no.1 (2011): 45–68.

Citron, Danielle Keats. *Hate Crimes in Cyberspace.* Cambridge, MA: Harvard Univer-sity Press, 2015.

Clay, Andreana. 2012. *The Hip-Hop Generation Fights Back: Youth, Activism, and Post-Civil Rights Politics*. New York: NYU Press.

Cobble, Dorothy Sue, Linda Gordon, and Astrid Henry. *Feminism Unfinished: A Short, Surprising History of American Women's Movements*. New York: Liveright, 2014.

Cochrane, Kira. "The Fourth Wave of Feminism: Meet the Rebel Women." *Guardian*, December 10, 2013. http://www.theguardian.com.

Cole, Elizabeth R., and Zakiya Luna. "Making Coalitions Work: Solidarity across Difference within U.S. Feminism." *Feminist Studies* 36, no. 1 (2010): 71–98.

Cooper, Marianne. *Cut Adrift: Families in Insecure Times*. Berkeley: University of California Press, 2014.

Correll, Shelley J. "Gender and the Career Choice Process: The Role of Biased Self-Assessments." *American Journal of Sociology* 106, no. 6 (2001): 1691–1730.

Correll, Shelley J., Stephen Benard, and In Paik. "Getting a Job: Is There a Motherhood Penalty?" *American Journal of Sociology* 112, no. 5 (March 2007): 1297–1339.

Corrigall-Brown, Catherine. "From the Balconies to the Barricades, and Back? Trajectories of Participation in Contentious Politics." *Journal of Civil Society* 8, no. 1 (2012a): 17–38.

Corrigall-Brown, Catherine. *Patterns of Protest: Trajectories of Participation in Social Movements*. Stanford, CA: Stanford University Press, 2012b.

Cotter, David, Joan M. Hermsen, and Reeve Vanneman. "The End of the Gender Revolution? Gender Role Attitudes from 1977 to 2008." *American Journal of Sociology* 117, no. 1 (2011): 259–89.

Crossley, Alison Dahl. "'When It Suits Me, I'm a Feminist': International Students Negotiating Feminist Representations." *Women's Studies International Forum* 33, no. 2 (2010a): 125–33.

Crossley, Alison Dahl. "Young Women's Feminist Identities: The Impact of Feminist Stereotypes and Heterosexual Relationships." In *Advances in Gender Research*, vol. 14, edited by Vasiliki Demos and Marcia Segal, 339–55. Bingley, UK: Emerald, 2010b.

Crossley, Alison Dahl. "Facebook Feminism: Social Media, Blogs, and New Technologies of Contemporary Feminism." *Mobilization* 20, no. 2 (2015): 253–68.

Crossley, Alison Dahl. "Women's Activism in Educational Institutions." In *Oxford Handbook of U.S. Women's Social Movement Activism*, edited by Holly McCammon, Lee Ann Banaszak, Verta Taylor, and Jo Reger. New York: Oxford University Press, forthcoming.

Crossley, Alison Dahl, and Verta Taylor. "Abeyance Cycles in Social Movements." In *Movements in Times of Democratic Transition*, edited by Bert Klandermans and Cornelis van Stralen. Philadelphia: Temple University Press, 2015.

Crossley, Alison Dahl, Verta Taylor, Nancy Whittier, and Cynthia Pelak. "Forever Feminism: Contemporary US Feminism from 1960–2011." In *Feminist Frontiers*, 9th ed., edited by Verta Taylor, Leila J. Rupp, and Nancy Whittier, 498–516. New York: McGraw Hill, 2011.

Crossley, Nick. *Contesting Psychiatry: Social Movements in Mental Health*. New York: Routledge, 2006.

Crossley, Nick. "Social Networks and Student Activism: On the Politicising Effect of Campus Connections." *Sociological Review* 56, no. 1 (2008): 18–38.

Crossley, Nick. "Student Protest: A Perspective from the UK." *Mobilizing Ideas*, May 2, 2012. http://mobilizingideas.wordpress.com.

Crowley, Helen. "Women's Studies: Between a Rock and a Hard Place or Just Another Cell in the Beehive?" *Feminist Review* 61 (1999): 131–50.

Currier, Ashley. *Out in Africa: LGBT Organizing in Namibia and South Africa*. Minneapolis: University of Minnesota Press, 2012.

Davalos, Karen Mary. "Sin Verguenza: Chicana Feminist Theorizing." *Feminist Studies* 34, nos. 1/2 (2008): 151–71.

Davis, Nancy J., and Robert V. Robinson. *Claiming Society for God: Religious Movements and Social Welfare*. Bloomington: Indiana University Press, 2012.

Diamond, Lisa. *Sexual Fluidity: Understanding Women's Love and Desire*. Cambridge, MA: Harvard University Press, 2008.

Dicker, Rory, and Alison Piepmeier, eds. *Catching a Wave: Reclaiming Feminism for the 21st Century*. Boston: Northeastern University Press, 2003.

Dill, Kim. 1989. "Qualified Feminism and Its Influence on College Women's Identification with the Women's Movement." An undergraduate thesis submitted at The Ohio State University.

Drake, Jennifer. "Third Wave Feminisms." *Feminist Studies* 23, no. 1 (1997): 30–39.

Duggan, Maeve. "Online Harassment." Pew Research Center, October 22, 2014. http://www.pewinternet.org.

Duncan, Barbara. "Searching for a Home Place: Online in the Third Wave." In *Different Wavelengths: Studies of the Contemporary Women's Movement*, edited by Jo Reger, 161–78. New York: Routledge, 2005.

Earl, Jennifer, and Katrina Kimport. *Digitally Enabled Social Change: Activism in the Internet Age*. Cambridge, MA: MIT Press, 2011.

Earl, Jennifer, and Alan Schussman. "The New Site of Activism: On-Line Organizations, Movement Entrepreneurs, and the Changing Location of Social Movement Decision Making." *Research in Social Movements, Conflicts, and Change* 24 (2002): 155–87.

Earl, Jennifer, and Alan Schussman. "The New Site of Activism: On-Line Organizations, Movement Entrepreneurs, and the Changing Location of Social Movement Decision-Making." *Research in Social Movements, Conflicts, and Change* 24 (2003): 155–87.

Edwards, Bob, and Sam Marullo. "Organizational Mortality in a Declining Social Movement: The Demise of Peace Movement Organizations in the End of the Cold War Era." *American Sociological Review* 60, no. 6 (1995): 908–27.

Einwohner, Rachel L. "Motivational Framing and Efficacy Maintenance: Animal Rights Activists' Use of Four Fortifying Strategies." *Sociological Quarterly* 43, no. 4 (2002): 509–26.

Ely, Robin, Pamela Stone, and Colleen Ammerman. "Rethink What You 'Know' about High-Achieving Women." *Harvard Business Review* 92, no. 12 (December 2014): 101–9.

England, Paula. "The Gender Revolution: Uneven and Stalled." *Gender and Society* 24, no. 2 (2010): 149–66.

England, Paula, Michelle Budig, and Nancy Folbre. "Wages of Virtue: The Relative Pay of Care Work." *Social Problems* 49, no. 4 (2002): 455–73.

England, Paula, and Su Li. "Desegregation Stalled: The Changing Gender Composition of College Majors, 1971–2002." *Gender and Society* 20, no. 5 (2006): 657–77.

Enke, Ann. *Finding the Movement: Sexuality, Contested Space, and Feminist Activism.* Durham, NC: Duke University Press, 2007.

Everyday Feminism. "Our Vision." Accessed May 25, 2016. http://everydayfeminism.com.

The Everyday Sexism Project. "Home Page." Accessed May 25, 2016. http://everyday-sexism.com.

Farmer, Ashley. "Black Women March on Washington: The Sojourners for Truth and Justice and Black Women's Lives Matter." African American Intellectual History Society, April 17, 2015. http://aaihs.org.

Faupel, Alison, and Regina Werum. "Making Her Own Way: The Individualization of First-Wave Feminism, 1910–1930." *Mobilization* 16, no. 2 (2011): 181–200.

Ferree, Myra Marx. "On-line Identities and Organizational Connections: Networks of Transnational Feminist Websites." In *Gender Orders Unbound? Globalization, Restructuring, and Reciprocity*, edited by Ilse Lenz, Charlotte Ullrich, and Barbara Fersch, 141–66. Opladen, Germany: Barbara Budrich Publishers, 2007.

Ferree, Myra Marx. *Varieties of Feminism: German Gender Politics in Global Perspective.* Stanford, CA: Stanford University Press, 2012.

Ferree, Myra Marx, and Beth B. Hess. *Controversy and Coalition: The New Feminist Movement across Four Decades of Change.* New York: Routledge, 1995.

Ferree, Myra Marx, and Patricia Yancey Martin, eds. *Feminist Organizations: Harvest of the New Women's Movement.* Philadelphia: Temple University Press, 1995.

Ferree, Myra Marx, and Carol McClurg Mueller. "Feminism and the Women's Movement: A Global Perspective." In *The Blackwell Companion to Social Movements*, edited by David A. Snow, Sarah A. Soule, and Hanspeter Kriesi, 576–607. Oxford: Blackwell, 2004.

Fillieule, Olivier. *Devenirs Militants: Approches Sociologiques du Désengagement.* Paris: Belin, 2004.

Findlen, Barbara. *Listen Up: Voices from the Next Feminist Generation.* New York: Seal Press, 1997.

Flacks, Dick. *Making History: The American Left and the American Mind.* New York: Columbia University Press, 1988.

Flores, Lisa Y., Maria D. Carrubba, and Glenn E. Good. "Feminism and Mexican American Adolescent Women: Examining the Psychometric Properties of Two Measures." *Hispanic Journal of Behavioral Studies* 28, no. 1 (2006): 28–64.

Fonow, Mary Margaret. *Union Women: Forging Feminism in the United Steelworkers of America*. Minneapolis: University of Minnesota Press, 2003.

Foster, Johanna E. "Women of a Certain Age: 'Second Wave' Feminists Reflect Back on 50 Years of Struggle in the United States." *Women's Studies International Forum* 50 (2015): 68–79.

Fox, Mary Frank, Gerhard Sonnert, and Irina Nikiforova. "Programs for Undergraduate Women in Science and Engineering: Issues, Problems, and Solutions." *Gender and Society* 25, no. 5 (2011): 589–615.

Franklin, Sekou M. *After the Rebellion: Black Youth, Social Movement Activism, and the Post–Civil Rights Generation*. New York: NYU Press.

Franklin, V. P. "Hidden in Plain View: African American Women, Radical Feminism, and the Origins of Women's Studies Programs, 1967–1974." *Journal of African American History* 87 (2002): 433–45.

Freedman, Janet. "Tools of the Movement: Democracy, Community, and Consciousness Raising." Presentation at the conference A Revolutionary Moment: Women's Liberation in the Late 1960s and 1970s, Women, Gender and Sexuality Studies Program, Boston University, March 27–29, 2014. http://www.bu.edu.

Freeman, Jo. *The Politics of Women's Liberation*. New York: David McKay, 1975.

Gamson, Joshua. "Must Identity Movements Self-Destruct? A Queer Dilemma." *Social Problems* 42, no. 3 (1995a): 390–407.

Gamson, Joshua. "The Organizational Shaping of Collective Identity: The Case of Lesbian and Gay Film Festivals in New York." *Sociological Forum* 11, no. 2 (1995b): 231–61.

Gamson, William. "The Social Psychology of Collective Action." In *Frontiers in Social Movement Theory*, edited by Aldon D. Morris and Carol McClurg Mueller, 53–76. New Haven, CT: Yale University Press, 1992.

Garcia, Alma M. "Voices of Women of Color: Redefining Women's Studies." *Race, Gender, and Class* 4, no. 2 (1997): 11–28.

Gelb, Joyce. "Feminist Organization Success and the Politics of Engagement." In *Feminist Organizations: Harvest of the New Women's Movement*, edited by Myra Marx Ferree and Patricia Yancey Martin, 128–34. Philadelphia: Temple University Press, 1995.

Gelb, Joyce, and Marian Lief Palley. *Women and Public Policies: Reassessing Gender Politics*. Charlottesville: University Press of Virginia, 1996.

Gerson, Kathleen. *The Unfinished Revolution: How a New Generation Is Reshaping Family, Work, and Gender in America*. Oxford: Oxford University Press, 2010.

Gerson, Kathleen. *The Unfinished Revolution: Coming of Age in a New Era of Gender, Work, and Family*. Oxford: Oxford University Press, 2011.

Gerson, Kathleen. "Why Are Young Women More Ambitious Than Men?" *CNN Opinion*, April 26, 2012. Accessed April 27, 2012. http://www.cnn.com.

Ghaziani, Amin. *The Dividends of Dissent: How Conflict and Culture Work in Lesbian and Gay Marches on Washington*. Chicago: University of Chicago Press, 2008.

Ghaziani, Amin, and Delia Baldassarri. "Cultural Anchors and the Organization of Differences: A Multi-Method Analysis of LGBT Marches on Washington." *American Sociological Review* 76, no. 2 (2011): 179–206.

Giddings, Paula. 2007. *In Search of Sisterhood: Delta Sigma Theta and the Challenge of the Black Sorority Movement.* New York: William Morrow.

Giffort, Danielle. "Show or Tell? Feminist Dilemmas and Implicit Feminism at Girls' Rock Camp." *Gender and Society* 25, no. 5 (2011): 569–88.

Gilmore, Stephanie. "Bridging the Waves: Sex and Sexuality in a Second Wave Organization." In *Different Wavelengths: Studies of the Contemporary Women's Movement,* edited by Jo Reger, 97–116. New York: Routledge, 2005.

Gilmore, Stephanie, ed. *Feminist Coalitions: Historical Perspectives on Second-Wave Feminism in the United States.* Urbana: University of Illinois Press, 2008.

Gittler, Alice Mastrangelo. "Mapping Women's Global Communications and Networking." In *Women@Internet: Creating New Cultures in Cyberspace,* edited by Wendy Harcourt, 91–101. New York: Zed Books, 1999.

Giugni, Marco G. "Personal and Biographical Consequences." In *The Blackwell Companion to Social Movements,* edited by David Snow, Sarah Soule, and Hanspeter Kriesi, 489–507. Oxford: Blackwell, 2007.

Goss, Kristin A., and Michael T. Heaney. "Organizing Women *as Women*: Hybridity and Grassroots Collective Action in the 21st Century." *Perspective on Politics* 8, no. 1 (2010): 27–52.

Gray, Gwendolyn. "Institutional, Incremental, and Enduring: Women's Health Action in Canada and Australia." In *Women's Movements: Flourishing or in Abeyance?* edited by Sandra Grey and Marian Sawer, 49–64. New York: Routledge, 2008.

Green, Adam I. "Queer Theory and Sociology: Locating the Subject and Self in Sexuality Studies." *Sociological Theory* 25, no. 1 (2007): 26–45.

Grey, Sandra, and Marian Sawer, eds. *Women's Movements: Flourishing or in Abeyance?* London: Routledge, 2008.

Guenther, Katja. *Making Their Place: Feminism after Socialism in Eastern Germany.* Stanford, CA: Stanford University Press, 2010.

Gusfield, Joseph R. "Social Movements and Social Change: Perspectives of Linearity and Fluidity." In *Research in Social Movements, Conflict, and Change,* vol. 4, edited by Louis Kriesberg, 317–39. Greenwich, CT: JAI Press, 1981.

Haenfler, Ross, Brett Johnson, and Ellis Jones. "Lifestyle Movements: Exploring the Intersection of Lifestyle and Social Movements." *Social Movement Studies* 11, no. 1 (2012): 1–20.

Hall, Stuart. *Encoding and Decoding in the Television Discourse.* Birmingham, UK: Centre for Contemporary Cultural Studies, 1973.

Hamilton, Laura. "Trading on Heterosexuality: College Women's Gender Strategies and Homophobia." *Gender and Society* 21, no. 2 (2007): 145–72.

Hamilton, Laura, and Elizabeth A. Armstrong. "Gendered Sexuality in Young Adulthood: Double Binds and Flawed Options." *Gender and Society* 23, no. 5 (2009): 589–616.

Haraway, Donna. "Situated Knowledges: The Science Question in Feminism and the Privilege of Partial Perspective." *Feminist Studies* 14, no. 3 (1988): 575–99.

Harding, Sandra. "Is There a Feminist Method?" in *Feminism and Methodology*, edited by Sandra Harding. Bloomington: Indiana University Press, 1987.

Harnois, Catherine. "Different Paths to Different Feminisms? Bridging Multiracial Feminism in Quantitative Sociological Gender Research." *Gender and Society* 19, no. 6 (2005): 809–28.

Harr, Bridget E., and Emily W. Kane. "Intersectionality and Queer Student Support for Queer Politics." *Race, Gender, and Class* 15, nos. 3/4 (2008): 283–99.

Harwarth, Irene, Elizabeth Debra, and Mindi Maline. *Women's Colleges in the United States: History, Issues, and Challenges.* Washington, DC: U.S. Government Printing Office, 1997.

Hasso, Frances S. "Feminist Generations? The Long-Term Impact of Social Movement Involvement on Palestinian Women's Lives." *American Journal of Sociology* 107, no. 3 (2001): 586–611.

Hawkesworth, Mary. "The Semiotics of a Premature Burial: Feminism in a Postfeminist Age." *Signs: Journal of Women in Culture and Society* 29, no. 4 (2004): 961–85.

Heaney, Michael T., and Fabio Rojas. "Hybrid Activism: Social Movement Mobilization in a Multi-Movement Environment." *American Journal of Sociology* 119, no. 4 (2014): 1047–1103.

Henry, Astrid. *Not My Mother's Sister: Generational Conflict and Third Wave Feminism.* Bloomington: Indiana University Press, 2004.

Henry, Astrid. "Solitary Sisterhood: Individualism Meets Collectivity in Feminism's Third Wave." In *Different Wavelengths: Studies of the Contemporary Women's Movement*, edited by Jo Reger, 81–96. New York: Routledge, 2005.

Henry, Astrid. "*Fittism* Feminists and Third Wave Feminists: A Shared Identity between Scandinavia and the United States?" *Feminist Studies* 40, no. 3 (2014): 659–87.

Hepburn, Aden. "Facebook: Facts, Figures & Statistics for 2010." *Digital Buzz Blog*, March 22, 2010. Accessed November 30, 2010. http://www.digitalbuzzblog.com.

Hercus, Cheryl. *Stepping out of Line: Becoming and Being Feminist.* New York: Routledge, 2005.

Hernández, Daisy, and Bushra Rehman, eds. *Colonize This! Young Women of Color on Today's Feminism.* New York: Seal Press, 2002.

Herold, Stephanie. "Young Feminists to Older Feminists: If You Can't Find Us, It's because We're Online." *Generation Progress*, July 19, 2010. http://genprogress.org.

Hess, Amanda. "Why Women Aren't Welcome on the Internet." *Pacific Standard*, January 6, 2014. http://www.psmag.com.

Hess, Amanda. "Why It's So Hard for Men to See Misogyny." *Slate*, May 27, 2014. http://www.slate.com.

Hesse-Biber, Sharlene, Margaret Marino, and Diane Watts-Roy. "A Longitudinal Study of Eating Disorders among College Women: Factors That Influence Recovery." *Gender and Society* 13, no. 3 (1999): 385–408.

Hirsch, Eric L. "Sacrifice for the Cause: Group Processes, Recruitment, and Commitment in a Student Social Movement." *American Sociological Review* 55, no. 2 (1990): 243–54.

Hoffnung, Michele. "Career and Family Outcomes for Women Graduates of Single-Sex versus Coed Colleges." *Sex Roles* 65, nos. 9/10 (2011): 680–92.

Holland, Laurel, and Sherry Cable. "Reconceptualizing Social Movement Abeyance: The Role of Internal Processes and Culture in Cycles of Movement Abeyance and Resurgence." *Sociological Focus* 35, no. 3 (2002): 297–314.

Hondagneu-Sotelo, Pierrette. *Domestica: Immigrants Cleaning and Caring in the Shadows of Affluence.* Berkeley: University of California Press, 2001.

Hull, Gloria T., Patricia Bell Scott, and Barbara Smith, eds. *All the Women Are White, All the Blacks Are Men, But Some of Us Are Brave: Black Women's Studies.* Old Westbury, NY: Feminist Press, 1982.

Hunter, Andrea G., and Sherrill L. Sellers. "Feminist Attitudes among African American Women and Men." *Gender and Society* 12, no. 1 (1998): 81–99.

Hurtado, Aida. "Relating to Privilege: Seduction and Rejection in the Subordination of White Women and Women of Color." *Signs: Journal of Women in Culture and Society* 14, no. 4 (1989): 833–55.

Hurwitz, Heather, and Verta Taylor. "Women Occupying Wall Street: Gender Conflict and Feminist Mobilization." In *100 Years of the Nineteenth Amendment: An Appraisal of Women's Political Activism*, edited by Lee Ann Banasak and Holly J. McCammon. New York: Oxford University Press, forthcoming.

Jasper, James M. *The Art of Moral Protest: Culture, Biography, and Creativity in Social Movements.* Chicago: University of Chicago Press, 1999.

Kane, Emily W. "Racial and Ethnic Variations in Gender-Related Attitudes." *Annual Review of Sociology* 26 (2000): 419–39.

Katzenstein, Mary Fainsod. *Faithful and Fearless: Moving Feminist Protest inside the Church and Military.* Princeton, NJ: Princeton University Press, 1998a.

Katzenstein, Mary Fainsod. "Stepsisters: Feminist Movement Activism in Different Institutional Spaces." *The Movement Society: Contentious Politics for a New Century*, edited by David S. Meyer and Sidney Tarrow. Lanham, MD: Rowman & Littlefield, 1998b.

Keller, Jessalynn Marie. "Virtual Feminisms: Girls' Blogging Communities, Feminist Activism, and Participatory Politics." *Information, Communication, and Society* 15, no. 3 (2012): 429–47.

Kendrick, Richard. "Swimming against the Tide: Peace Movement Recruitment in an Abeyance Environment." In *Social Conflicts and Collective Identities*, edited by Patrick G. Coy and Lynne M. Woehrle, 189–206. Lanham, MD: Rowman & Littlefield, 2000.

Kim, Mikyong Minsun. "Institutional Effectiveness of Women-Only Colleges: Cultivating Students' Desire to Influence Social Conditions." *Journal of Higher Education* 72, no. 3 (2001): 287–321.

Kim, Mikyong Minsun, and Rodolfo Alvarez. "Women-Only Colleges: Some Unanticipated Consequences." *Journal of Higher Education* 66, no. 6 (1995): 641–48.

Klandermans, Bert. "New Social Movements and Resource Mobilization: The European and American Approach." *Mass Emergencies and Disasters* 4, no. 2 (1986): 13–38.

Klandermans, Bert. "Transient Identities: Changes in Collective Identity in the Dutch Peace Movement." In *New Social Movements: From Ideology to Identity*, edited by Hank Johnston, Joseph Gusfield, and Enrique Larana, 168–85. Philadelphia: Temple University Press, 1994.

Klandermans, Bert. "Legacies from the Past: Eight Cycles of Peace Protest." In *The World Says No to War: Demonstrations against the War on Iraq*, edited by Stefaan Walgrave and Dieter Rucht, 61–77. Minneapolis: University of Minnesota Press, 2010.

Klandermans, Bert, and Suzanne Staggenborg, eds. *Methods of Social Movement Research*. Minneapolis: University of Minnesota Press, 2002.

Klawiter, Marin. *The Biopolitics of Breast Cancer: Changing Cultures of Disease and Activism*. Minneapolis: University of Minnesota Press, 2008.

Kuperberg, Arielle, and Pamela Stone. "The Media Depiction of Women Who Opt Out." *Gender and Society* 22, no. 4 (2008): 497–517.

Laughlin, Kathleen A., Julie Gallagher, Dorothy Sue Cobble, Eileen Boris, Premilla Nadasen, Stephanie Gilmore, and Leandra Zarnow. "Is It Time to Jump Ship? Historians Rethink the Wave Metaphor." *Feminist Formations* 22, no. 1 (2010): 76–135.

Lemon, Don. "Hollywood and Violence: Is Misogyny a Growing Concern?" *CNN*, May 28, 2014. http://transcripts.cnn.com.

Levin, Amy K. "Questions for a New Century: Women's Studies and Integrative Learning: A Report to the National Women's Studies Association." Northern Illinois University, 2007. http://www.niu.edu.

"LGBTQ Issues, Gender-Related Violence Call AS Senate to Action." *Bottom Line Student Newspaper* 7, no. 5 (October 31–November 6, 2012).

Lind, Rebecca Ann, and Colleen Salo. "The Framing of Feminists and Feminism in News and Public Affairs Programs in the U.S. Electronic Media." *Journal of Communication* 52, no. 1 (2002): 211–28.

Liss, Miriam, Mary Crawford, and Danielle Popp. "Predictors and Correlates of Collective Action." *Sex Roles* 50, nos. 11/12 (2004): 771–79.

Lovejoy, Meg. "'You Can't Go Home Again': The Impact of Women's Studies on Intellectual and Personal Development." *NWSA Journal* (1998): 119–38.

Luker, Kristin. *Abortion and the Politics of Motherhood*. Berkeley: University of California Press, 1985.

Maatz, Lisa M. "The Awful Truth behind the Gender Pay Gap." *Forbes*, April 7, 2014. http://www.forbes.com.

MacKay, Fiona. "The State of Women's Movement/s in Britain: Ambiguity, Complexity, and Challenges from the Periphery." In *Women's Movements: Flourishing or in Abeyance?* edited by Sandra Grey and Marian Sawer, 17–32. New York: Routledge, 2008.

Maddison, Sarah, and Greg Martin. "Introduction to 'Surviving Neoliberalism: The Persistence of Australian Social Movements.'" *Social Movement Studies* 9, no. 2 (2010): 101–20.

Mansbridge, Jane. *Why We Lost the ERA*. Chicago: University of Chicago Press, 1986.

Mansbridge, Jane, and Katherine Flaster. "The Cultural Politics of Everyday Discourse: The Case of 'Male Chauvinist.'" *Critical Sociology* 33 (2008): 627–60.

Martin, Courtney E., and J. Courtney Sullivan. *Click: When We Knew We Were Feminists*. Berkeley, CA: Seal Press, 2010.

Marwell, Gerald, Pamela Oliver, and Ralph Prahl. "Social Networks and Collective Action: A Theory of the Critical Mass." *American Journal of Sociology* 94, no. 3 (1988): 502–34.

McAdam, Doug. *Political Process and the Development of Black Insurgency, 1930–1970*. Chicago: University of Chicago Press, 1982.

McAdam, Doug. *Freedom Summer*. Chicago: University of Chicago Press, 1988.

McAdam, Doug. "The Biographical Consequences of Activism." *American Sociological Review* 54, no. 5 (1989): 744–60.

McAdam, Doug, Sidney Tarrow, and Charles Tilly. *Dynamics of Contention*. Cambridge, UK: Cambridge University Press, 2001.

McCabe, Janet. "What's in a Label? The Relationship between Feminist Self-Identification and 'Feminist' Attitudes among Young Women and Men." *Gender and Society* 19, no. 4 (2005): 480–505.

McCammon, Holly J., and Karen E. Campbell. "Allies on the Road to Victory: Coalition Formation between the Suffragists and the Woman's Christian Temperance Union." *Mobilization* 7, no. 3 (2002): 231–51.

McCammon, Holly J., Courtney Sanders Muse, Harmony D. Newman, and Teresa M. Terrell. "Movement Framing and Discursive Opportunity Structure: The Political Successes of the U.S. Women's Jury Movements." *American Sociological Review* 72, no. 5 (2007): 725–49.

McCarthy, John D., and Mayer N. Zald. "Resource Mobilization and Social Movements: A Partial Theory." *American Journal of Sociology* 82, no. 6 (1977): 1212–41.

McCaughey, Martha. *Women's Studies Program Administrators' Handbook*. 2006. http://www.nwsa.org.

McCaughey, Martha, and Michael D. Ayers. *Cyberactivism: Online Activism in Theory and Practice*. New York: Routledge, 2003.

McCaughey, Martha, and Cat Warren. "Responding to Right-Wing Attacks on Women's Studies." *Women's Studies Program Administrators' Handbook*. 2006, 43–47, http://www.nwsa.org.

McRobbie, Angela. "Post-Feminism and Popular Culture." *Feminist Media Studies* 4, no. 3, (2006): 255–64.

McRobbie, Angela. *The Aftermath of Feminism: Gender, Culture, and Social Change*. Thousand Oaks, CA: Sage, 2009.

Medina, Jennifer. "Campus Killings Set Off Anguished Conversation about the Treatment of Women." *New York Times*, May 26, 2014. http://www.nytimes.com.

Melucci, Alberto. *Nomads of the Present: Social Movements and Individual Needs in Contemporary Society*. Philadelphia: Temple University Press, 1989.

Melucci, Alberto. "The Process of Collective Identity." In *Social Movements and Culture*, edited by Hank Johnston and Bert Klandermans, 41–63. Minneapolis: University of Minnesota Press, 1995.

Messner, Michael, Max. A. Greenberg, and Tal Peretz. *Some Men: Feminist Allies and the Movement to End Violence against Women*. Oxford, UK: Oxford University Press, 2015.

Meyer, David S., and Nancy Whittier. "Social Movement Spillover." *Social Problems* 41, no. 2 (1994): 277–98.

Minkoff, Debra C. "The Sequencing of Social Movements." *American Sociological Review* 62, no. 5 (1997): 779–99.

Minneapolis Plan. "Community Data Profile." Accessed May 25, 2016. http://www.minneapolismn.gov.

Mooney, Patrick H., and Theo J. Majka. *Farmers' and Farm Workers' Movements: Social Protest in American Agriculture*. New York: Twayne, 1995.

Moraga, Cherríe, and Gloria Anzaldua. *This Bridge Called My Back: Writings by Radical Women of Color*, 4th ed. Albany: SUNY Press, 2015.

Morris, Aldon. "Black Southern Sit-in Movement: An Analysis of Internal Organization." *American Sociological Review* 46, no. 6 (1981): 744–67.

Morris, Aldon. "Birmingham Confrontation Reconsidered: An Analysis of the Dynamics and Tactics of Mobilization." *American Sociological Review* 58, no. 6 (1993): 621–36.

Myaskovsky, Larissa, and Michele Andrisin Wittig. "Predictors of Feminist Social Identity among College Women." *Sex Roles* 50, nos. 11/12 (1997): 861–83.

Myers, Daniel J. "Communication Technology and Social Movements: Contributions of Computer Networks to Activism." *Social Science Computer Review* 12, no. 2 (1994): 251–60.

Naples, Nancy. *Feminism and Method: Ethnography, Discourse Analysis, and Activist Research*. New York: Routledge, 2003.

Oaks, Laury. "What Are Pro-Life Feminists Doing on Campus?" *Feminist Formations* 21, no. 1 (2009): 178–203.

Office of Human Resources, University of Minnesota. "Find a Job." Accessed May 25, 2016. http://www1.umn.edu.

Office of Institutional Research. "All Enrollment Data for Spring 2011." Accessed August 9, 2015. University of Minnesota. http://www.oir.umn.edu.

Olesen, Virginia. "Early Millennial Feminist Qualitative Research: Challenges and Contours." In *The Sage Handbook of Qualitative Research*, edited by Norman K. Denzin and Yvonna S. Lincoln, 235–78. Thousand Oaks, CA: Sage, 2005.

Oliver, Pamela. "Bringing the Crowd Back In: The Nonorganizational Elements of Social Movements." *Research in Social Movements, Conflict, and Change* 11 (1989): 1–30.

Orr, Catherine M. "Tellings of Our Activist Pasts: Tracing the Emergence of Women's Studies at San Diego State College." *Women's Studies Quarterly* 27, nos. 3/4 (1999): 212–29.

Parker, J., and J. Freedman. "Women's Centers/Women's Studies Programs: Collaborating for Feminist Activism." *Women's Studies Quarterly* 27, nos. 3/4 (1999): 114–21.

Pelak, Cynthia Fabrizio. "Women's Collective Identity Formation in Sports: A Case Study from Women's Ice Hockey." *Gender and Society* 16, no. 1 (2002): 93–114.

Pelak, Cynthia Fabrizio. "Contesting Collective Memory: Grassroots Resistance to the Privatization of the National Civil Rights Museum." Paper presented at the American Sociological Association Annual Meeting, Atlanta, GA, August 14, 2010.

Peltola, Pia, Melissa A. Milkie, and Stanley Presser. "The 'Feminist' Mystique: Feminist Identity in Three Generations of Women." *Gender and Society* 18, no. 1 (2004): 122–44.

Pepitone, Julianne. "Facebook Traffic Tops Google for the Week." *CNN Money*, March 16, 2010. Accessed November 30, 2010. http://money.cnn.com.

Percheski, Christine. "Opting Out? Cohort Differences in Professional Women's Employment from 1960–2005." *American Sociological Review* 73, no. 3 (2008): 497–517.

Piepmeier, Alison. *Girl Zines: Making Media, Doing Feminism.* New York: NYU Press, 2009.

Pino, Andrea, and Annie E. Clark. *The Hunting Ground.* DVD. Directed by Kirby Dick. New York: Radius/TWC Films, 2015.

Polletta, Francesca. "'It Was Like a Fever': Narrative and Identity in Social Protest." *Social Problems* 45, no. 2 (1998): 137–59.

Polletta, Francesca. "'Free Spaces' in Collective Action." *Theory and Society* 28 (1999): 1–38.

Polletta, Francesca, and James M. Jasper. "Collective Identity and Social Movements." *Annual Review of Sociology* 27 (2001): 283–305.

Pomerantz, Shauna, Rebecca Raby, and Andrea Stefanik. "Girls Run the World? Caught between Sexism and Postfeminism in School." *Gender and Society* 27, no. 2 (2013): 185–207.

Pudrovska, Tetyana, and Amelia Karraker. "Gender, Job Authority, and Depression." *Journal of Health and Social Behavior* 55, no. 4 (2014): 424–41.

Raeburn, Nicole C. *Changing Corporate America from Inside Out: Lesbian and Gay Workplace Rights.* Minneapolis: University of Minnesota Press, 2004.

Ray, Raka. *Fields of Protest: Women's Movements in India.* Minneapolis: University of Minnesota Press, 1999.

Reger, Jo. "Organizational Dynamics and the Construction of Multiple Feminist Identities in the National Organization for Women." *Gender & Society* 16, no. 5 (2002): 710–27.

Reger, Jo, ed. *Different Wavelengths: Studies of the Contemporary Women's Movement.* New York: Routledge, 2005.

Reger, Jo. "Drawing Identity Boundaries: The Creation of Contemporary Feminism." In *Identity Work in Social Movements*, edited by Jo Reger, Daniel J. Myers, and Rachel Einwohner, 101–20. Minneapolis: University of Minnesota Press, 2008.

Reger, Jo. *Everywhere and Nowhere: Contemporary Feminism in the United States.* Oxford: Oxford University Press, 2012.

Reger, Jo, Daniel J. Myers, and Rachel Einwohner, eds. *Identity Work in Social Movements*. Minneapolis: University of Minnesota Press, 2008.

Reger, Jo, and Lacey Story. "Talking about My Vagina: Two College Campuses and *The Vagina Monologues*." In *Different Wavelengths: Studies of the Contemporary Women's Movement*, edited by Jo Reger, 139–60. New York: Routledge, 2005.

Reinharz, Shulamit. *Feminist Methods in Social Research*. New York: Oxford University Press, 1992.

Reskin, Barbara. "Bringing Men Back In: Sex Differentiation and the Devaluation of Women's Work." *Gender and Society* 2, no. 1 (1988): 58–81.

Reynolds, Michael, Shobha Shagle, and Lekha Venkataraman. "A National Census of Women's and Gender Studies Programs in U.S. Institutions of Higher Education." *National Opinion Research Center*, 2007. http://082511c.membershipsoftware.org.

Ridgeway, Cecilia L., and Shelley J. Correll. "Unpacking the Gender System." *Gender and Society* 18, no. 4 (2004): 510–31.

Riordan, Cornelius. "The Value of Attending a Women's College: Education, Occupation, and Income Benefits." *Journal of Higher Education* 65, no. 4 (1994): 486–510.

Rivers, Caryl, and Rosalind C. Barnett. *The New Soft War on Women: How the Myth of Female Ascendance Is Hurting Women, Men—and Our Economy*. New York: Penguin Books, 2013.

Robnett, Belinda. *How Long? How Long? African American Women in the Struggle for Civil Rights*. New York: Oxford University Press, 1997.

Robnett, Belinda. "We Don't Agree: Collective Identity Justification Work in Social Movement Organization." In *Research in Social Movements, Conflicts, and Change*, vol. 26, edited by Patrick G. Coy, 199–237. Bingley, UK: Emerald, 2005.

Rohlinger, Deana. *Abortion Politics, Mass Media, and Social Movements in America*. Cambridge: Cambridge University Press, 2015.

Rojas, Fabio. *From Black Power to Black Studies: How a Radical Social Movement Became an Academic Discipline*. Baltimore, MD: Johns Hopkins University Press, 2007.

Rojas, Fabio, and Michael T. Heaney. "Social Movement Mobilization in a Multi-Movement Environment: Spillover, Interorganizational Networks, and Hybrid Identities." Unpublished paper, February 13, 2008. https://www.hks.harvard.edu.

Ronen, Shelly. "Grinding on the Dance Floor: Gendered Scripts and Sexualized Dancing at College Parties." *Gender and Society* 24, no. 3 (2010): 355–77.

Roscigno, Vincent J., and William F. Danaher. *The Voice of Southern Labor: Radio, Music, and Textile Strikes, 1929–1934*. Minneapolis: University of Minnesota Press, 2004.

Rosen, Robyn L., ed. *Women's Studies in the Academy: Origins and Impact*. Upper Saddle River, NJ: Pearson/Prentice Hall, 2004.

Rosen, Ruth. *The World Split Open: How the Modern Women's Movement Changed America*. New York: Penguin Books, 2000.

Rosenthal, Naomi, Meryl Fingrutd, Michele Ethier, Roberta Karant, and David McDonald. "Social Movements and Network Analysis: A Case Study of Nineteenth-

Century Women's Reform in New York State." *American Journal of Sociology* 90, no. 5 (March 1985): 1022–54.

Rosin, Hanna. "Marissa Mayer Thinks Feminists Are a Drag: Is She Right?" *Slate*, March 4, 2013. http://www.slate.com.

Roth, Benita. *Separate Roads to Feminism: Black, Chicana, and White Feminist Movements in America's Second Wave.* Cambridge: Cambridge University Press, 2004.

Roth, Benita. "'Organizing One's Own' as Good Politics: Second Wave Feminists and the Meaning of Coalition." In *Strategic Alliances: Coalition Building and Social Movements*, edited by Nella Van Dyke and Holly J. McCammon, 99–118. Minneapolis: University of Minnesota Press, 2010.

Roth, Silke. "Developing Working-Class Feminism: A Biographical Approach to Social Movement Participation." In *Self, Identity, and Social Movements*, edited by Sheldon Stryker, Timothy Owens, and Robert White, 300–323. Minneapolis: University of Minnesota Press, 2000.

Roth, Silke. *Building Movement Bridges: The Coalition of Labor Union Women.* Westport, CT: Praeger, 2003.

Rowe, C. J. "Cyberfeminism in Action: Claiming Women's Space in Cyberspace." In *Women's Movements: Flourishing or in Abeyance?* edited by Sandra Grey and Marian Sawer, 128–39. London: Routledge, 2008.

Rowe-Finkbeiner, Kristin. *The F Word: Feminism in Jeopardy.* Berkeley, CA: Seal Press, 2004.

Ruby, Jennie. "Workshop: Rethinking the Master's Tools: The Impact of Institutionalization on the Movement Vision of Women's Studies." *Off Our Backs* 27, no. 8 (1997): 8.

Rudman, Laurie A., Corinne A. Moss-Racusin, Julie A. Phelan, and Sanne Nauts. "Status Incongruity and Backlash Effects: Defending the Gender Hierarchy Motivates Prejudice against Female Leaders." *Journal of Experimental Social Psychology* 48 (2012): 165–79.

Rupp, Leila J. "The Women's Community in the National Woman's Party, 1945 to the 1960s." *Signs: Journal of Women in Culture and Society* 10, no. 4 (1985): 715–40.

Rupp, Leila J. *Worlds of Women: The Making of an International Women's Movement.* Princeton, NJ: Princeton University Press, 1997.

Rupp, Leila J. "Forging Feminist Identity in an International Movement: A Collective Identity Approach to Twentieth-Century Feminism." *Signs: Journal of Women in Culture and Society* 24, no. 2 (1999): 363–86.

Rupp, Leila J. "Is Feminism the Province of Old (or Middle-Aged) Women?" *Journal of Women's History* 12, no. 4 (2001): 164–73.

Rupp, Leila J. *Drag Queens at the 801 Cabaret.* Chicago: University of Chicago Press, 2003.

Rupp Leila J. "Foreword." In *Different Wavelengths: Studies of the Contemporary Women's Movement*, edited by Jo Reger, xi–xiv. New York: Routledge, 2005.

Rupp, Leila J. "The Persistence of Transnational Organizing: The Case of the Homophile Movement." *American Historical Review* 116, no. 4 (2011): 1014–39.

Rupp, Leila J. "Sexual Fluidity 'Before Sex.'" *Signs: Journal of Women in Culture and Society* 37, no. 4 (2012): 849–56.

Rupp, Leila J., and Verta Taylor. *Survival in the Doldrums: The American Women's Rights Movement, 1945 to the 1960s.* New York: Oxford University Press, 1987.

Rupp, Leila J., and Verta Taylor. "Forging Feminist Identity in an International Movement: A Collective Identity Approach to Feminism." *Signs* 24 (1999): 363–86.

Rupp, Leila J., and Verta Taylor. *Drag Queens at the 801 Cabaret.* Chicago: University of Chicago Press, 2003.

Rupp, Leila J., Verta Taylor, Shiri Regev-Messalem, Alison Fogarty, and Paula England. "Queer Women in the Hookup Scene: Beyond the Closet?" *Gender and Society* 28, no. 2 (2013): 212–35.

Saleem, Muhammad. "By the Numbers: Facebook vs. the United States [INFOGRAPHIC]." *Mashable,* April 5, 2010. Accessed November 30, 2010. http://mashable.com.

Salime, Zakia. *Between Feminism and Islam: Human Rights and Sharia Law in Morocco.* Minneapolis: University of Minnesota Press, 2011.

Sandberg, Sheryl. *Lean In: Women, Work, and the Will to Lead.* New York: Knopf, 2013.

Sandberg, Sheryl. *Lean In for Graduates.* New York: Knopf, 2014.

Santoro, Wayne A., and Gail M. McGuire. "Social Movement Insiders: The Impact of Institutional Activists on Affirmative Action and Comparative Worth Policies." *Social Problems* 44, no. 4 (1997): 503–19.

Sawyers, Traci M., and David S. Meyer. "Missed Opportunities: Social Movement Abeyance and Public Policy." *Social Problems* 46, no. 2 (1999): 187–206.

Schilt, Kristen. "'The Punk White Privilege Scene': Riot Grrrl, White Privilege, and Zines." In *Different Wavelengths: Studies of the Contemporary Women's Movement,* edited by Jo Reger, 39–56. New York: Routledge, 2005.

Schnittker, Jason, Jeremy Freese, and Brian Powell. "What Are Feminists and What Do They Believe? The Role of Generations." *American Sociological Review* 68, no. 4 (2003): 607–22.

Seidler, Victor. "Transforming Masculinities: Bodies, Power, and Emotional Lives." In *Gender in Flux,* edited by Anne Boran and Bernadette Murphy, 13–34. Chester, UK: Chester Academic Press, 2004.

Seidman, Gay W. "Gendered Citizenship: South Africa's Democratic Transition and the Construction of a Gendered State." *Gender and Society* 13, no. 3 (1999): 287–307.

Shaw, Frances. "'HOTTEST 100 WOMEN': Cross-Platform Discursive Activism in Feminist Blogging Networks." *Australian Feminist Studies* 27, no. 74 (2012): 373–87.

Sherkat, Darren E., and T. Jean Blocker. "Explaining the Political and Personal Consequences of Protest." *Social Forces* 75, no. 3 (1997): 1049–76.

Silva, Eduardo. "The Winter Chilean Students Said, Enough!" *Mobilizing Ideas,* May 2, 2012. http://mobilizingideas.wordpress.com.

Simi, Pete, and Robert Futrell. "Negotiating White Power Activist Stigma." *Social Problems* 56, no. 1 (2009): 89–110.

Smith College. "Smith College Common Data Set, 2011–2012." Accessed May 25, 2016. http://www.smith.edu.

Smith College. "Smith History." Accessed May 25, 2016. http://www.smith.edu.

Snow, David A., and Robert D. Benford. "Master Frames and Cycles of Protest." In *Frontiers in Social Movement Theory*, edited by Aldon D. Morris and Carol Mc-Clurg Mueller, 133–55. New Haven, CT: Yale University Press, 1992.

Snow, David A., and Dana Moss. "Protest on the Fly." *American Sociological Review* 79, no. 6 (2014): 1122–43.

Snow, David A., E. Burke Rochford Jr., Steven K. Worden, and Robert D. Benford. "Frame Alignment Processes, Micromobilization, and Movement Participation." *American Sociological Review* 51, no. 4 (1986): 464–81.

Snow, David A., and Sarah A. Soule. *A Primer on Social Movements*. New York: Norton, 2010.

Snow, David A., Louis A. Zurcher Jr., and Sheldon Ekland-Olson. "Social Networks and Social Movements: A Micro-Structural Approach to Differential Recruitment." *American Sociological Review* 45, no. 5 (1980): 787–801.

Snyder, Margaret. "Unlikely Godmother: The UN and the Global Women's Movement." In *Global Feminism: Transnational Women's Activism, Organizing, and Human Rights,* edited by Myra Marx Ferree and Aili Mari Tripp, 24–50. New York: NYU Press, 2006.

Solnit, Rebecca. *Men Explain Things to Me.* Chicago: Haymarket Books, 2014.

Soule, Sarah A. "The Student Divestment Movement in the United States and Tactical Diffusion: The Shantytown Protest." *Social Forces* 75, no. 3 (1997): 855–82.

Soule, Sarah A., and Jennifer Earl. "A Movement Society Evaluated: Collective Protest in the United States, 1960–1986." *Mobilization* 10, no. 3 (2005): 345–64.

Spar, Debora L. *Wonder Women: Sex, Power, and the Quest for Perfection.* New York: Sarah Crichton Books, 2013.

Sprague, Joey. *Feminist Methodologies for Critical Researchers.* Walnut Creek, CA: Altamira Press, 2005.

Springer, Kimberly. "Third Wave Black Feminism." *Signs: Journal of Women in Culture and Society* 27, no. 4 (2002): 1059–82.

Springer, Kimberly. *Living for the Revolution: Black Feminist Organizations, 1968–1980.* Durham, NC: Duke University Press, 2005.

Stacey, Judith. "Sexism by a Subtler Name? Postindustrial Conditions and Post-Feminist Consciousness in the Silicon Valley." *Socialist Review* 17, no. 6 (1987): 7–28.

Staggenborg, Suzanne. "Coalition Work in the Pro-Choice Movement: Organizational and Environmental Opportunities and Obstacles." *Social Problems* 33, no. 5 (1986): 374–90.

Staggenborg, Suzanne. "The Consequences of Professionalization and Formalization in the Pro-Choice Movement." *American Sociological Review* 53, no. 4 (1988): 585–605.

Staggenborg, Suzanne. "The Survival of the Women's Movement: Turnover and Continuity in Indiana." *Mobilization* 1, no. 3 (1996): 143–58.

Staggenborg, Suzanne. "Social Movement Communities and Cycles of Protest: The Emergence and Maintenance of a Local Women's Movement." *Social Problems* 45, no. 2 (1998): 180–204.

Staggenborg, Suzanne, Donna Eder, and Lori Sudderth. "Women's Culture and Social Change: Evidence from the National Women's Music Festival." *Berkeley Journal of Sociology* 38 (1993–1994): 31–56.

Staggenborg, Suzanne, and Amy Lang. "Culture and Ritual in the Montreal Women's Movement." *Social Movement Studies* 6, no. 2 (2007): 177–94.

Staggenborg, Suzanne, and Josée Lecomte. "Social Movement Campaigns: Mobilization and Outcomes in the Montreal Women's Movement." *Mobilization* 14, no. 2 (2009): 405–22.

Staggenborg, Suzanne, and Verta Taylor. "Whatever Happened to the Women's Movement?" *Mobilization* 10, no. 1 (2005): 37–52.

Stake, Jayne E., and Frances L. Hoffman. "Changes in Student Social Attitudes, Activism, and Personal Confidence in Higher Education: The Role of Women's Studies." *American Educational Research Journal* 38, no. 2 (2001): 411–36.

Stein, Arlene. *Sex and Sensibility: Stories of a Lesbian Generation.* Berkeley: University of California Press, 1997.

Stoecker, Judith L., and Ernest T. Pascarella. "Women's Colleges and Women's Career Attainments Revisited." *Journal of Higher Education* 62, no. 4 (1991): 394–406.

Stone, Pamela. *Opting Out? Why Women Really Quit Careers and Head Home* Berkeley: University of California Press, 2008.

Stryker, Sheldon. "Identity Salience and Role Performance: The Relevance of Symbolic Interaction Theory for Family Research." *Journal of Marriage and Family* 30, no. 4 (1968): 558–64.

Stryker, Sheldon, Timothy J. Owens, and Robert W. White, eds. *Self, Identity, and Social Movements.* Minneapolis: University of Minnesota Press, 2000.

Sulik, Gayle. *Pink Ribbon Blues: How Breast Cancer Culture Undermines Women's Health.* Oxford: Oxford University Press, 2010.

Taft, Jessica. "'I'm Not a Politics Person': Teenage Girls, Oppositional Consciousness, and the Meaning of Politics." *Politics and Gender* 2, no. 3 (2006): 329–52.

Taft, Jessica. *Rebel Girls: Youth Activism and Social Change across the Americas.* New York: NYU Press, 2010.

Taylor, Judith, and Kim de Laat. "Feminist Internships and the Depression of Political Imagination: Implications for Women's Studies." *Feminist Formations* 25, no. 1 (2013): 84–110.

Taylor, Verta. "Social Movement Continuity: The Women's Movement in Abeyance." *American Sociological Review* 54, no. 5 (1989): 761–75.

Taylor, Verta. "Watching for Vibes: Bringing Emotions into the Study of Feminist Organizations." In *Feminist Organizations: Harvest of the New Women's Move-*

ment, edited by Myra Marx Ferree and Patricia Yancey Martin, 223–33. Philadelphia: Temple University Press, 1995.

Taylor, Verta. *Rock-a-by Baby: Feminism, Self-Help, and Postpartum Depression*. New York: Routledge, 1996.

Taylor, Verta. "Gender and Social Movements: Gender Processes in Women's Self-Help Movements." *Gender and Society* 13, no. 1 (1999): 8–33.

Taylor, Verta. "Emotions and Identity in Women's Self-Help Movements." In *Self, Identity, and Social Movements*, edited by Sheldon Stryker, Timothy J. Owens, and Robert W. White, 271–99. Minneapolis: University of Minnesota Press, 2000.

Taylor, Verta. "Crossing Boundaries in Participatory Action Research: Performing Protest with Drag Queens" In *Rhyming Hope and History: Activism and Social Movement Scholarship*, edited by David Croteau, William Hoynes, and Charlotte Ryan, 239–264. Minneapolis: University of Minnesota Press, 2005.

Taylor, Verta. "Culture, Identity, and Emotions: Studying Movements as If People Really Matter." *Mobilization* 15, no. 2 (2010): 113–34.

Taylor, Verta. "Social Movement Participation in the Global Society: Identity, Networks, and Emotions." In *The Future of Social Movement Research*, edited by Jacquelien van Stekelenburg, Conny Roggeband, and Bert Klandermans. Minneapolis: University of Minnesota Press, 2013.

Taylor, Verta, Katrina Kimport, Nella Van Dyke, and Ellen Andersen. "Culture and Mobilization: Tactical Repertoires, Same-Sex Weddings, and the Impact on Gay Activism." *American Sociological Review* 74, no. 6 (2009): 865–90.

Taylor, Verta, and Lisa Leitz. "From Infanticide to Activism: Emotions and Identity in Self-Help Movements." In *Social Movements and the Transformation of American Health Care*, edited by Jane Banaszak-Holl, Sandra Levitsky, and Mayer N. Zald, 446–75. New York: Oxford University Press, 2010.

Taylor, Verta, and Nikki Raeburn. "Identity Politics as High-Risk Activism: Career Consequences for Lesbian, Gay, and Bisexual Sociologists." *Social Forces* 42, no. 2 (1995): 252–73.

Taylor, Verta, and Leila J. Rupp. "We Make Our Own History, but Not Just as We Please." In *Beyond Methodology: Feminist Scholarship as Lived Experience*, edited by Mary Margaret Fonow and Judith A. Cook, 119–32. Bloomington: Indiana University Press, 1991.

Taylor, Verta, and Leila J. Rupp. "Women's Culture and Lesbian Feminist Activism: A Reconsideration of Cultural Feminism." *Signs* 19, no. 1 (1993): 32–61.

Taylor, Verta, and Leila J. Rupp. "Loving Internationalism: The Emotion Culture of Transnational Women's Organizations, 1888–1945." *Mobilization* 7 (2002): 141–58.

Taylor, Verta, Leila J. Rupp, and Joshua Gamson. "Performing Protest: Drag Shows as Tactical Repertoires of the Gay and Lesbian Movement." *Research in Social Movements, Conflict, and Change* 25 (2004): 105–37.

Taylor, Verta, and Nella Van Dyke. 2007. "Get Up, Stand Up: Tactical Repertoires of Social Movements." In *The Blackwell Companion to Social Movements*, edited by David Snow, Sarah Soule, and Hanspeter Kriesi, 262–93. Oxford: Blackwell, 2007.

Taylor, Verta, and Nancy Whittier. "Collective Identity in Social Movement Communities: Lesbian Feminist Mobilization." In *Frontiers in Social Movement Theory*, edited by Aldon D. Morris and Carol McClurg Mueller, 104–29. New Haven, CT: Yale University Press, 1992.

Taylor, Verta, and Mayer N. Zald. "Conclusion: The Shape of Collective Action in the U.S. Health Sector." In *Social Movements and the Transformation of American Health Care*, edited by Jane Banaszak-Holl, Sandra Levitsky, and Mayer N. Zald, 300–337. Oxford: Oxford University Press, 2010.

Thompson, Becky. "Multiracial Feminism: Recasting the Chronology of Second Wave Feminism." *Feminist Studies* 28, no. 2 (2002): 336–60.

Tidball, M. E. "Perspectives on Academic Women and Affirmative Action." *Educational Record* 54, no. 2 (1973): 130–35.

Tidball, M. E. "Baccalaureate Origins of Entrants into American Medical Schools." *Journal of Higher Education* 56, no. 4 (1985): 385–402.

Tidball, M. E. "Baccalaureate Origins of Recent Natural Science Doctorates." *Journal of Higher Education* 57, no. 6 (1986): 606–20.

Tidball, M. Elizabeth, Daryl G. Smith, Charles S. Tidball, and Lisa E. Wolf-Wendel. *Taking Women Seriously: Lessons and Legacies for Educating the Majority.* Washington, DC: ACE/Oryx Press, 1999.

Tilly, Charles. *From Mobilization to Revolution.* New York: Random House, 1978.

Tilly, Charles. *The Contentious French.* Cambridge, MA: Belknap Press of Harvard University Press, 1986.

Tilly, Charles. *Contentious Repertoires in Great Britain, 1758–1834.* In *Repertoires and Cycles of Collective Action*, edited by Mark Traugott, 15–42. Durham, NC: Duke University Press, 1995.

Tilly, Charles. *The Language of Contention: Revolutions in Words, 1688–2012.* New York: Cambridge University Press, 2013.

Traister, Rebecca. "How the 'War on Women' Squashed Feminist Stereotypes." *Washington Post Opinion*, May 11, 2012.

"2014 Isla Visa Killings." *Wikipedia.* Last modified May 9, 2016. https://en.wikipedia.org.

University of Minnesota. "Women's Center: About Us." Accessed May 20, 2016. https://diversity.umn.edu.

University of Minnesota. "Women's Center: Why a Women's Center." Accessed May 20, 2016. https://diversity.umn.edu.

Valocchi, Steve. "The Class-Inflected Nature of Gay Identity." *Social Problems* 46, no. 2 (1999): 207–24.

Van Dyke, Nella. "Hotbeds of Activism: Locations of Student Protest." *Social Problems* 45, no. 2 (1998): 205–20.

Van Dyke, Nella. "Crossing Movement Boundaries: Factors That Facilitate Coalition Protest by American College Students, 1930–1990." *Social Problems* 50, no. 2 (2003): 226–50.

Van Dyke, Nella. "The Return of Student Protest." *Mobilizing Ideas*, May 2, 2012. http://mobilizingideas.wordpress.com.

Van Dyke, Nella, and Holly J. McCammon, eds. *Strategic Alliances: Coalition Building and Social Movements.* Minneapolis: University of Minnesota Press, 2010.

Van Dyke, Nella, Sarah A. Soule, and Verta Taylor. "The Targets of Social Movements: Beyond a Focus on the State." In *Authority in Contention*, vol. 25 of *Research in Social Movements, Conflict, and Change*, edited by Daniel J. Meyers and Daniel M. Cress, 27–51. Oxford: JAI Press, 2004.

Walker, Rebecca. *To Be Real: Telling the Truth and Changing the Face of Feminism.* New York: Anchor Books, 1995.

Weigand, Kate. *Red Feminism: American Communism and the Making of Women's Liberation.* Baltimore, MD: Johns Hopkins University Press, 2001.

White, Robert W. "Structural Identity Theory and the Post-Recruitment Activism of Irish Republicans: Persistence, Disengagement, Splits, and Dissidents in Social Movement Organizations." *Social Problems* 57, no. 3 (2010): 341–70.

Whittier, Nancy. *Feminist Generations: The Persistence of the Radical Women's Movement.* Philadelphia: Temple University Press, 1995.

Whittier, Nancy. "Political Generations, Micro-Cohorts, and the Transformation of Social Movements." *American Sociology Review* 62, no. 5 (1997): 760–78.

Whittier, Nancy. "The Consequences of Social Movements for Each Other." In *The Blackwell Companion to Social Movements*, edited by David A. Snow, Sarah A. Soule, and Hanspeter Kriesi, 531–51. Oxford: Blackwell, 2004.

Whittier, Nancy. "From the Second to the Third Wave: Continuity and Change in Grassroots Feminism." In *The US Women's Movement in Global Perspective*, edited by Lee Ann Banaszak, 45–67. Lanham, MD: Rowman & Littlefield, 2006.

Whittier, Nancy. *The Politics of Child Sexual Abuse: Emotion, Social Movements, and the State.* New York: Oxford University Press, 2009.

Whittier, Nancy. "The Politics of Coming Out: Visibility and Identity in Activism against Childhood Sexual Abuse." In *Strategies for Social Change*, edited by Gregory M. Maney, Rachel V. Kutz-Flamenbaum, Deana A. Rohlinger, and Jeff Goodwin, 145–69. Minneapolis: University of Minnesota Press, 2012.

Whose University? Campaign, Film Project, and Event. "About the Project." Accessed December 20, 2012. https://sites.google.com.

Williams, Christine. *Still a Man's World: Men Who Do Women's Work.* Berkeley: University of California Press, 1995.

Williams, Joan C., and Rachel Dempsey. *What Works for Women at Work: Four Patterns Working Women Need to Know.* New York: NYU Press, 2014.

Williams, Rachel, and Michele Andrisin Wittig. "'I'm Not a Feminist, but . . .': Factors Contributing to the Discrepancy between Pro-Feminist Orientation and Feminist Social Identity." *Sex Roles* 37, nos. 11/12 (1997): 885–904.

Wolf, Naomi. "What Really Lies Behind the 'War on Women.'" *Guardian*, May 24, 2012. http://www.guardian.co.uk.

YouGov. "Omnibus Poll." *Huffington Post*, April 11–12, 2013. http://big.assets.huffing-tonpost.com.

Zald, Mayer, and Roberta Ash. "Social Movement Organizations: Growth, Decay, and Change." *Social Forces* 44, no. 3 (1966): 327–41.

Zeisler, Andi. "On Our Radar: Today's Feminist News Roundup" *Bitch,* March 8, 2013. https://bitchmedia.org.

INDEX

abeyance theory, critique of wave framework, 19, 151; definition, 19; updated, 151–58; and wave framework, 17–21

activism, 2, 7, 8, 10–11, 20–22, 25, 45–47, 56–58, 91, 95, 98, 103, 104–5, 108, 111, 116, 122, 128, 135, 138, 142–44, 146, 147–48, 150, 152–53, 156, 166, 171–73, 176, 179, 184; institutional fields of, 61–90

antifeminist, 21, 27, 79, 89, 102, 148, 161–62, 169

appendix: campuses, 178–86; interviews, 172–74; methods, 170–78; participant age, 171–72; participant observation, 174–75; Smith College, 178–81; survey, 176–78; University of Minnesota–Twin Cities, 181–83; University of California–Santa Barbara, 183–86

beauty norms, 133–34. *See also* everyday feminism: typology

Blee, Kathleen, 10–11

classism, 145, 165, 177

Clinton, Hillary, 110

consumption habits, 134–35. *See also* everyday feminism: typology

Correll, Shelley, 15–16, 57–58

coalitions, 22–23, 49, 61, 83, 85, 107–8, 116, 135–46, 148–50, 162–63, 171

collective identity: definition, 92–93; elements needed for formation of, 93; in interactional process, 93; offering definition of feminist, 93

consciousness raising groups, 8–9

everyday abeyance structure, 128–35; definition, 154

everyday feminism: beauty norms, 133–34; consumptive habits, 134–35; definition, 127; interactionally, 130; language, 130–31; part of abeyance theory, 154–58; personalities, 129–30; perspective, 128–29; relation to intersectionality, 128; relationships, 131–33; typology, 128–35, 154; understanding own privilege, 133

everyday sexism: invisible even to women, 3, 25–26, 31–33, 39; masked by progress, 32–33; in personal life, 34–35; in school, 36; in society, 31–32; at work, 37–38, 42, 67

everywhere and nowhere feminism, definition, 93, 128

Facebook: boundary contestation, 124–25, 158; education, 124–26, 174; feminist resource, 123; fundraising through, 123; organize events and projects, 124

false feminist death syndrome, 3, 4

feminism, generational differences in: admiration for second wave feminists, 111–15; definition, 6, 29, 45, 46, 47, 53, 93; extreme, 55; feminism is dead, 3, 25–26; fourth wave, 18–19, 108–11; history, 18; key to social change, 9, 13; as mental framework, 129; pervasive 101; proposed by collective identity typology, 93; sexuality and gender prominence, 49, 133; shaping relationships, 132; third wave, 17–18, 22, 25, 58, 77, 92, 94, 108–11, 117, 136, 156, 159–60

online feminism, 19, 122–27, 158, 162
oppositionally oriented feminism, 95; as
  organizational collective identity, 92; at
  University of Minnesota–Twin Cities,
  95–98

pathways to feminism: click moment, 28;
  consciousness-raising groups, 8–9,
  127, 155; feminist student organizations, 118, 153–55; friends, 45, 100, 103,
  134, 158, 171; mainstream media, 3, 4,
  10–12, 31, 57, 61, 158, 163; mothers, 24,
  34, 42 45; online, 8–9, 12–13, 24, 45,
  59, 121, 125–27, 145, 150, 157–58, 163,
  174; school, 28–30, 45, 61–62, 64–69,
  75, 129, 148, 152; women's centers,
  70–74
personal is political, 8, 67, 128, 135, 155
personalities, 129. See also everyday feminism: typology
perspectives, 128–29. See also everyday
  feminism: typology
Polletta, Francesca, 19, 171

racism, 3, 6, 8, 18, 28, 30, 35, 75, 107, 125,
  129, 145, 151, 165, 177
rape culture, 32, 51–52, 147, 149, 169
Reger, Jo, 66, 102, 144
relationships, 131–33. See also everyday
  feminism: typology
reproductive justice, 9, 16, 28, 30–31, 51,
  53, 87, 96, 107, 114–15, 118, 122, 149–50,
  169
reproductive rights, 16, 18, 28, 30,
  53, 86–87, 96, 114–15, 118, 122,
  169
resistance to gendered beauty norms,
  133–34. See also everyday feminism:
  typology
"rose-colored glasses syndrome," 25, 29,
  41, 45, 60, 163
Roth, Benita, 12, 136, 159–60
Rupp, Leila J., 11, 93, 136, 149

sexual assault, 3, 9, 25, 51, 52, 59, 61–62,
  70, 72, 84–86, 88, 95, 124, 131, 145, 149,
  162, 185
situational feminism, 101
Smith College: cupcake social, 137–40;
  history of empowering women, 178–79;
  history of institutional feminism, 99,
  131; institutionally oriented feminism,
  99–104; no acknowledgment of gender,
  162; perception of disproportionate
  funding, 81; relationship between feminist student organizations and school,
  80; response to funding issues, 82;
  selection for research study, 21; sexuality and gender issues and feminism,
  55–56, 132; student interviews, 30–32,
  34–39, 41–56, 68, 77–78, 80–82, 98, 100–
  104, 109–15, 124–26, 128–29, 130–35,
  137–40; student pride in gender, 129–30,
  tensions between feminist student
  organizations and school, 80–81; "we"
  over "I" feminism, 99–104
Staggenborg, Suzanne, 17
stalled gender revolution, 4; cooexistence
  of gender advancement and stagna-
  tion, 35; expectations that disproportionately negatively affect mothers, 15;
  family devotion schema at odds with
  work devotion schema, 14–15, 41; feminization of poverty, 4; mental health
  rates, 16; "motherhood penalty," 15–16,
  42; no urgency for equality, 5; proof
  that progress is not permanent, 13–14;
  reproductive justice, 9, 16, 31; under-
  representation in media, 31; worsening
  wage gap, 4, 14, 31, 43
street harassment, 10, 13, 25, 38–40, 44, 52,
  57, 59, 120
student activism (male), 53, 132–33, 136–
  38, 147–48
surfacing, definition, 66
study of women and gender programs.
  See women's studies programs

ABOUT THE AUTHOR

Alison Dahl Crossley is the Associate Director of the Clayman Institute for Gender Research at Stanford University. She has published research about social movements, women's movements, and online feminism.